Can the Prizes Still Glitter?

The Future of British Universities in a Changing World

Edited by Hugo de Burgh, Anna Fazackerley
and Jeremy Black

THE UNIVERSITY OF BUCKINGHAM PRESS

First published in Great Britain in 2007 by
The University of Buckingham Press
Buckingham MK18 1EG
www.ubpl.co.uk

© The University of Buckingham Press

The moral right of the authors has been asserted.

A CIP catalogue record for this book is available at the British
Library

ISBN-10   0-9554642-0-X
ISBN-13   978-0-9554642-0-1

The Forum for
Culture and Education

"Can the prizes still glitter?" has been published to mark the launch of
Agora - a new independent think tank whose mission is to promote
serious and searching discussion about higher education and its roles
in our society.

Contents

Part 1
Facing The Future: Thorny Issues for British Universities

Editors: Hugo de Burgh, Anna Fazackerley, Jeremy Black

Part 2
Looking Further Afield: The New Global Higher Education Market

Part 3
Case Studies: How Are Universities Changing To Fit The New Market?

Editors: Hugo de Burgh, Anna Fazackerley, Jeremy Black

Part 4
Mickey Mouse And The Death Of Science: What Should Universities Be Teaching?

PREFACE

Anna Fazackerley

Anna Fazackerley is the Director of Agora. Her background is in Higher Education Journalism. She spent three years as a reporter for the Times Higher Education Supplement, and has also written about universities for The Guardian, The Financial Times and The Scientist.

Agora is an independent think tank whose mission is to promote serious and searching discussion about higher education and its roles in our society.

The media and politicians have long been preoccupied with what is happening to our schools, and with good reason. But what about higher education? As a broadsheet education correspondent commented to me at a party full of bearded academic types recently: "Well come on, no one is really interested in what is going on in universities are they?" If true, this is a sorry state of affairs. For while we have taken our eye off the ball universities have undergone massive and rapid change - and there is more to come. Whereas in the early 1960s only 6% of under-21 year-olds went to university, last year nearly 42% of 18 to 30 year olds went into higher education and the government is pushing for the iconic target of 50%. There are now 168 higher education institutions operating in the UK – with most voicing a desire to compete locally, nationally and internationally. British Higher Education is an exciting and thrusting place to be.

Yet there is a growing discomfort amongst many academics that in all of the rush for progress there has been little time for reflection, or indeed for proper strategic thought about where we are going. In the race to expand, to think global, and to compete, are we losing some of the values that we used to consider core to the academic experience? In today's world, what is a university actually for? It is a big and obvious question – and one that hasn't been addressed adequately. There may be a number of different answers. It seems clear that different institutions could excel at different things. But we mustn't dodge the issue completely.

Editors: Hugo de Burgh, Anna Fazackerley, Jeremy Black

Agora was set up to provide a new space in which people from different educational, personal and political backgrounds could question and investigate the key issues and trends that are shaping higher education. We aim to ask the difficult questions that other groups in higher education are unable to tackle because they are committed to a certain type of answer. I think this book is an excellent beginning.

Vice chancellors, politicians, business people and academics from a range of disciplinary backgrounds and a range of institutions have written personal essays about where universities are now and where they ought to be. Between them they tackle an impressively broad range of topics – from declining standards and student selection to the management of a university, and from the future of science and media studies to the dual missions of teaching and research. Britain can no longer afford to think of itself in isolation, or to rest on its laurels, and we have asked our contributors to think hard about the global context in all of this.

Each essay is intended as a starting point for reflection and discussion. Our writers have explained clearly the main concerns in often complicated areas. We are grateful to them for their time. I hope you will find this volume both enlightening and thought-provoking. The future of our universities will have profound consequences for the future of society as a whole. These are issues that demand a proper debate.

CAN THE PRIZES STILL GLITTER?
The Future of British Universities in a Changing World

INTRODUCTION
THE CHINA CONNECTION[1]

Hugo de Burgh

Professor Hugo de Burgh is Director of the China Media Centre at the University of Westminster. He Chairs Agora. He has recently taken up an Honoured Professorship at Tsinghua University under the Ministry of Education Leading International Scholar Programme.

Shakespeare set plays in Venice, according to Sisci,[2] because the alert Englishmen of his day saw Venice as the powerhouse from which to learn. They were wrong. It was the Venetians who ought to have been studying England to understand the future. In telling us this, Sisci is suggesting that we are being lulled, by all those visiting delegations of Chinese and 60,000 students in the UK alone, into getting everything wrong; China, though only at the early stages of its development, has much to teach us. By contrast, in his more pessimistic tôme, Hutton[3] is convinced that China cannot go further without adopting our Enlightenment norms and institutions. Yet both, along with many captains of industry, some politicians and perhaps a few culture vultures, share the insight that the rise of China obliges us to rethink the world. This thought is echoed by many of the contributors to this volume on higher education. How we should do so is not clear.

This stimulus arrives at a time when, for unrelated domestic reasons, many of us in British universities fear that our profession is not working at full capacity, not realising all of which it is capable and that our institutions may not be able to match progress elsewhere. Several developments – the globalisation of research, described here by Peter Atkins, the successes of private universities, shown to us by

---

[1] I should like to record my thanks to Oliver Letwin for suggesting the idea of the book, and for many other encouragements and kindnesses, and to Martha Varney for her stimulating help in the initial stages of getting it together. I have greatly benefited from the insights of my students Zeng Rong and Tong Jingrong..

[2] Sisci, Francesco (2006) *Chi ha paura della Cina?* Milan: Ponte all Grazie p18

[3] Hutton, Will (2007) *The Writing on the Wall, China and the West in the 21st Century* London: Little, Brown *passim*

James Tooley and Terence Kealey, the achievements of the US model of university management referred to by David Palfreyman, the use of English by competitors abroad, the implications of which are dealt with by Susan Bassnett and, finally, the rapid march of Asia[4] – have further increased our unease. This book deals with some of the issues we need to face, exhibits some of the solutions of which individual institutions are proud and infers the kind of decisions politicians need to make. But first, China.

The Chinese Way

In recent years we, like our counterparts in many other countries, have congratulated ourselves upon the large numbers of Chinese that have chosen to study in the UK. They have been welcomed for subsidising the uneconomic fees paid by UK students and have become necessary to the survival of some departments and courses. Chinese families are famously prepared to pay fabulous sums to prepare their children for glorious futures, and Chinese institutions have paid for many others.

The reasons why they choose the UK are various, but one important reason – the lack of appropriate courses at home – is fast becoming obsolete as Chinese higher education develops. The traditional elite universities have taken stock of international examples, welcomed new staff out of foreign postgraduate training, recruited foreign lecturers, begun to reform teaching and curricula and developed new courses.

In the early 1980s the academics persecuted by Mao were rehabilitated, foreign staff were brought in to introduce them to modernity and tens of thousands of students were sent abroad. From 1985 to 2000 the government addressed other problems by decentralising, giving the regions and localities responsibility for education and by depoliticising education, or giving academic bodies power over their own affairs and telling the Party committees to confine themselves to limited tasks. There are now 1800 state

---

[4] Parts of this introductory chapter are taken from de Burgh, Hugo (2006) *China: Friend or Foe?* Cambridge: Icon and from de Burgh, Hugo (2005) 'Introduction' in de Burgh, Hugo (ed) *China and Britain: the potential impact of China's development* London: The Smith Institute

universities, including both general ones covering most subjects and subject-specific ones, such as China University of Communications (formerly the Beijing Broadcasting Academy) or Beijing Sports University. 'Normal Universities' provide teacher training. In the state universities students pay fees, though there is a scholarship and loans programme for poorer students. [5] Vice Chancellors are keen to increase fees from the well-off.

The government has simultaneously exhorted local authorities to partner industry in creating vocational and technical skill courses at every level. The push for vocational training is partly an answer to a skills shortage, partly to limit the number of academic or 'academicised' courses and partly to provide places for all those who still want to attend HE after public funds are exhausted. Some 1,300 private universities have been established, usually with flexible, practical and very work-orientated courses and modules. Fees are high by Chinese standards but the subjects of study, the teaching and learning techniques and the emphasis on contact with employers through work placements and in curriculum design can make them a good career investment.

In 1997 'Project 211' was launched to ensure that key branches of learning in the state sector were adequately resourced and that resources were not frittered on non-performers. 100 elite institutions were identified into which the government pours money for research; they include those that were seeking to emulate Harvard, Yale and Oxbridge until 1949. Today these universities, such as Tsinghua, Peking and Fudan, are ambitious to be world leaders in scholarship and are also fired with enterprise: they are using their estate holdings as collateral in establishing money-making ventures such as science parks and business services, whose profits support further research and innovations. Tsinghua University's Ziguang Corporation, Xian Jiaotong University's Kaiyuan Corporation, Peking University's Founder Corporation are models. Moreover, like the science academies and other state institutions, the universities are often

---

[5] Tuition paid by students at state institutions now accounts for 15-20% of the total cost of his or her higher education. Bank loans are available

incubating enterprise, particularly in bioengineering, information and digital technology applications.[6]

Far from allowing the elite institutions to cut back on science and technology courses, the government has insisted on their primacy. The number of science and engineering PhDs doubled between 1996 and 2001,[7] although higher degrees may be offered by only a small minority of institutions, lest too many become too theoretical.

Foreign corporate investors in higher education have been welcomed: the China Europe Business School is funded by, among others, Philips, Bayer, Alcatel, Colgate, AXA and LVMH. Some foreign institutions have established campuses in China, notably Nottingham University at Ningbo and Liverpool University at Suzhou.

What China's Development Means For Us

China's advances present several challenges to us: they show us that we are not immune from competition and that we need to know what we can offer that stands out; the very scale of Chinese education invites us to ask what our tiny number of graduates can do better, or differently; the focus on the sciences is a warning – Harry Kroto writes here that our 'laissez-faire attitude to science education has resulted in a disaster'; the ability of Chinese to operate in different cultures contrasts with the collapse of language learning in England; the discipline and rigor for which Chinese institutions strive, and which the best achieve, is salutary. Finally, the mix of institutions, academic and vocational, state and private, with different priorities, target populations, prices and public investment, seems better suited to the modern world than our pretense of uniformity.

International Students and Reputation

Our ability to recruit overseas students has made it possible for many departments, and a few entire institutions, to survive our

---

[6] See also Wilsdon, James and Keley, James (2006) *China: The next science superpower?* London: Demos

[7] Newcomb, Amelia "China Goes to College – in a Big Way" in *Christian Science Monitor* (29 July 2005)

governments' failure adequately to fund us, or cause us to be funded. Yet, as the market place becomes truly global, our advantages, the English language and the good reputation of our leading institutions, may not be enough. Robert Boucher assesses the various modes by which higher education is likely to be obtained in the years ahead, with more overseas campuses, more blended learning and more franchised and twinned provision.[8]

China sends 120,000 abroad to study each year; it receives 110,000 international students to study in China. Worldwide some 10,000[9] take the Chinese language proficiency test, the gateway to studying at a Chinese university. Some courses are taught in English, as they increasingly are in universities elsewhere. If you are one of the many unsuccessful English applicants to read medicine who find that there is no place for you in England, you may not choose China yet, but you can enroll in Prague or several north European universities as well as the Anglosphere; if you choose to work in another language you can go anywhere. A truly international market is emerging, and the growth of private universities, described here by Robert Boucher and James Tooley, will sharpen the competition when what these new operations lack in breadth they make up for in focus.

While the proportion of foreign students in China is still small, the fact that universities are both increasing the number and quality of preparatory Chinese language programmes and also introducing courses taught in English means that this will change. Wealthy individuals and cadets of multinationals such as IBM and Volkswagen, now attend business schools in China; formerly they would have chosen Harvard. Governments are following suit. The Singapore government, long an important customer of UK universities, now funds as many students in China as in the UK.

---

[8] He describes the potential dangers of (currently fashionable) twinned provision and his caveats accord with my own experiences as Validator, Verifier and External Examiner abroad where I have seen UK universities struggle to impose homegrown procedures and criteria upon partners.

[9] Figures from the Ministry of Education, also available on its websites.

Scale and USPs

As to scale: '23 million students' apologised the Chinese Ministry of Education, 'but of course this must quintuple'. The occasion was a visit by Shadow HE Spokesman Boris Johnson.[10] As Johnson, with characteristic brio, put it, leaping onto his bicycle in the lanes nearby: 'if even a small percentage of these have first-rate education and can use English, they will compete with us in everything'.

In such a competitive climate we need to preserve our reputation. Yet in China we are forever being told that it is too easy to get into our universities to read for Master courses; too easy to pass them and much easier to earn a UK PhD than a Chinese one. We are too keen to shovel them in, and lack of discrimination is 'spoiling the brand'. Even if this is only partly true, and only true of a few institutions, nevertheless it may damage us and make it yet more necessary to reduce our dependence on international students. International students are not, anyway, our raison d'être. It is English and European culture that it is our task to preserve and enrich, the quest for knowledge at home that we want pursued and our own public sphere that we should be responsible to and for. These points are made eloquently in their own words by Kenneth Minogue and Frank Furedi. Their reflections also point to a serious deficiency in our ability to compete: we ought to be able to say that independence of thought, intellectual inquiry, un-orthodoxy are what make our universities different from those groaning under statist micromanagement, but we cannot. There is an ugly spirit of conformism at home, conformism to a set of assumptions about the world which smother reflection and debate. Tim Birkhead relates this to changes in the way English universities are now forced to operate, and Michael Shattock points to management pressures and their influences.

Science

Numbers are not all. Two reports have estimated that only small proportions of the huge numbers of engineers qualified in Chinese

---

[10] Boris Johnson MP at the Ministry of Education, Peking, 15 April 2005. Of the 23m, 16m are full-time.

universities are up to Western standards. [11] Yet what impresses qualified visitors such as Imperial's Richard Sykes [12] are the high standards at the top, the climate of respect for science and technology, the vast numbers of graduates being produced, the courses for which are constantly improving such that we can expect that they will overcome current limitations, the widespread enthusiasm for science and a rational outlook. Government investment in R&D, science education, the popularization of science and its commercial application are phenomenal. 59% of undergraduates study science and engineering, compared to 32% in the USA and 36% in the UK [13]. Universities aside, the state owns well over 4000 research institutions, headed by the Academy of Sciences (CAS). In the light of this, the wreck of our scientific tradition, described by Harry Kroto, indeed seems to put our future in jeopardy.

Languages and Cultures

Many, perhaps most, of our universities are already global, whether in the sense of being part of a global research community, as Peter Atkins describes from Oxford, or as institutions with international customers, activities and campuses, such as Geoffrey Copland's Westminster. Where we fail, as Susan Bassnett reminds us, is in ensuring that our students are as competent internationally as those of many other countries. It is not just that the Chinese elite use foreign languages, particularly English, effectively, but that its members can operate capably in other cultures, a more complicated requirement. She draws our attention to the decline of language learning in England. Those whose professions require contact with other cultures are convinced that successful relationships do not use one language. To work with the Arab, Hispanic, Chinese, Russian and Turkic worlds, just to point to cultures that are mighty different from ours but underpin huge economies, we need people equipped to do so – especially at a time when the prestige of the Anglosphere is falling and the fastest growing second language is not English but Chinese.

---

[11] Hutton op cit, p321

[12] Sir R Sykes made his admiration for the Chinese popularization of science clear in an AGORA seminar, March 2005. I have attempted to summarise the prevailing approach to science in China in my introductory volume (2006) *China: Friend or Foe?* Cambridge: Icon pp77-82.

[13] http://www.ucas.com/figures/ucasdata/subject/index.html#analyse

The English will never be as polyglot as Uighurs or Danes or Indians, but if they are to prosper as a trading nation in a world where other cultures are as influential as ours has been, then we need a policy on learning about and from other cultures.

Rigour

About rigour and discipline it is difficult to say anything empirically verifiable, but it is worth noting the anecdotes of visitors to Chinese schools as different as David Held, David Willetts and Elizabeth Reid, were equally impressed [14] by them. Do we have anything to learn from Chinese schooling? There are many deficiencies and many children do not get school at all. But at least they are not going backwards as many of our state schools have done (the effects of this on our universities are highlighted in Chris Patten's chapter), and the best Chinese schools are remarkable. They have to be rigorous; at the beginning of the HE ladder access is tough; it is regularly said that entrants all have the equivalent of a maths A level. [15] There's no nonsense about admitting students who don't know their grammar, spelling or essay composition. Access is wide, but never at the expense of standards in the way that is the case now in England, according to John Stein (the Admissions Tutor at Oxford to whom Laura Spence applied) and, in his politic way, Minister Rammell.

As a marker of essays and an External examiner in several universities of different types I have satisfied myself that better thinking is likely to be done and better English written by students whose second language is English than by those educated at a substantial number of English schools. Employers are right to complain of this, and Bernard Lamb right to remind us that standards in maths too are bad. The proposals for dealing with this are either that we provide remedial attention or that universities lower their standards,

---

[14] Held, David, author of, *inter alia* 'Globalisation: The Argument of Our Time.' www.opendemocracy.net; David Willetts MP, Shadow Education Secretary and Elizabeth Reid, Director of the Specialist Schools and Academies Trust. Conversations with the author.

[15] At the time of going to press I have not been able to find any UK mathematician who can confirm this to me. However, the blogs of Chinese students in the UK give further credence to this. See, for example, a student at ICST on http://lkcn.net/bbs/index.php?showtopic=41111

neither of which tactic is good for reputation, morale or efficacy. Nor are they good for our long-term future. David Lathbury, referring to our deficiencies in basic science education, believes that because of the failures of our schools today we will miss out on the growth industries of the century; that our grandchildren could work only in call centres.

Mix of Institutions

There is common ground, at first sight, in the mix of institutions. In England we have, in addition to thoroughly academic education, varied and enterprising professional courses, as Sally Feldman's essay reminds us, courses which respond to the rapid changes and demands for multiskilling required in today's economy. China's private institutions want to do the same and team up with English institutions to provide the kind of media, arts and design courses which she manages. However, many academics are concerned lest the exigencies of business come to dominate research and teaching. Business is not the only external influence on courses and their content: Gary Day worries that the main aim of many institutions has become to please students, not to educate them. 'For the first time in history what the student wants, not what the student needs to know, has apparently become the driving force of education'. Is not this the case in the private institutions in China, trumpeted as the world's most dynamic economy, and therefore *a good thing*? Is this not proof that market forces know best? The utilitarian might so argue, yet where the Chinese approach to the mix differs from ours, it would seem, is (first) that the state now intends only to involve itself with those areas of study where very high investment or national needs are concerned and (second) that the Chinese market choices may be informed by more hard-headed judgments, simply because life itself is much harder. Chinese families pay for courses which provide the liklihood of a rice bowl; the state (and, in the future, private foundations) must therefore support the less immediately realisable investments. In England, as Lathbury concludes, weaknesses in schooling condition the choices children make. If there is little or no science or maths then pupils are unlikely to seek university courses based on them so that they make choices which may be bad; the state then subsidises these bad choices. In this manner can schools determine what universities offer, and which the public purse will pay. The failures of state schooling exact another fearsome price.

An answer to the issue of whether universities should specialise or be generalist is provided here by Alec Reed, who regards the notion that universities provide an essential branding as being hopelessly out of date. Universities offer products, very different products for very different purposes, and it is those products which the rest of us, whether taxpayer or employer, are interested in.

As we have seen China encourages a varied array of institutions to flourish, with the most vocational courses supplied through private provision. The state restricts itself to key areas. In our country, as Chris Patten writes, 'universities are left in a No Man's Land, in which they neither get enough funding from the state nor are they allowed to raise money themselves beyond the ridiculously low limits of the tuition fee.' Eric Thomas tells us that, at present the USA spends 2.5 times what we spend on HE; because they too encourage realistic funding, China and India may soon be close behind.

So, these are some areas in which we are challenged to do better by China's rise. Our dependence on overseas students has come about because governments have made demands upon universities without funding them adequately. The contraction of sciences and languages results from market failure where it is the responsibility of government to step in and selectively promote some subjects, preferably by supporting those who are competent to study them rather than by subsidising departments. As to the issue of schooling standards, from a Chinese perspective it is incomprehensible to address the low standards of large numbers of state schools by obliging universities to lower their entry requirements. As to the refusal to accept that institutions should be different in what they offer and as to whom they recruit, this will damage the long-term interests of the universities.

Paradoxically, what in the end may diminish us is the very attitude to higher education that informs our fearful competitiveness, most recently exhibited in the Leitch Report. Almost all talk of higher education in our public life is pitifully utilitarian; no value is found for it except as it directly contributes to the economy. Such contempt for learning for its own sake – because it civilises us – would have shocked our dynamic Victorian forbears. It is also contrary to the traditional attitude to learning that is behind the expansion of education in China, that education is quite different from skill training, it is an end in itself. The fact that we no longer defend learning as part of humankind's search for understanding, but pare it down to what has an immediate economic payback, reflects a wider malaise that is undermining our educational institutions. If England, a rich country with long traditions of modern scholarship, does not realise that what must make its universities different is that which developing and less free countries envy, learning for the sake of understanding, then we have given up our greatest advantage.

Sub specie aeternitatis, the prizes that glitter most are the scientific advances, the wisdom from the arts and the understanding we gain from the social sciences. What reforms are needed that our universities continue to make such contributions? China's achievements, of the past few years, offer a warning that we need to think through how to maintain our value in a changing world. This book will help.

Editors: Hugo de Burgh, Anna Fazackerley, Jeremy Black

Part 1

FACING THE FUTURE

THORNY ISSUES FOR BRITISH UNIVERSITIES

Editors: Hugo de Burgh, Anna Fazackerley, Jeremy Black

DO ACADEMICS STILL THINK?

Frank Furedi

Professor Frank Furedi is a sociologist based at the University of Kent in Canterbury. His commentaries on culture and society frequently serve as focus for public debate. His recent book, 'Where Have All The Intellectuals Gone: Confronting 21st Century Philistinism' explores the problem of politicising intellectual life. His other books include "Politics of Fear" and "Paranoid Parenting".

Recently a colleague at a redbrick university asked me to provide my views on the suitability of a group of applicants to an academic post. The applicants had clearly done their homework. They all stressed the importance of their potential contribution to THE department's RAE. They emphasised their commitment to 'diversity', 'inclusive teaching' and 'critical thinking'. They boasted of the many research skills that they had acquired. They clearly talked the talk expected of them. But what struck me as particularly depressing was the fact that none of them attempted to present themselves as scholars or thinkers. Their account of their research profile was perfunctory and technical. From the information they provided it was evident that they applied for grants, sometimes got one, did the research, published a couple of monographs and went on to apply for a further round of grants. In the story they offered of their research career there was barely a mention of an idea that they thought was important nor did they transmit a statement of intellectual interest. Obviously the way we present ourselves on an application form tells only part of the story. And for all I know every one of these applicants was a closet thinker and scholar. But they clearly did not believe that thinking is part of the job description of an academic. They also understood that their prospective employer was not looking for thinkers. And in this respect they were right.

Of course academics still think, and fortunately world class thinkers can be found in the corridors of many British universities. But thinking takes place despite the powerful trends that seek to downsize the academic into a teacher of further education. Increasingly thinking has become a freelance activity to be pursued when we are not teaching, administrating or researching. Universities still attach some value to thinking but the value associated with it tends to be rhetorical rather than substantive. It is difficult to disagree with the diagnosis offered by Mary Evans, who describes the university as a site for 'battery farming of the mind'.[1]

The Infantalisation of Academics

Academics seem to be in a constant state of list making. I don't just mean designing reading lists. We are continually asked to provide lists of publications, lists of teaching commitments, lists of administrative duties, lists of grants etc. List making has become an important by-product of the growing trend towards the formalisation of university life. So the lists are not even the product of an academic's imagination or thought. There is now a ready made template that instructs how the list should be constructed, what language should be used and what values should be promoted. Forms dominate every aspect of university life and little is left to chance or professional discretion. The performance of academic list making is evaluated on the ability to follow instructions rather than on creative thinking.

The micro-management of university life has become an accomplished fact. This form of governance is achieved through the homogenisation, standardisation and quantification of university life. That is why there needs to be a proverbial template for every dimension of the academic experience. And forms need to be filled in and literally followed to the letter. As every academic can testify this regulation of higher education leads to its bureaucratisation. In turn bureaucratisation leads inexorably to the deprofessionalisation and infantilisation of academics.

In the army, soldiers follow orders, in a bureaucracy civil servants live by the rule-book, and in the university academics are forced to work to a template. Academics may have their PhDs and published monographs but their managers do not trust them to pursue their work

---

[1] Evans, M. (2005) *Killing Thinking: The Death of the Universities*, Continuum: London.

as mature and responsible scholars. Nor are they encouraged to think for themselves. There is now growing pressure on academics – particularly those who are newly appointed – to internalise the values of their managers. From this perspective academics are perceived as immature and unworldly employees who need to be socialised and trained by experts who know a thing or two about the management of higher education. Consequently academics, like precocious children, are offered 'support' to realise their potential. One way that this condescending view of the academic is transmitted is through the mechanism of staff development.

In recent years, many academics have discovered that attending staff development courses has assumed the character of a contractual obligation. Checking out how many of these courses you have attended is often part of the appraisal process. Along with listing your publications, grant applications and conference papers, you have to provide evidence that you have been a busy staff-development course attendee. And if you think that you have better things to do than spend an afternoon getting whiteboard training - think again. As the University of Brighton's staff development website indicates: "The university has the right to expect that each member of staff as part of the individual's contractual obligation will develop his/her competencies and capability, which are aligned to the university's strategy as it may be operationalised at faculty, departmental, school, section, team or individual level." Quite a mouthful, but the message is clear. Attendance will be policed. Brighton requires that "each member of staff keeps a record of staff development activity, which is monitored and evaluated in collaboration with the line manager".

A review of British university staff development programmes indicates that their objective is to ensure that staff are fully socialised into accepting the bizarre technocratic ethos that prevails on campuses. "Staff development exists to maximise the potential of each individual to support the university in achieving its strategic goals," declares the human resource home page of Brunel University. Clearly, this is not a statement celebrating the individual's potential to develop, but an attempt to ensure that employees know the institution's line. The University of Leicester's declaration on this subject is no less subtle: "One of the main responsibilities of the university's Staff Development Centre is to provide a central programme of developmental activities for all categories of staff to support developments and the university's institutional plan." One of the main aims of staff development at the University of Sheffield is "to enable the university to improve its institutional performance". It can be argued that there is nothing objectionable about mobilising staff to promote the corporate plans of a university. But why call it staff development? Why pretend that these initiatives are for the benefit of staff?

The premise of staff development is literally that academics are not quite developed adults. That is why so many of the programmes are oriented towards what is euphemistically characterised as "personal development". At Loughborough University, personal development courses deal with topics such as "assertiveness, financial advice, meditation, relaxation, etc". The learning outcome of one assertiveness communication course at a leading university is to gain the ability to "differentiate between different types of behaviour". Aside from its patronising assumption that staff cannot do this already, the training course is wholly objectionable because it seeks to impose an insidious form of emotional conformism. At least in the old days, the military had no inhibitions about letting everyone know that soldiers were not expected to think for themselves. University bureaucrats prefer to hide behind the Kafkaesque language of staff development when they transmit the same message to human resources.

At the University of Nottingham, staff are offered a course patronisingly titled "Looking after yourself". Participants are told that they will have an opportunity to "recognise the importance of good nutrition and exercise". They will also learn to "identify a range of techniques for reducing the effects of stress and increasing self-esteem". Thankfully, it will also "plan ways of improving their personal image". At Cambridge University, a course "Navigator: A programme for men" is "designed for those who wish to progress to develop themselves", while its "Springboard: A women's development programme" aims "to value what you have got going for you and build on your strengths". Cambridge also runs "Assertiveness in action". The objective of this course is to allow yourself "to find out how you see yourself in relation to others". Or at least to see yourself through the eyes of your trainer.

Diminishing Institutional Integrity

Thankfully in terms of time and effort staff development plays only a marginal role in the lives of most academics. But it symbolises the university's attitude towards its academics. Academics are not trusted to construct their own professional culture. They need to internalize a system of values cobbled together by business consultants and higher education experts. Like so many dimensions of university life this is certainly not the product of academic thinking.

University teachers are increasingly forced to work according to rules and practices that do not derive from an academic culture but from a managerial one. The standardisation of evaluation procedures, benchmarking, auditing and quality assurance procedures all compel academics to work according to an externally imposed script. University teaching needs to be consistent with bureaucratically devised 'learning outcomes'. We do not yet have the equivalent of a 'literacy hour', but it is only a matter of time before lecturers are advised to teach certain 'key skills' at a designated time in the academic calendar.

Back in the nineties, the author of the *McDonaldization Thesis* noted that soon the university will adopt many of the managerial models and practices associated with the spread of this hamburger chain. According to the American sociologist George Ritzer, new forms of quality control and consumer orientation would be integrated into the existing structure of the university.[2] My initial reaction to Ritzer's thesis was that although it was a clever idea, the arrival of McUniversity was far off. Today, when virtually every university brochure, mission statement and web-site is indistinguishable from one another, I am not so sure. Of course, we don't quite do the same thing and we try to pursue our work in accordance with the demands of our discipline. However the pressure towards homogenisation, standardisation and quantification works towards the constant diminishing of academic judgement.

---

[2] Ritzer, G (1998) *The McDonaldization Thesis: Explorations and Extensions*, Sage: London.

The rationalisation of intellectual life in universities necessarily encroaches on the process of thinking. Creative and open-ended thinking invariably collides with bureaucratic norms. It is difficult to quantify or audit thinking. That is why the new breed of academic experts have not been able to resist the temptation of attempting to devise a template for managing thinking. In the social sciences and humanities, academics are encouraged to become 'reflexive' and adopt 'critical thinking'. What the template demands can be best described as formulaic thinking since neither genuine thought or criticism can be performed by rote. In line with the prevailing pedagogic ethos of higher education thinking is transformed into a skill. Along with study skills, listening skills, time management skills, telephone conversation skills, information gathering skills, evaluating skills, analyzing skills, and integrating skills, we have thinking skills. The breaking down of thinking into a series of skills may assist the trainer and business consultant but it is entirely alien to what academics do when they seek to know and understand. It actually dispossesses academics from thinking according to their own inclination and in a way that is integral to the pursuit of knowledge. Academic thinking evolves in a constant interaction with the problems they address. It is open-ended and moves in unexpected directions.

Bureaucratically convenient practices like the skills agenda serve to erode the institutional integrity of the university. These are practices that others have thought up for the academic. One unfortunate consequence of this development is that the predominant ideas about the purpose of the university are not the product of academic thinking. Academics have no right to have a monopoly on defining the purpose of a university.

There is nothing wrong with society having a wide divergence of opinion about the purpose of higher education. A clash of strongly held views can stimulate all parties to develop important insights into the role of higher education and society. But instead of reflection or informed debate what we have are decrees dreamt up by invisible bureaucrats and officials.

There was a time when the metaphor of living in an Ivory Tower could be used to describe the behaviour of some academics. Today academics live in an open plan institution and are continually forced to account for themselves to officials who have no real concern with the substantive content of their work. Increasingly academic life is subjected to norms and values that are external to it. As Gordon Graham notes, academics are 'no longer, or only rarely, formers of public opinion and more usually subject to opinions and hence policies formed elsewhere'.[3] Academics still possess a visible profile but when they speak in public they frequently talk to a script written by someone outside the university.

It is tempting to blame the rise of template culture on the forces from without. But universities have always been subject to some form of external pressure and yet did not necessarily tow the line. In recent times academics have often been accomplices to the demise of the integrity of their profession. Many of the regrettable trends outlined above have become institutionalised without provoking much opposition from academics. In recent decades academics have become consummate grumblers but not very articulate foes of the McDonaldization of their institution. Nor have academics sought to influence the public and win support for their ideal of what a university is about. Academics can demonstrate that they are still thinking by taking responsibility for initiating a public debate about the purpose of their work.

---

[3] Graham, G (2002) *Universities; The Recovery Of An Idea*, Imprint Academic: Thorverton, p 121.

FOREIGN STUDENTS: THEIR EFFECTS ON UK HIGHER EDUCATION

Bernard Lamb

Dr Bernard Lamb is a Reader in Genetics at Imperial College London, where he has taught since 1968. He takes a special interest in overseas students, introducing some of them to aspects of British life such as Gilbert and Sullivan operettas and sheep farms. He does research on human diversity and on fungal genetics, and is Chairman of the London Branch of the Queen's English Society.

Students from abroad have a variety of effects on UK higher education, some beneficial, some detrimental. They influence the UK students socially and culturally by direct personal interaction and by example. They affect potential UK undergraduates and postgraduates by competing with them for places in higher education.

In this article, the term "Overseas students" excludes "Other EU", which means non-UK EU students such as Germans and Greeks. "Foreign students" will be used collectively for Other EU and Overseas students. Most of the data analysed is from The Higher Education Statistics Agency (HESA, website www.hesa.ac.uk), but I have also used my own unpublished observations and survey data on students from Imperial College London, and data from Imperial College official and student sources.

Fees, Costs and Benefits

Other EU students pay the same fees as Home students, providing competition for places but no fee advantage. Overseas students pay higher fees, which is a financial disadvantage to them, their families or sponsors, but it makes them more desired than are Home or Other EU students by our cash-deficient universities. The Rector of Imperial College, Sir Richard Sykes, stated that he wanted to increase the proportion of Overseas students because the college needs their higher fee income, as government funding is quite inadequate for running advanced courses. He estimates that the college lost about £2,500 a year on each Home student. According to a HESA Press Release of 13th March, 2006, the UK vice-chancellors, through Universities UK, stated that two thirds of British universities were increasing their overseas recruitment efforts. As student numbers have gone up to meet the Government's requirements over nearly a decade, the unit of resource per student has dropped disastrously.

Typical undergraduate fees a year for England for 2006/07 are: Home and Other EU students, £3,000; Overseas students, £6,000 to £16,000. Typical taught postgraduate course fees are: Home and Other EU students, £3,000 to £8,000; Overseas students £7,500 to £15,000. Fees are less at some institutes and very much more at others, especially business schools.

Although Overseas students pay higher fees, Overseas and Other EU students also bring extra costs. UK universities have to employ specialist staff to give remedial English tuition and advice to Foreign students. Especially in first year, lecturers sometimes have to go more slowly and/or give extra out-of-lectures help for Foreign students struggling to keep up, even though the latter have passed the necessary English tests for entry. There may be other extra costs, as in provision of additional welfare or accommodation advice to Foreign students.

The undergraduates and taught course postgraduates are mainly recipients of information, wherever they come from, but their research projects benefit their institutions. Research students receive some course instruction, some research instruction, and contribute substantially to their departments' research output, providing much of the labour and some of the ideas in staff research projects. These contributions are made by Home and Foreign students. My genetics research has benefited enormously over many years from the work of Sri Lankan, Egyptian, Pakistani, Iranian, Greek and Polish research students.

Numbers of Students of Different Types, and Competition for Places Between Them

The Higher Education Statistics Agency (HESA) gives the following figures for UK universities in academic year 2004/05. There were 1,754,905 undergraduates, of which 91.3% were Home students, 3.1% were Other EU and 5.6% were Overseas students. There were 532,630 postgraduates, including research and taught course students, with 68.9% Home, 8.6% Other EU and 22.5% Overseas students. According to the Universities and Colleges Admissions Service (UCAS) in August 2006, the number of Other EU students accepted rose by 10% to 13,357 for 2006 admissions, while that for English students went down by 4.7%.

The proportion of Home, Overseas and Other EU students varies enormously between UK universities, depending on their reputation, subject mix, geographical location, traditions, and recruiting efforts. Some typical figures for undergraduates are given in Table 1 for universities of different types in different parts of the country. The high percentage of Foreign students at Imperial College reflects one of its original aims, to be "the sword and shield of the Empire"; it has been high for many years, being 9% in 1919, 25% in 1929, 22% in 1939, 15% in 1949, 22% in 1959, 21% in 1969, and 21% in 1979. The high proportion of EU students at Brighton perhaps reflects its proximity to the Continent, and its many continental visitors and language schools.

In many institutions, as at Chester (98.3% Home undergraduates), the relatively low number of Foreign students suggests that there is not a high level of competition with Home students for places there, but at other institutions, such as Imperial College (70.4% Home undergraduates), there is much more competition between Home, Other EU and Overseas students. According to the Imperial College London Statistics Pocket Guide 2005-06, Overseas students (excluding Other EU ones) made up 28.9% of the 11,490 full-time students, including 26.6% of undergraduates, 39.8% of taught postgraduates and 29.5% of research postgraduates there in 2005-06. According to the London School of Economics and Political Science Profile (May 2004), their undergraduates were 50% Home, 8.1% Other EU and 41.9% Overseas, while their postgraduates were Home 25.5%, Other EU, 20.4% and 54.1% Overseas, showing a very high proportion of Foreign students. The LSE and Imperial College have high standards of entry.

However, one cannot accurately judge the degree of competition for places in different institutions or on different courses solely from

CAN THE PRIZES STILL GLITTER?
The Future of British Universities in a Changing World

Table 1. The proportions of Home, Other EU and Overseas undergraduate students in a range of UK universities, calculated from HESA data for 2004-05

University	Home, %	Other EU, %	Overseas, %	Total under-graduates
Aston	86.5	2.0	11.4	6,160
Bath	86.2	4.6	9.2	9,775
Birmingham	92.4	1.8	5.8	18,785
Bournemouth	94.6	2.2	3.2	13,315
Bradford	83.8	3.1	13.1	8,545
Brighton	89.2	6.3	4.5	15,935
Bristol	92.0	2.3	5.7	15,470
Cambridge	90.4	3.4	6.2	16,160
Central Lancashire	92.8	2.0	5.2	23,660
Chester	98.3	1.3	0.4	10,055
City	86.6	4.0	9.4	14,845
De Montfort	95.8	1.3	2.9	18,990
East London	85.7	5.3	9.0	11,505
Gloucestershire	95.5	1.2	3.4	7,145
Greenwich	86.9	3.8	9.3	16,095
Huddersfield	95.0	2.0	2.9	14,475
Hull	90.5	2.3	7.1	17,490
Imperial College	70.4	7.6	22.0	7,850
King's College London	87.7	4.6	7.7	14,995
Leicester	88.9	2.8	8.2	9,890
Lincoln	94.6	4.3	1.1	11,435
London Metropolitan	80.7	6.3	13.0	22,060
LSE	54.9	9.3	35.4	4,015
Middlesex	82.7	4.0	13.3	18,755
Oxford	91.0	3.5	5.6	15,490
Queen Mary London	82.5	3.2	14.3	8,225

the relative numbers of Home, Other EU and Overseas students. Some courses, such as pesticide spray techniques for the tropics, are largely designed for Foreign students or for seconded agricultural extension officers sponsored by their governments. A very important consideration is that many undergraduate and postgraduate taught courses would not be run at all if it were not for the Foreign students keeping the numbers up and providing much of the necessary fee income. Having sufficient numbers of Foreign students therefore enables places to be available for Home students on such courses, which would not otherwise run. That applies to very prestigious and less prestigious universities.

The competition for places varies widely with subject area and university: some departments in top universities are overwhelmed with well-qualified Home and Foreign applicants, while some departments in poorer universities are desperate to fill places, for financial reasons. They get many or most of their students from the UCAS Clearing Scheme, accepting students with just one A-level, even at D or E grade. The degree of competition between Home and Foreign students is generally strongest in the best universities, especially the Russell Group, and much weaker in the less popular ones, which are often former technical colleges elevated to university status in 1990s.

The best measure of competition comes from the number of applicants per place for particular subject areas at particular universities. According to the Imperial College London Statistics Pocket Guide 2005-6, the numbers of applicants there per undergraduate place for the 2005 entry were: aeronautics, 7.5; bioengineering, 4.3; chemical engineering and technology, 4.3; civil and environmental engineering, 5.7; computing, 5.8; earth science and engineering, 4.3; electrical and electronic engineering, 5.3; materials, 3.2; mechanical engineering, 5.0; life sciences, 5.8; medicine, 7.9; chemistry, 6.0; mathematics, 6.3; physics, 3.7; overall average, 5.7. The overall number of applicants there per postgraduate place in 2005 was 5.3. Given that Imperial College has a high proportion of Other EU and Overseas students (Table 1), these figures show that there is a real competition between Home, Other EU and Overseas students for undergraduate and postgraduate places there. Competition for places in arts subject such as English and History, say at Bristol University, and in subjects leading to professional qualifications such as medicine, veterinary science and law, is also often very strong.

Overseas student numbers are rising in the UK, faster than the number of places available. The following information comes from the HESA Press Release, 13th March, 2006. Overseas student numbers rose by 6.1% to 318,400 in 2004/05, whereas the increase in the previous year had been 9%. Other EU numbers rose by 3.2% to 100,005, partly due to the accession of new member states in May 2004. Cyprus was the largest contributor from new member states (5,675), while Poland more than doubled its numbers from 965 to 2,185. Of the non-EU countries, China was the largest contributor of Overseas students, with a rise of 10.3%, following a huge rise of 35.8% between 2002/03 and 2003/04. Increases were 14.1% for India and 37.1% for Nigeria, while Canada replaced Singapore as the 10th largest contributor of overseas students, with 4,190.

Background to my Data

I have taught genetics at Imperial College since 1968, interacting with a wide range of Home and Foreign undergraduates and postgraduates. In 1966-67, I spent a year as a postdoctoral fellow at the California Institute of Technology in Pasadena, so have some experience of studying in a Foreign country.

Some of my research has been on human diversity. Each year I give the first year students a questionnaire about their physical features, medical conditions, country of birth, nationality and ancestry. I also ask about social mixing between Overseas and Home students. There is a nearly 100% response from those present. While my results from one department in one university may not be typical, the data are relevant.

What are the Origins of Different Types of Student?

One has to be careful in generalising about Foreign and Home students since there are such large racial and cultural differences between different Overseas students and between different Home students. Home students may well be Pakistani Muslims, Sri Lankan Buddhists, Spanish Catholics, Chinese atheists, Indian Hindus, traditional English, or of many other kinds, some of them very similar in ancestry and culture to those counted as Foreign students. Quite a high proportion of Overseas students, especially from China or Hong

Kong, go to British schools for their A-levels, so are partly British-educated and partly culturally assimilated. A smaller proportion of Home students is educated at least partly abroad.

One point which is often ignored in debates about Foreign students is the extent to which many students defined for the purposes of higher education as Home students are of overseas origin, either born abroad, or brought up here as part of an immigrant culture. For example, one racially Chinese student I taught was born in London to parents who arrived here from China about 22 years ago and run a Chinese take-away food outlet. The father still speaks no English and the mother has a little English, so the student has grown up in family which always speaks Chinese at home, reads Chinese books and newspapers, watches Chinese TV and videos and very largely has Chinese friends. I assumed that she was brought up in China until she told me her background. The number of overseas Chinese at Imperial College has increased dramatically from 200 in 2001-02 to 1,133 in 2005-06, and even more in 2006-07.

The Higher Education Statistical Agency[1] gave these figures for UK-domiciled students of known ethnicity in 2004-05:undergraduates, 615,995, 83.9% white, 5.3% black, 5.9% Indian, Pakistani or Bangladeshi, 0.8% Chinese; postgraduates, 156,850, 86.0% white, 4.0% black, 5.2% Indian, Pakistani or Bangladeshi, 1.2% Chinese.

Trevor Phillips, Chair of the Commission for Racial Equality, was interviewed for the Imperial College student newspaper, *Felix* (No. 1356, 15/6/2006, p 7). He said that: "Although there are a lot of [British] ethnic minorities in higher education, they are in the poorest, least prestigious places. When you separate the Russell group from everywhere else, it is like two countries. There is under representation in the Russell group and a huge over representation in the big municipal universities." The same article mentioned that: "Earlier this year the Higher Education Statistics Agency revealed 'a deeply worrying racial divide amongst British universities' and singled out Imperial as having one of the smallest populations of [home] students of Afro-Caribbean descent – only 15."

---

[1] www.hesa.ac.uk/holisdocs/pubinfo/student/ethnic0405.htm

CAN THE PRIZES STILL GLITTER?
The Future of British Universities in a Changing World

Table 2 shows much more detailed data on the countries of birth of Home and Foreign students in my surveys of the 2003, 2004 and 2005 biology undergraduate intakes at Imperial College. Of 180 Home students, 15% were born outside the British Isles. For the Foreign students, Singapore (13%) and Hong Kong (9%) occurred most frequently, followed by China, France, Germany, England and Finland.

Table 2. Countries of birth of Home and Foreign students, 2003, 2004 and 2005 Imperial College Biology intakes

Home students:
England, 146; Hong Kong, 7; China, 6; Scotland, 4; Japan, 2; Wales, 2; one each, Bermuda, France, Germany, Guyana, Ireland, Jersey, Mexico, Netherlands, Portugal, Singapore, Spain, Taiwan, Trinidad.
Overseas and Other EU students:
Singapore, 12; Hong Kong, 8; China, 5; France, 5; Germany, 5; England, 4; Finland, 4; Belgium, 3; Cyprus, 3; Netherlands, 3; South Korea, 3; Spain, 3; Taiwan, 3; USA, 3; Canada, 2; Iran, 2; Japan, 2; Malaysia, 2; one each, Bermuda, Brazil, Brunei, Colombia, Czech Republic, Greece, India, Indonesia, Italy, Ivory Coast, Mauritius, Nigeria, Poland, Portugal, Russia, Saudi Arabia, Slovakia, Sri Lanka, Switzerland, Trinidad, Uzbekistan, Zimbabwe.

Countries of birth are often indicative of ancestry and culture, but direct figures on ancestry of these students are even more useful. They are shown in Table 3.

Excluding trace amounts, 181 Home students had about 52 different ancestries, with English, Chinese, Irish, Scottish, Welsh and Indian predominant, and in total, less than 50% English ancestry in this London institute. The 95 Foreign students had about 47 different ancestries, with Chinese, French, Japanese and Indian predominant. Chinese, including Hong Kong, was the most frequent ancestry in the Foreign students and the second most frequent in the Home students, where they include ones born abroad and the offspring of Chinese immigrants. The Chinese students often refer to a "BBC", meaning a British-born Chinese.

Taking figures from different years, it is clear that students classified as "Home" are increasingly more diverse in their ancestry, departing more and more from the traditional "White Anglo-Saxon

Protestant" archetype. A school photograph of the author's school (Tiffin School, Kingston-Upon-Thames) in the late 1950s shows about 750 white boys, one brown Asian and no black pupils, whereas today the school has about 35% non-white boys. In inner London schools, non-whites now predominate, with a huge range of different languages spoken and many different cultures and religions represented. The large and varied amount of immigration into Britain and the high immigrant birth rate are progressively "racially globalising" it and its Home students, as clearly shown in Table 3, upper panel.

Table 3. Ancestries of Home and Foreign students, 2003, 2004 and 2005 Imperial College Biology intakes, in percentages

Home students:
English, 48.8; Chinese, 9.5; Irish, 6.7; Scottish, 4.8; Welsh, 4.0; Indian, 3.0; American, 1.5; Italian, 1.4; Pakistani, 1.3; South African, 1.3; French, 1.2; German, 1.2; Portuguese, 1.2; Australian, 1.0; Greek, 0.9; Iranian, 0.8; Japanese, 0.8; Jewish, 0.8; Lebanese, 0.6; Turkish, 0.6; Cypriot, 0.5; Ghanaian, 0.5; Polish, 0.5; Sudanese, 0.5; Belgian, 0.4; Filipino, 0.4; Israeli, 0.4; Sri Lankan, 0.4; Thai, 0.4; Danish, 0.3; Dutch, 0.3; Egyptian, 0.3; Grenadian, 0.3; Mexican, 0.3; Spanish, 0.3; St. Vincent, 0.3; Vietnamese, 0.3; Bangladeshi, 0.2; Colombian, 0.2; Hainanese, 0.2; Malaysian, 0.2; Anglo-Indian, 0.1; Arab, 0.1; Canadian, 0.1; Channel Islands, 0.1; Hungarian, 0.1; Maltese, 0.1; Russian, 0.1; Russian Jewish, 0.1; Singaporean, 0.1; Unknown, 0.1; Romany, 0.03.
Overseas and Other EU students:
Chinese, 34.3; French, 4.5; Japanese, 4.5; Indian, 4.1; Finnish, 3.7; Dutch, 3.5; Italian, 3.3; English, 3.2; Spanish, 3.1; German, 2.9; Korean, 2.9; Cypriot, 2.5; Iranian, 2.1, Sri Lankan, 2.1; Polish, 1.7; Greek, 1.6; Colombian, 1.3; Malaysian, 1.2; Lebanese, 1.1; Slovak, 1.1; Swiss, 1.1; Brazilian, 1.0; Czech, 1.0; Portuguese, 0.9; Angolan, 0.8; Nigerian, 0.8; Uzbek, 0.8; Ghanaian, 0.6; Hebrew, 0.6; Irish, 0.6; Romanian, 0.6; Scottish, 0.6; Venezuelan, 0.6; Zimbabwean, 0.6; Thai, 0.5; Corsican, 0.4; Hungarian, 0.4; Luxembourgeois, 0.4; Russian, 0.4; Ukrainian, 0.4; Indonesian, 0.2; Mongolian, 0.2; Swiss, 0.2; Welsh, 0.2; Amerindian, 0.1; Australian, 0.1; Belgian, 0.1.

Social Mixing Between Groups

The amount of influence Foreign students have on Home students depends to a large extent on social mixing. Since 1998 I have used my annual human diversity forms for first year biology students to record their views on the amount of social mixing between Overseas and Home students. The question asked is: *"In general, home students do not mix much socially with overseas students."* Do you think that this statement is true, partly true, untrue? Most Home and Foreign students, of either sex, think that the statement is partly true. In the last five years, the percentage of the class putting that the statement is untrue has varied from 26% in the 2000 intake, when there were 18% of Foreign students, to only 9% in the 2005 intake when there were 34% of Foreign students.

The respondents mentioned that the lack of mixing was more on the part of the Overseas students than of the Home students, with the Asians the least likely to mix with Home students, and Europeans the most likely to mix. It was noted that large groups of Asian students often socialised within national, geographical or language groups. The Japanese students seemed to have the most difficulty in conversing in English, and the Chinese students – of whom there are many – tended to keep to themselves in class and out of it. It was very noticeable in my 2006 third-year practicals that the racially Chinese (including Chinese-speakers from the UK, Singapore and Malaysia) wanted to sit and work together, and formed an extended social group, even though some spoke Mandarin and others Cantonese. In my second-year practicals, most of the Chinese chose to work with other Chinese or other Asians. One does however see some intimate relations developing between students of different ancestries. Students from countries with very few students at a university, and perhaps only one in any department in any year, have little choice but to mix with others.

The Imperial College student newspaper, *Felix* (No. 1356, 15/6/2006, pp 4-5, www.felixonline.co.uk) reported an interview with the Rector, Sir Richard Sykes, who said:

"When [overseas] students come here they must interact and be part of the community. What we don't want is to set up ghettos."

The student interviewer, Rupert Neate, commented that:

"... most students believe that there is already a degree of ghettotisation and that interaction between Home and International students is minimal at best. Some students told Felix 'that coming to Imperial has made us less inclined to engage with overseas students.' Different ethnic groups on campus rarely mix, and many students are perfectly comfortable within their own cultural groups. Friendships rarely form between them, Felix was told. The Rector also admitted that the English language competence of overseas students was big problem."

The Influence of Overseas and of Other EU Students on Home students

Sources of influence include social chatting, talking at lectures, practicals, seminars, field courses, in libraries, student unions, food outlets, bars, working together on projects, working in the same lab group, sharing student accommodation, joining the same clubs, or recreation, religious or sports groups, reading others' opinions in the student press, student events such as discos, going on holiday together, becoming romantically involved, or set-piece events such as International Nights where national societies put on displays for all to see. At Imperial College, the students I observe at International Night and national events such as Malaysian Night are mainly foreign, not British.

Foreign students often talk to Home students about their own countries and compare aspects of different ways of life, thus broadening the Home students' knowledge. The Foreign students often influence Home students to visit their own countries and homes, and in Britain may encourage them to try a wider range of foods and cultural experiences.

Some Home students undergo a large change in outlook at university, especially those who become converts to Islam, but the students who change them can be Foreign or Home students. That is why I stressed the racial mix of nominally Home students above in

Table 3. Conversely, actions and attitudes of Foreign students can be affected by the Home students, especially when the former are freed from their usual parental and cultural influences, perhaps adopting some of the local habits in a less religious and looser moral atmosphere here. A lot of Home students also get much more involved in drink and sex when away from family supervision. Some students from atheistic countries like China take up Christianity, for example, with converts often being more zealous than those brought up in a faith, and trying to inspire Home students with their new religion.

Academic Examples

Students from different cultures tend to have different attitudes to hard work and academic success. In a number of Asian countries such as Singapore and Korea, working hard and achieving high marks are admired, with social esteem to some extent reflecting the grades obtained. By contrast, many British students perversely seem to admire those who slack and do poorly. As the British long-distance runner Paula Radcliffe told *The Daily Telegraph* (11/9/2006, p 27), "Being good at school gets you picked on, so I would never put up my hand when I knew the answers because I didn't want to draw attention to myself. But being good at sport doesn't get you picked on. I never worried about winning a race." It is noticeable at Imperial College how many of the degree prize winners are Asians, especially in areas of technology.

Shortened Versions of Comments from Imperial College Biology Students

- Overseas Chinese male from Beijing. *There are very difficult exams to get into the top universities in China, so parents with enough money send their children to UK and other universities instead. Similar reasons apply to students from Taiwan, Korea and Japan. Some of the newer UK universities have whole classes full of Chinese not good enough for prestigious Chinese universities.*
- Overseas Chinese female from Beijing. *My room mate is Chinese and doing maths here. She says that 60% of the maths students are Chinese.*

- Home female, Indian ancestry but brought up in UK. *My room mate last year was Malaysian and worked extremely hard. She did not socialise with me but spent a lot of time with other Malaysian students, often speaking their home language. In the library, some Chinese students segregate themselves off and speak loudly in Chinese. Many people find it irritating because they talk loudly and because you can't understand it.*
- Overseas Chinese female from Shenzen. *There are differences in performance and competitiveness between officially sponsored and family-sponsored overseas students. On our course, government-sponsored Singaporean and Malaysian students are in many cases much better than family-sponsored ones, and that is true in other departments such as maths and electrical and electronic engineering. Students from different countries are good at different subjects. The Chinese are especially good at maths, engineering, physics, IT and finance, subjects more about figures, formulae and graphs, needing less skill in English. Biology has a higher English requirement than those subjects, needing the ability to write whole sentences. The mixing of people of different nationalities largely depends on how easily they can understand each other and how much they have in common. The degree of mixing of overseas and native students depends on how good the overseas person's English is. To talk with people from different backgrounds and mother tongue needs much courage. There is a larger mixing of Chinese with other Foreign students (especially Malaysian and Singaporean) than with native students; it is easier to communicate and understand each other's minds if your backgrounds are similar. Foreign students from different countries can become friends easily since they are all staying in a foreign city. We need to encourage the native students to talk to overseas students and overseas students to be confident enough to talk to native students.*
- Overseas male from Hong Kong. *Some Chinese students like sticking together and this makes it very hard for Home students to talk to them. I have managed to know more people (overseas and home) by trying not to stay in a group. I have more difficulty in communicating with British students. I have discussed these issues with other international students and*

we all end up asking the same question – why are Home students not interested in talking to us? If a foreigner comes to Hong Kong, I am very interested in knowing where they were born, their home country culture and family background. When I was in the UK doing A-levels in Surrey, one of the British boarding staff asked why were we always saying that international students didn't integrate with Home students, when it was the home students not integrating with the international students? This staff member told me that for 10 years in the boarding house, she had not seen a Briton who was willing to start a conversation with a Chinese student. I have rarely seen a Home student willing to come forward to start a conversation with me. But there is a time when the barrier between international and Home university students breaks: when we are all having alcohol. In hall, we had much more mixing when there was a party in the bar.

Conclusions

Foreign students compete for places in UK universities with Home students, but to very different degrees in different institutions. Overseas students, but not Other EU students, bring substantially higher fees, and both types bring some additional costs. Their presence actually keeps some courses and departments going, thereby increasing the choices for Home students. While Foreign students do have some culturally broadening effects on Home students, there is already a large and increasing diversity of cultures and racial ancestries among the Home students. The degree of mixing between Home and Foreign students can be small, especially if large groups of Asian students keep largely to themselves. The increasing "globalisation" of the ancestry and culture of Home students reduces the cultural benefits of meeting Foreign students.

Editors: Hugo de Burgh, Anna Fazackerley, Jeremy Black

UMBILICAL CULTURE: STANDARDS AND GRADE INFLATION*

Tim Birkhead

Tim Birkhead is professor of behaviour and evolution at the University of Sheffield. He took his first degree at the University of Newcastle, followed by a doctorate at the University of Oxford. He joined Sheffield in 1976 and worked as a Lecturer, Senior Lecturer and Reader in Zoology before gaining his chair in 1992. He is a fellow of the Royal Society. His popular science books include "The Red Canary" and "Promiscuity"

Among lecturers of my generation and in certain types of university there is a strong sense, real or otherwise, that the huge expansion of higher education has been accompanied by a decline in academic standards among undergraduates. Whether standards have declined, and if so by how much, is difficult to assess, not least because there have been so many other changes since the 1980s. Standards matter. In a recent edition of the *Times Higher Education Supplement* (22 September 2006) writer Fay Weldon bemoaned the lack of critical thinking among arts undergraduates. The necessity of standards is especially obvious in my own field of science where sloppy thinking won't do. Without good science planes would fall out of the sky and many more of us would die from dental abscesses.

Of the many changes that create a sense of declining standards the most important is grade inflation at both school and university level. It seems bizarre that having admitted a higher proportion of school leavers into higher education, and hence taken a greater number of what might be considered less able or less motivated individuals, the proportion of students now achieving upper second class or first degrees has actually increased. One cause of grade inflation is undoubtedly modularisation and the mechanisation of marking, themselves the consequences of increased undergraduate numbers. The irony is that politicians have turned this on its head and tell us

---

* I am grateful to Miriam Birkhead, Pat Butler, Len Hill, Robert Montgomerie and Malcolm Press for valuable discussion.

now that standards cannot have fallen because more students than ever are getting upper seconds or first class degrees and that the third class degree is virtually extinct. In this respect, we've been our own worst enemies; either naïve victims of a scam, or simply too scared of retribution to stand up and shout 'dumbing down'. But things are starting to improve.

A careful analysis of how much undergraduate standards have changed is needed, but a truly objective assessment will be difficult. What we do need however, is an admission that there is a problem and an admission that not all universities are, nor should be, the same. Let's accept that some universities are simply better or at least better at some things, than others. No-one claims that football clubs are all the same, nor do they accuse them of being elitist when they rise to top of the premiership. Let's give everyone an equal educational opportunity but accept that some individuals are more able than others (and have had better opportunities) and get into the better universities in their particular field of interest. Pretending otherwise is naïve.

Some of those I have talked to refuse to accept either that standards have changed or that standards differ between universities, claiming instead that things are merely 'different'. This reminds me of a statement made by a government fisheries biologist, who in response to the accusation of over-fishing and extirpation of cod, said: 'you cannot damage a fishery, you can only change it'. I don't want to dwell here on declining standards or grade inflation, instead I will focus on a related topic, the issue of whether students are less able to think for themselves than they were ten or twenty years ago. Convinced of this, many academics blame the prescriptive spoon-feeding culture in school. Some have gone one further, describing the current school system as a breast-feeding culture. In my opinion it is worse than that. It is umbilical: a culture of total dependence.

I will discuss three aspects of how this umbilical culture affects universities: (i) evidence that the average undergraduate is less able to think independently than previously, (ii) some possible causes, and (iii) possible solutions.

(i) Evidence for an Inability to Think

There are several lines of evidence, all anecdotal. The first is my own subjective assessment based on thirty years of teaching undergraduates (assuming age and experience are not confounding factors). My overwhelming impression is that the majority of undergraduates (but not all) are much more dependent than they were previously. They are less able to think and scared of taking intellectual risks. Another line of evidence becomes apparent if we look at the nature of the information we now provide for undergraduates: endless lists of what they should and should not learn, so-called 'learning outcomes'. Of course, it is possible that this particular change in educational policy preceded any demise in undergraduate independence and is the cause rather than a consequence of our culture of dependence. Since a lot of education is conceptual and requires a depth and breadth of understanding, providing students with tick-lists of info-bites misses the point. The third and most compelling line of evidence that undergraduates are less independent than before comes from employers themselves. As the main 'users' of undergraduates, employers feel that the graduates universities are currently producing are not adequate, particularly in terms of their ability to think outside the box.

(ii) Causes

What are the causes of this lack of independence? The problem undoubtedly starts at school. Teaching is a demoralised, under-funded and over-bureaucratised profession that now educates in a prescriptive manner designed to meet targets and league tables. The umbilical culture starts here. By recruiting teachers too often from the lower strata of undergraduates, it may even be self-perpetuating. Learning targets, lists of facts at the expense of independent thought in order to maximise schools' rankings conspire to create a fear of failure and a culture of dependency. Another factor contributing to the inability to think is the change in the way English is taught in school, the main consequence of which is a staggering inability of students to express themselves cogently in writing – now well established.[1]

---

[1] www.rlf.org.uk/fellowshipscheme/research.cfm

CAN THE PRIZES STILL GLITTER?
The Future of British Universities in a Changing World

At university the umbilical trend continues. But this is hardly surprising given the three major constraints under which universities operate: (a) increased undergraduate numbers, (b) inadequate funding, and (c) in the UK the over-arching dominance of the Research Assessment Exercise. Although many academics enter higher education because of a passion for research, many also recognise the absolute necessity of inspiring undergraduates by research-led teaching. Even in those universities not at the forefront of research, teaching still needs to be driven by scholarship. The conflict between teaching and research (and scholarship) is a long-standing one with no easy solutions, but in recent years it has been exacerbated by the obsession with research performance. Mass education, limited resources and rewards mainly for research has meant that at some universities teaching comes second. Ironically, the very bodies set up to prevent this (the Quality Assurance Agency (QAA) and Independent Evaluation of Teaching (IET),) focus primarily on audit trails rather than on the quality of teaching itself. Remarkably, in their current form these organisations do not observe any teaching directly as part of their assessment. Instead, they rely on a paper trail – meeting performance indicators via easily quantifiable but meaningless indices - a costly sidestep that achieves little more than keeping assessors employed.

In my opinion, one of the main casualties of all these changes is contact time. Providing the opportunities for undergraduates to break free from the umbilical ties of school and begin to develop their ability to think for themselves requires time, and in particular, quality contact time. Not that long ago university staff had an open-door policy, interested students would drop by for a chat, and we would be happy to spend time discussing things. This still happens, but less often and staff are more likely to avoid students in case it detracts from their grant and manuscript writing.

Although the main cause of insufficient contact time is the huge increase in student:staff ratios and increased emphasis on research, the boom in bureaucracy is also partly responsible. A less bureaucratic system would provide more time for teaching, research and scholarship.

A particularly unfortunate aspect of mass education and a major factor impinging upon the ability of undergraduates to think is the drive for uniformity imposed by educationalists. Safe, steady uniformity in the way teaching is delivered and in both what and how students are taught crushes independent thought, and often any thought at all - in students and staff alike. Uniformity is dull. Variety is the spice of a university education and forcing academics to structure and deliver their lectures in a similar way is the kiss of death. Luckily, many lecturers still retain some independence of thought and many have resisted the educationalists' demands, and deliver their teaching with passion and individuality, inspiring undergraduates – at least those that can cope with the challenge. Intellectual mediocrity is also fostered by the short-term goals engendered by continuous assessment and modular teaching. Asking students to write an account of something that requires information from different modules or (heaven forbid!) across different years, exposes their limitations. So we dodge the issue, requiring only short answers and short-term memory. Synthesis is hard! In the past when students were more independent they would challenge their teachers, but now they are as docile as babies, passively ingesting a gentle flow of nutrients that they later regurgitate – largely undigested - in their exams a few weeks later. Little wonder their intellectual growth is stunted.

(iii) Solutions

The changes in schools and universities have undoubtedly provided opportunities for more students and probably raised the overall level of education, but at what cost? According to employers the cost is that we produce undergraduates who cannot think. What is the solution? Assuming no major overhaul of the entire education system, we can either carry on much as we are doing and continue to produce a large pool of rather uniform but largely uninspiring graduates. Alternatively, we could modify the system to help students better realise their potential. In statistical terms the averages would be the same but in the first case the variability in real achievement would be low, whereas in the second it is higher. The latter scenario produces a higher proportion of graduates able to think independently. What is better for the country? If employers are demanding more graduates who can think independently, then the answer is obvious.

The reality is actually a little more complex. As all university teachers know, the very brightest students will rise to the top regardless. But it isn't these we need to focus on it is the next tier: those that require a little extra input. How do we get this group to the top? The key, I believe, is by increasing contact time. For this there needs to be less emphasis on research (or more accurately, grant acquisition), and rewards for quality teaching comparable to those for quality research. By this I do not simply mean the competent delivery of information, but inspired, individualistic and effective teaching of a standard that is on a par with top research. In the sciences at least, the most cost-effective way of teaching is the lecture: several hundred students sitting in front of one lecturer. It may be economic, but with a few exceptions this is an unexciting way to transmit information. I would abandon half of all lectures and replace them with more small-group teaching. Of course, some of this happens already in the form of tutorials, but this can also become victim of bureaucratisation. In many systems, unless the tutorial is formally classed as a module and undergraduates get credits for their tutorial performance, they don't count and students won't attend and lecturers won't deliver. Credit-acquisition, like an embryo's procurement of nutrients has fostered the umbilical culture.

The best solutions to the lack of contact time have been four-year degree courses and masters programmes. In these the better undergraduates continue their studies for an additional year during which they enjoy an improved student:staff ratio, and the close supervision of intellectually challenging projects or dissertations in their final year.

Despite the problems associated with mass education, I am optimistic. Top-up fees will almost certainly drive a change in the quality of education, as parents and students demand better value for money. Four-year degrees and masters programmes will help to improve the quality of education. It is also encouraging that after almost a generation of despair, academics and others (including employers, parents and students themselves) are finally speaking out. For years academics have been reluctant to admit publicly that university courses have been dumbed down, and the quality of independent thought sacrificed on the false altar of "equality" (*Observer* 20 August 2006). We can no longer ignore the weight of evidence that the current education system has failed in many important respects. Nor can we ignore the fact that well-trained academics are the best hope for improving the system.

Editors: Hugo de Burgh, Anna Fazackerley, Jeremy Black

STUDENT SELECTION FOR UNIVERSITIES OF THE FUTURE

John Stein

John Stein is Professor of Physiology and Fellow of Magdalen College Oxford. His primary research interest is the neurological basis of dyslexia. He chaired the medicine selection panel that rejected state schoolgirl Laura Spence in 2000, prompting accusations of elitism from Chancellor Gordon Brown. Yet he believes strongly that the benefits of Oxford's tutorial-based teaching should be made available to all those with the ability to benefit from it, irrespective of income, class, colour or creed.

One of the biggest threats to the universities of the future is political interference over whom they may select. We only have to look at the downward trend of the great 19th Century universities on the European Continent that our Victorian forbears used to admire so much, to see that this is true. In the name of equality everyone with a minimum qualification was allowed to attend university in the 20th C., and inevitably standards slipped. In contrast some UK and US universities were able to maintain very high entrance criteria and their performance has remained high. For example despite overall income from fees and endowments that is less than 10% of that which Harvard receives (generally regarded as the 'best' university in the world), Oxford and Cambridge punch much above their weight internationally, because they have retained very high standards at entry, together with individual tuition. Highly able students taught individually attract highly able teachers. Highly able teachers produce well educated and enthusiastic students, many of whom go on to contribute productively to research and so to become the next generation of teachers. Thus a virtuous circle is fertilised that can to some extent compensate for poor funding.

However this happy state of affairs is already under the same kind of attack on 'elitism' in the UK, as that to which our European cousins succumbed. Since the universities receive the major part of their income directly or indirectly from Government, Governments expect them to be accountable and to conform to the explicit or implicit requirements of the State. Under the old 'binary' system in the UK, universities were left under 'donnish dominion' to pursue scholarship and basic research with no particular requirement for economic return, and the polytechnics were required to provide the technocratic meritocracy to man the new information technology and service industries. Now all the polytechnics have become universities and there are over 1 million students at UK universities. So pressure has been mounting on the older universities to be more accountable, more like the old polytechnics, and to contribute more directly to the economy.

One way in which this has manifested itself is by frequent political criticism of the 'elitism' of some universities. Intellectual elitism is deliberately confused with social elitism and strongly attacked. An example was the allegation that some of Oxford's medical tutors turned down Laura Spence, a girl from a comprehensive school, because she was 'working class'. The Magdalen College tutors concerned were easily able to show that their procedures provided true 'equality of opportunity' for those with the requisite abilities, irrespective of irrelevant factors such as race, religion, colour or class. Nevertheless the criticism was damaging. Even selection purely on the basis of merit is deemed to be unfair by some; they argue that high quality university education is so important to all that it should be provided for all, irrespective of ability. Maybe in an ideal world this might be possible, but in a world of limited resources it makes no sense to provide highly academic training for all, many of whom would not be able to benefit from it. Nobody would dream of training any but elite footballers for a football team.

We should therefore be proud of and defend intellectual elitism, but argue strongly for the distinction of this from social elitism. We can successfully defend ourselves from such attacks only if we can show that we select only those who will profit most from high quality undergraduate education, and therefore are likely to benefit society most. These students must be selected to have the highest motivational, intellectual and academic potential, and we must be able to show that we pay no attention at all to irrelevant factors such as their colour, religion, race, social class or ability to contribute financially. If we can demonstrate with clear evidence that our systems achieve these aims, then the attacks should lose all force.

But here we run into a serious social problem, namely inequality of educational opportunity further back in children's development. Governments tend to expect universities to compensate for deficits in schooling and to blame us if we fail. But fail we will, because really we have no power to correct primary and secondary educational inequality; and it is serious. 93% of UK children are educated at schools supported by the State; and only 7% go to fee paying, 'independent' schools. But most independent schools have a selective entry system, and this, coupled with their generally better facilities and higher staff-pupil ratio compared with state-maintained schools accounts for the fact that independent schools almost always occupy the top places in league tables of academic achievement at GCSE and A-level.

At Oxbridge entrants are required to achieve the highest standards in their school leaving exam and over 95% of those admitted have obtained at least AAA, 3As, at A-level. In 2005 only c. 3% of the 723,000 UK pupils who stayed on at school to take A levels or equivalent, i.e. only 22,000 school leavers, obtained this high standard of 3 As. The problem for elite universities is that of these, 9,000 (40%) were educated at fee-paying schools, even though these schools only educate 7% of the population. Thus the elite pupils who achieve the highest standards at A-level are six times over represented at fee-paying schools and equivalently under-represented at state schools.

There is a further aspect to this social problem that is not revealed by these figures. Simple calculations derived from the way intelligence is 'normally' distributed suggest that probably many more pupils than 22,000 per year are capable of obtaining 3 As at A-level. There is a high and highly significant correlation ($r = 0.5$) between IQ and school performance.[1] A number of studies have shown that anybody with an IQ that is 1.5 standard deviations above average or more (ie having an IQ of 122.5 or greater) should be capable of achieving the highest standards in school leaving exams. This means that c. 51,000 of the UK school leavers in 2005 were probably capable of achieving AAA at A level, whereas less than half these actually did so.

---

[1] Mackintosh, N, IQ and Human Intelligence. 1998 Oxford: OUP, UK

What these calculations also imply is that most fee-paying schools are remarkably successful in helping their pupils to gain 3 As if they are potentially capable of achieving this standard. They educate only 50,000 of our 18 year olds; yet they helped 9,000 of these to achieve 3As. If IQ were normally distributed among Independent pupils we would only expect 3,500 to achieve this standard.

Unfortunately, in contrast however, State schools appear to fail to help c.30,000 of their pupils who might have gained the highest scores, to actually achieve them. This is not intended to be a criticism of any State school teachers, most of whom are incredibly dedicated, conscientious and hard working. It is a problem of numbers and lack of the resources that fee-paying schools can provide. Of course also these calculations are very rough; but they support what many people suspect, that many State schools are to some extent failing their most able pupils.

There is yet another problem for Oxbridge and other elite universities. A-levels seem to have been getting easier and they do not have enough discriminatory power for selection. Even 22,000 applicants with 3 As at A-level are too many for the c. 6000 places per year that Oxbridge has to offer. Hence we have to introduce a further layer of discrimination, which currently takes the form of a further examination in the applicant's subject together with two or more interviews. But as implied above, these methods of selection for interview and entry may well miss out students from state-maintained schools who have the potential to do well at university but have not achieved high enough grades in examinations so far.

However our further layer of discrimination actually offers us some flexibility to attempt to compensate to some extent for the failings of State education. But political attacks should not lead us to travel supinely down the path of 'positive discrimination' in favour of State applicants. We believe that it would be totally unfair to penalise applicants from fee paying schools in this way; at the margin that would mean depriving better fee paying applicants of their rightful places. If we believe in education at all then the fact that fee paying schools probably achieve the best for their pupils should be encouraged, not penalised.

Nevertheless our Entrance procedures allow us the possibility of trying to devise a means of identifying the students who have the highest academic potential, despite relatively poor teaching. We want to find, from whatever source, the students who have the most enthusiasm for their subject, the highest intelligence, the most searching critical ability, the most fertile imaginations and the strongest motivation. These talents are not particularly well captured by A-level or even current scholastic aptitude type (SAT) exams. But if we could develop techniques for identifying academic potential in those who have not been so well taught, we would be able to select the elite students we want who have the highest academic potential, even if they might seem at first sight inferior as regards current exam achievement, due to inferior schooling.

Before we can do this we have to decide what abilities and skills we think will be really important for success in the future university. At present we can all agree that we would like to be able to test imagination, motivation, enthusiasm and ability to think clearly and logically, and critically evaluate evidence. At Oxbridge, tutors use extensive interviews to look for these qualities. But interviews have well known drawbacks. However careful we are to structure them fairly, they tend to benefit the articulate, outgoing and self confident product of fee paying schools at the expense of the less well educated, less experienced, possibly more introverted, but maybe deeper thinker from a State school.

Ideally therefore we would like to have more objective instruments to test thinking ability and motivation. These should not just test a student's ability to regurgitate factual information, so called 'surface learners', since knowledge of facts does not necessarily imply understanding, and most facts are but provisional anyway, liable to be modified by later discoveries. Instead we need to develop means of assessing students' motivation, thinking processes and learning styles that will reveal academic potential rather than just current achievement.

Could a simple IQ test be sufficient? Unfortunately although IQ does predict academic success it is well known that young people from disadvantaged backgrounds tend on average to get poorer scores on IQ tests than those from more privileged backgrounds and this difference is likely to be due to the nature of the tests rather than intrinsic differences in intelligence. Furthermore standard IQ tests simply do not have the discriminating power at the upper end of the range to be useful for selection for elite universities.

Jane Mellanby and I therefore set out to develop a technique for university applicants to assess the ability to think open-endedly. In particular we were looking for evidence of 'deep' learning, the desire not just to learn the facts about a situation, but also to actively dig deeper and understand how those facts arise and fit together. We know that active involvement is the most effective way of teaching – getting people to teach themselves, whether discovering the effects of gravity by playing with water and sand in nursery school, measuring and weighing things in primary school, pipetting acid against base in secondary school, or writing and testing computer programmes at university. Such active learning fosters a deep learning style that is well known to be advantageous to teaching yourself at university.

We therefore developed a pilot test in which we gave a sample of candidates for places at Oxford University a short passage to read and then asked questions on it designed to get them to produce their own ideas about how to validate the evidence, pick out key points and see how to use them in arguing a case; all features that are particularly valued in the majority of courses at the most academic universities. The passage was about the Green Revolution, a subject that we thought most lively sixth-formers would find interesting and of which they were likely to have some awareness. So as not to favour those who had had the opportunity to be taught essay-writing, the answers were to be written in short notes rather than essay form. We also asked them some standardised questions that have been developed to determine learning style.[2]

Our main objective was to develop a test that we could use to assess thinking skills without being biased in favour of students who came from schools where more intensive teaching might have given them a more extensive knowledge base. And we were gratified to find that our test did achieve these aims at least to some extent. Importantly there were no differences between the State and Independent students' results, either on average or in distribution,

---

[2] 2 Biggs, J B, *Student approaches to learning and studying.* 1987, Melbourne: Australian Council for Educational Research.

confirming that the test did not favour Independent school students particularly.

Since it is generally agreed that a deep learning style is advantageous for high level academic achievement, we hoped that the commentary test would actually probe students capacity for deep learning. We realised that it would not be possible to use the standardised questions about learning style themselves for selection by examination, because they are too transparent; the students would very soon learn what we were looking for and learn not to answer them honestly. Again we were pleased to find that those who did well on the commentary displayed a clear deep learning style in the standardised questions. Furthermore the one third of the sample who were ultimately accepted at Oxford had significantly higher deep learning scores than those who were not offered places.

Two of the questions in the commentary were: 'How would you know how generally applicable the findings described in the text were?' and 'How would you persuade people to change their practices in the light of these findings'. The candidates who scored highly on these open-ended commentary questions and also highly on the learning style questionnaire (questions about enjoying their studies and enjoying seeing how things fit together) had a 75% chance of obtaining a place at Oxford. Thus it seems that the Oxford Tutors who admitted these students were using (intentionally or unconsciously) similar criteria to those identified by our test. Therefore they were probably tapping into the same deep learning values: enjoyment of the subject, actively fitting different parts of their knowledge together and the ability to see how to validate empirical findings in a wider context. These are indeed qualities that most university teachers value in their students and which they try to explore in interviews.

We also found that scores on the commentary questions at interview time predicted quite well who was going to get a First Class degree 3 years later. Indeed, high scores on the commentary question, 'How would you persuade people to change their practices in the light of the reported findings?' produced a greater than 70% chance of obtaining a first class degree 3 years later.

We concluded from our study that questions designed to identify deep learners could be used to select high flying students, to some extent independently of their previous academic attainment. In short, our results suggested that identifying deep learning could indeed help us to detect unusual ability in those who have not been so well taught at State schools. Reassuringly they also showed us that even our current interview procedures, for all their faults, are already to some extent identifying deep learners, although not explicitly, to the benefit of our accurate selection of an intellectual elite, irrespective of race, religion, colour or class. Being able to show that this is what we actually achieve should help to defuse criticism of the selection practices of elite universities

But perhaps we should worry that all our efforts may be irrelevant to the selection of students for the universities of the future. As information technology changes their nature towards 'virtual' 'Universities of the Air' with perhaps no physical buildings at all, will deep learning lose its importance? After all 'computers will soor be able to work out how everything works'.

I believe that precisely the opposite will be the case. As simple factual knowledge becomes more and more easily accessible from the Internet and other information resources, the ability to memorise facts, which at present enables surface learners to pass exams very successfully without necessarily attaining much understanding, will become less and less important. Instead we will urgently need the deep learners, people who can work out the potential consequences of change, and therefore help to cope with the effects of man's closer and closer interface with computers and other electronic inhabitants of cyber space. Knowing that 1066 is the date of the Battle of Hastings or that eicosapentanoic acid has a 20 carbon atom chain and 5 double bonds between them, will carry less status, as these facts will be more or less instantly available from information resources. However the thinking skills provided by deep learning will be at a premium to enable us to see parallels and connections that computers cannot see, and hence to help us to adapt to the changes that are being driven by the rapid rise of information technology.

The main danger of the information technology age from the point of view of education will probably be its tendency to convert learners into increasingly passive spectators. This may foster the opposite of active deep learning habits, a tendency to lazily wait to be told about things, which we know to be a very inefficient way of learning, rather than going out and actively finding out. Also computer games, distance education and internet searches are all solitary pursuits; yet man is a naturally gregarious species. Less and less involvement in collective learning, in team sports or other group activities will provide a recipe for the disevolution of active learning that may spell disaster for our future.

Even our individuality may be at risk; information machines may become, like other tools such as the violinist's bow, incorporated into our own self images. This could change our personalities in totally unpredictable ways. Our only hope is to foster the one thing that humans still have over computers: the ability for creative thought and deep understanding. It will take highly talented deep thinkers educated at elite institutions to work out effective ways of harnessing the advance of information technology for our future well being and to obviate what at present seem more like a train of unremittingly adverse consequences of the onward march of the computer age.

NATIONAL RESEARCH ASSESSMENT IN HIGHER EDUCATION*

Eric Thomas

Professor Eric Thomas has been Vice Chancellor of the University of Bristol since 2001. He studied Medicine at the University of Newcastle, and trained as an Obstetrician and Gynaecologist. In 1991 he was appointed Professor of Obstetrics and Gynaecology at the University of Southampton and became Dean of the Faculty of Medicine, Health and Biological Sciences in 1998. He was a Consultant Gynaecologist from 1987 to 2001. Professor Thomas is Chair of the Worldwide Universities Network and of the Research Policy Committee of Universities UK. He is a member of Agora's Advisory Council.

Intermittent assessment of research quality through a formal national exercise, the Research Assessment Exercise (RAE), is arguably the most powerful intervention in UK higher education of the last 20 years. The exercise has both its supporters and its opponents and is a continuing topic for heated debate both inside and outside HE. Supporters argue that the net effect of the successive exercises has been to improve UK research output and the management and leadership of research and thus ensure that the UK remains internationally competitive. Other beneficial secondary effects identified are that it has highlighted the quality of UK research to the government and acted as a benchmark for institutional leaders and managers. Critics argue that the improvement in quality and management would have occurred without the exercise, that it carries a large and unnecessary administrative burden, it distorts institutional research leadership and planning, it malignly influences behaviour particularly through the academic transfer market and that all the improvement in the outcome of the exercise is a result of universities learning to play the game better. In this chapter I shall try and tease out the beneficial and negative impacts of the RAE on UK universities

* Acknowledgements. I am grateful for advice received from Dr Sian Thomas and Dr David Pilsbury

and then consider whether the continuation of such a national exercise in a globalised world continues to be logical and, if so, in what form.

The use of the word national in the title of this chapter is quite deliberate because there has been plenty of research assessment taking place outside the national context for a long time. The refereeing of both grant applications and papers submitted for publication is a major process of research assessment. The impact of publications both in citation and in longevity is a further assessment. Invitations to give keynote addresses and plenary presentations to major meetings are a secondary assessment of the quality of an individual's research output, as are invitations to join editorial boards and to lead learned societies. Finally promotion and appointment to research leadership positions, or being given tenure, are mechanisms of assessment. This type of assessment is the bedrock of the United States research system, which is the most successful in the world. It has also proved to be academically fit for purpose and ensured that the UK was at the forefront of discovery all of the last century. There would appear to be no imperative in the 1980s that the UK needed an RAE to improve its research ambitions or output. In which case why was such an exercise deemed necessary?

The main clue lies in the name of the first two exercises – the Research Selectivity Exercise. In its publication "The Strategy for Higher Education into the 1990s",[1] the University Grants Committee (UGC) recommended a "more selective allocation of research support among universities in order to ensure that resources are used to best advantage". The first two exercises only informed a very small proportion of the distribution of funding, In 1992, however, the dissolution of the binary funding regime meant that all the research funding was informed by the exercise thus ensuring that selectivity was strong and that the funding did not flow from the research intensive universities to the new universities on the basis of student numbers alone. In short, the exercise was initiated to distribute funding in particular the block grant from the UGC, which is now distributed as QR by the funding councils. There appears to be no evidence of an imperative in the 1980s to initiate national assessment

---

[1] University Grants Committee (1984) "A Strategy for Higher Education in to the 1990s" London. Her Majesty's Stationery Office.

either to improve the quality of UK research or its management or to inform policy about research funding.

There can be little doubt that the RAE has fulfilled the purpose for which it was initiated; the funding of research, through all potential streams, has become more selective. QR has become increasingly concentrated in a small number of universities, particularly those with a strong science, engineering and medical base. In 1997–98 approximately 56% of QR funding went to 5 and 5* units of assessment and this increased to just over 82% in 2002–3 after the 2001 RAE. Part of this increase reflects the increased volume of staff in 5 and 5* units but part also reflects increased selectivity. Selectivity has further increased with changes to the funding variables meaning that 86% of QR in 2006–7 went to 5 and 5* units. This selectivity also concentrates other forms of funding, particularly research council and charitable funding, to those institutions. This is not necessarily because of a perception that they are high quality as a result of the outcome of the RAE but because it is only those institutions that can afford the investment in infrastructure, including cutting edge equipment, and staff to perform such research and thus attract further funding. Furthermore such concentration also enables more opportunities for interdisciplinarity and for the creation of more ambitious research agendas. There is a predictable upward spiral here for those institutions. It is not the purpose of this chapter to analyse whether such an outcome is best for UK universities but it is clear that the exercise has delivered its main objective.

Furthermore the design of RAE 2008 will inevitably increase this selectivity. Research output and environment will be graded with percentages of four star, three star, two star and one star work. One star is work of national significance and two star and above is defined as clearly international. As previous RAEs have shown the lowest grade receives either little or no funding so this exercise will inevitably focus funding in two star or above. Essentially RAE 2008 will focus on the assessment and funding of only a proportion of the work that would have been graded as 5 and 5* in 2001.

There are many publications testifying that the quantity and quality of the UK's research output has improved over the last 20 years. Many also cite the Research Assessment Exercise as one of the main reasons for this. There is, of course, no proof of a causal relationship here and such evidence would be almost impossible to produce. The rebased average impact factor (RBI) for UK output has improved since 2000 although it remained static from 1995 to 2000. Germany's average is approximately the same and has shown a greater improvement from a lower base since 1995. Germany has no RAE. More detailed analysis of the data shows that the distribution of impact is highly skewed with a very small proportion of the publications having between 4 to 8 times greater impact and thus increasing the average. In fact more than half the UK's output is never cited or has an RBI of less than 1.[2]

The conclusion must be that the main increase in the quality of UK research has been in a small amount of top quality output. It is perfectly rational to explain this as a result of increased selectivity. The more infrastructure, resources and staff are concentrated in fewer locations it more likely that, in general, the output will be high quality, especially in science. There is no evidence that the process that is used to concentrate those resources increases quality; the explanation is the concentration itself.

Another benefit claimed of the RAE is that it has led to better leadership and management of research within institutions. Certainly preparation for an audit exercise will identify both academic areas and staff who are not research active and those who are most productive in research income and output. Managers will then be able to focus resources into those productive areas and re-arrange job plans so that they reflect the real activity of staff. Such managerial actions should be routine and not require an external audit exercise to initiate them, particularly if the university has a system of regular departmental review. However, if the RAE has forced all institutions to do this that must be a significant benefit. Furthermore the audit will have produced an institutional map of research activity which will have enabled leaders to think about collaborative research and interdisciplinarity in innovative ways – for example, the emergence of interdisciplinary themes as the structure prosecuting research has probably been amplified by the managers knowing how the research maps in their universities. Some argue that such a thematic approach

---

[2] Adams J 2006. How Good is the UK Research Base? Higher Education Policy Institute

is inappropriate but in a world where the research problems are increasingly complex and require multiple intellectual approaches many would support them as the best was forward.

It is much more debatable whether these benefits have translated into more logical research strategies over the whole university. Firstly there is the impact on individual behaviour. Clearly the existence of RAE will mean that individual academics will be focussing on their own profile for both assessment and promotion. This may well deter them from long term and riskier projects and may also decrease their desire for inter-disciplinary work which will lead to multi-author publications that they perceive will not carry so much weight in the assessment. If this individual behaviour is collectivised it will create a risk averse institution in which inter-disciplinarity carries less imperative.

Certainly the existence of an RAE will have been one factor that will have concentrated strategic thinking and planning of research at institutional level but it is possible that other variables would have forced universities into such strategic planning anyway. The most important variables are the increasing expense, complexity and interdisciplinarity of research in an environment where resources are constrained. Even the very largest universities globally are not resourced to fund any research in any discipline and have to focus their resources on their strengths. The highest performing research environment in the world, the United States of America, has not required an RAE to get it to that position although it is possible that some funders do use some metrics to inform their decisions. Furthermore, a single national and inflexible RAE will squeeze out strategic thinking that could have given much more weight to local, regional and international variables working on individual universities.

What is clear is that the RAE has led to some irrational planning behaviour in institutions. Knowledge generation is a long-term activity. The lead time between considering and deciding strategic direction, initiating and completing the changes needed, finding the funds, performing the research, generating and publishing the output and that output having some impact will be in the order of ten years. It cannot be rational to base such strategic planning on an irregular, retrospective, external audit exercise with a shorter cycle than that described above, over which the institution has no control, and the methodology of which will unpredictably change. In addition the outcome has an unknown and unpredictable link to future funding formula.

However, certainly over the last 15 years, it has been common to hear institutional leaders talking about "investing for the RAE". Even superficial analysis shows such investment incapable of producing an economically sustainable return. The quantum of QR is finite and all universities will be ensuring they maximise the possible returns. The financial outcome of successive RAEs has been to increase the selectivity of funding and there is usually one university that does very well and one rather badly; all the others see a marginal change one way or another. What doesn't happen is that a large number of universities see a large increase in QR unless the total amount of money allocated by the funding councils increases. However, the investment strategy leading up to the RAE leaves universities with large recurrent costs, particularly in salaries. Even large universities find this deficit difficult to manage and for smaller institutions it can be particularly damaging. A sort of boom and bust cycle occurs with major investment before the RAE and significant retrenchment afterwards because the outcome has not delivered the expected increase in income.

There seems to be no learning curve over this perverse behaviour. Many university leaders are investing in staff in the run up to RAE 2008 to improve their outcome, in spite of the fact that the new assessment procedures mean that even the most outstanding researcher can only add marginal financial benefit. There can be no economic benefit for attracting an expensive research star. In fact the outcome is entirely the opposite unless that individual can generate massive indirect cost recovery on research grants. It bears repetition that the financial position for the English Higher Education sector is a surplus of 1.1% in 2004–5 when the minimum for financial sustainability is in the order of 3% to 5%. Only two out of the twenty largest universities in turnover have a surplus that exceeds 3% and six are in deficit, including three of the largest five. Of course there are many reasons why this financial position exists but to continue to have an intermittent exercise that stimulates such damaging investment behaviour is certainly one powerful force.

CAN THE PRIZES STILL GLITTER?
The Future of British Universities in a Changing World

The retrospective and intermittent nature of the exercise means that current research funding is predicated on work that was performed many years before. In certain disciplines in RAE 2001 work could be submitted for assessment that had been published in 1994. The outcome of RAE 2001 will continue to inform QR funding until 2008–9 i.e. the funding will be based on work that was published 15 years ago and actually written a longer time before then. Furthermore, staff who were assessed may have left their universities and whole research groups may have ceased and others have started without any of those changes affecting QR funding. Many argue that such a profound disconnect between the basis of QR funding and the current research activity of a university is nor only inappropriate but also inequitable and perversely fails to reward those investing in physical and human research infrastructure in a timely manner.

Perhaps the behaviour precipitated by the current RAE structure that is most discussed and disliked is the creation of a transfer market in the very best researchers. Academics have always moved between universities but the decision to structure the RAE so that it is a snapshot on a single date has led to a very competitive transfer market with the big and financially powerful universities aggressively seeking staff in the year or two before the assessment date. The university who loses the member of staff receives no credit for the work they had done prior to the transfer. Some have likened this to a situation whereby when a Premiership footballer transfers to another club, he takes all the goals he scored with him and they are then credited to his new club thus affecting the league position of both clubs. It has also created a wage spiral for these highly desirable staff, which may not be a bad outcome but adds to costs. Senior managers have had to learn to deal with staff playing one institution off against another, an unedifying experience at best. The imperative for this activity is less with RAE 2008 because a single individual can only add an incremental increase under the new assessment structure rather than move a whole unit to a higher grade. However the behaviour still continues even when there is no chance of a positive economic output. It is, of course, entirely right for a university to attempt to attract staff to an area of research that it has identified as important strategically so that they can maximise the academic output and creativity. That is the business of universities. What is not right is when such transfers are solely led by a potential but actually unrealisable, economic RAE benefit.

There is a remaining question about whether the RAE serves a purpose for the UK in the current globalised world of Higher Education. It can be argued that the award of a high assessment will ensure that worldwide competitors recognise the excellence of the research in that discipline in that university. However there is not a great deal of evidence that it will influence peer behaviour. In spite of small numbers of international academics sitting on panels, the RAE is essentially a parochial exercise. In fact its parochial nature means that it does not influence global league tables. RAE scores may influence the choices of overseas postgraduate research students but peer assessment of research quality will be based on the latest publications and presentations from an academic department not a historical score that many do not even understand. A clear case could be made that the position of a university in one of the three current global league tables will have much more impact - and those positions are predominantly based on metrics.

In conclusion, evidence of a causal relationship between the RAE audit process and improvement in research quality and leadership and management cannot be proved and it is logical to suppose that these improvements have occurred as a result of managerial necessity and the increasing selectivity of research funding. On the other hand, there is evidence that the current RAE audit process precipitates behaviours which can be damaging to universities and their staff. The key policy issue for the future is not the shape of the audit process, although this receives the lion's share of debate, but how far selectivity of funding should be taken. Clearly extreme selectivity would lead to a situation whereby the intellectual environment of many universities would radically change and the capacity to produce an important workforce would decrease. A very few universities cannot provide all the career research scientists needed for the UK. On the other hand low selectivity would simply spread the funding too thinly and ensure that the very best research environments cannot flourish and compete in a globally competitive sector.

The decision over the degree of selective funding is for government, in discussion with the sector, to take. Once that decision is clear then a mechanism whereby those institutions or groups who receive this selective funding are identified needs to be designed. Ideally the mechanism should be timely and relevant, have a low administrative burden and not precipitate inappropriate management and investment decisions. There is no *a priori* reason why metrics of research income and output could not mostly or wholly fulfil this task. Even if they were averaged over a three-year period they would be much more timely than the current process and represent current peer review. They would enable funding to reflect current changes in a university's research environment. They would create some different behaviours but they would not precipitate the boom and bust investment cycle described earlier and the transfer market would be based on academic imperatives alone. Finally, the administrative burden inside universities would be much less.

Whether the RAE is an emperor without clothes will remain an unknown but it is certainly a child of its time. Even if it is portrayed as having many positive effects, there is little evidence that there is much to gain from continuing it in its current form because those effects are now hard wired into institutional practice and are counter balanced by the damage of the behaviours it precipitates. A well-managed, incremental transition over a few years to a more metric-based approach will surely serve higher education in the UK better.

Editors: Hugo de Burgh, Anna Fazackerley, Jeremy Black

THE GREAT WHITE LIES

Boris Johnson

Boris Johnson is Shadow Minister for Higher Education. He has been the Conservative MP for Henley-on-Thames since 2001, and has served as Shadow Minister for the Arts and Vice Chairman of the Conservative Party. He was educated at Eton and Balliol College, Oxford. He worked for The Times and The Wolverhampton Express and Star before joining The Daily Telegraph, where he was successively a leader and feature writer, EU Correspondent, and Assistant Editor. He was Editor of the Spectator from 1999-2005. He writes a weekly column for The Daily Telegraph, and has published five books.

I was looking at a child's homework the other day, and wondering how I should react, when it hit me that I was teetering slap bang in the middle of the central dilemma of all educational policy.

On the one hand the homework wasn't bad; on the other hand, it was very far from brilliant. So what did I do? Did I pretend that it was a work of genius, in order to boost the morale of my offspring? Or did I tell the child to pull its socks up and try harder?

There are many on the right of the argument who think we have gone too far with all this praise. Look here, they say, let's stop this "All Must Have Prizes" nonsense. Let's call a spade a spade and admit that some people are just less successful than others, and less academically gifted than others, and some people, frankly, should pull their finger out.

It is a deep conservative insight that there can be no success without failure, no triumph without disaster, no breakthrough without effort, and so these conservative figures demand a bit more chiaroscuro in the educational landscape, a bit more black and white, because realism, they say, is the only way to bring out the best in our children.

Then there are those on the left who think that life is frankly a bit short, and nature a bit too cruel in her distribution of brains and talent, and that on the whole we are better off if we connive in some polite fictions. It is their instinct that we will all get more out of our children if we are encouraging, and big them up, and make them feel happy and confident, and that is why they think there is little point in getting in a grump about some shoddy piece of work - far better to say the glass is half-full, even if it is only actually a quarter full.

All these thoughts flashed through my head as I looked at the piece of homework, and eventually, because I am a loving parent, pronounced it really jolly good in what I hoped were tones at once encouraging but not delusively flattering. And if I lied at all about my true feelings, I hope all will agree that it was a white lie, offered in the hope of progress.

We all approve of such white lies. Hypocrisy is the indispensable handmaiden of civilisation; and yet we are all now collaborating in a series of white lies - huge white lies - about our educational system, and the trouble is that these white lies are well meant, but they are increasingly allowing the privileged to hold back the underprivileged in such a way as to cause serious social injustice.

I thought of our tendency to collective hypocrisy the other day, when a group of university Vice-Chancellors were discussing the problems of access to Higher Education. It was a gloomy discussion. Everybody wanted to encourage more kids from the lowest socio-economic groups to get to university. Huge efforts were being made to reach out to schools and families that did not traditionally see themselves as university feeders. Undergraduates were all out proselytising and evangelising for the benefits of a university education, in a way that never happened 20 years ago; and quite right that they should be. We all agreed that encouraging access would be a top priority for any new Tory government.

I mean it. Be in no doubt that the Cameroon Tories are enthusiasts for universities as mobilisers of British society. I believe a university education is a wonderful thing in itself, and also has the potential to be culturally, intellectually and materially enriching. It is still true that the average graduate earns 58 per cent more than the average non-graduate. To a very large extent, the story of the expansion of British higher education (in which Conservative governments played a distinguished role) is the story of the rise of the British middle classes.

It is the story of female emancipation in this country. It is in many ways a triumph; and it is one of the few disappointments that we have been so unsuccessful, so far, in recruiting university candidates from the bottom quintile of the income groups.

In spite of all the outreach programmes, and the money spent on Aim Higher, we are still stuck on 14 per cent of Group D who make it to university, and 77 per cent from Group A, and that position has been unchanged for about 20 years. That does not mean that Aim Higher is futile; far from it. But it does mean that we need to look at the problems in schools, and I was slightly taken aback when at the end of the discussion every Vice-Chancellor made the same lugubrious observation.

These Vice-Chancellors were by no means reactionaries; many of them were lefties of one kind or another. But they all agreed, with sad shakings of the head, that it was much simpler when we had Grammar Schools. When there were Grammar Schools, they said, there was a ladder for poor bright kids, and it was a doddle for top universities to recruit from the maintained sector. That was why 60 per cent of Oxbridge students were from the state sector in the 1960s, they said, when those universities struggle to manage 50 per cent state school entry today.

Of course they were being smart, these Vice-Chancellors, and subtly throwing the problem back at me, the politician; because they know there is not a cat's chance in hell of any party bringing back Grammar Schools, en masse, across the educational landscape. It wasn't Tony Crosland who was mainly responsible for the extermination of the Grammar Schools, nor was it Shirley Williams. It was Margaret Thatcher who closed the largest share of them, and that was because millions of Tory voters had become thoroughly disgruntled with being told that their little Johnny or Samantha was not bright enough, and would have to go to the secondary modern; and though they might in theory approve of the concept of failure in the classroom, and academic differentiation, they jolly well didn't want it applied to their own children - or not at the age of 11, at any rate.

The Grammar School solution was too brutal, and so we took that option away in most of the country, and in so doing removed both the unpleasant divisiveness and, of course, the ladder for the bright poor. But it is just not true that in abolishing most of the Grammar Schools we have done away with selection in our schools, or with people's ineradicable desire to do the best for their children. That is the Great White Lie number one: that the British ruling classes are prepared to see equality of opportunity for children of all socio-economic backgrounds. And to see how the British elites collaborate in this deceit - whatever their ostensible political convictions - let us take three people of unimpeachable liberal credentials: Tony Blair, Polly Toynbee and myself.

What do we have in common? Well, we all products of Oxford, far and away the most politically successful educational institution in Britain. We are all beneficiaries, therefore, of a highly selective education, and we are all (why not admit it?) members of the ruling elite of this country.

Much more important, however: we all USE selective education. Tony Blair just about kept up the fiction that he and Cherie used state education until it was revealed in the Spectator that he hired private tutors from Westminster, one of the most expensive and brutally selective schools in the country, to get his children ready for university entrance. I use fee-paying schools for at least some of my children, since generations of Labour misrule have not been good for secondary education in Islington. As for darling Polly Toynbee, who, with her former co-Guardianista Melanie Phillips now forms one of the ideological book-ends of the modern Conservative party, she appears to be in the same position as me, in that she has sent at least some of her offspring to fee-paying schools. This is not a fact that she makes much of in her newspaper philippics against educational selection.

If you wanted evidence that even the hard left is willing to collaborate in this hypocrisy, then I would cite Diane Abbott MP. Faced with a choice between the reality of the educational system in Hackney and the deep unbeatable maternal instinct to do as well as possible by her children, she did the same as Polly and Tony - she talked left but acted right. She went for the fee-paying option, and quite rightly put her children before her credentials as a lefty. More and more are following her lead. At least 7 per cent of the population now uses fee-paying education, and then there are the 190-odd grammar schools still in existence, and we still have not exhausted the relentless cunning of the middle classes in maximising their advantages - to make sure that their children get into the good schools, and therefore (by mathematical necessity) to reduce the opportunities for those children who are not blessed with rich or pushy parents.

In polite lefty circles it is still taboo to talk, for instance, about the boom in tutoring for children in primary school. Well-heeled Islington parents will feel all warm inside because they are doing the local primary school the favour of sending it their well-adjusted middle class progeny. But all the while they stealthily ensure that when the moment comes they will be ready to flee the benighted borough (like Tony and Cherie) by providing them (like Tony and Cherie) with private tutoring. In some Islington schools about half the children are receiving tutoring after hours, at great expense, from fancy tutor groups. No one in the liberal intelligentsia who extols this system - one thinks of Margaret Hodge, who did so much to wreck education in Islington, and who used tutors for her own children - has given any thought to the deep injustice this entails for the 50 per cent of the class whose parents cannot afford private tuition.

These lefties rail against the independent sector, and charitable status for private schools; but it does not seem to occur to them that they are introducing serious division and injustice into state school classrooms, and using money to do it. Instead of taking an interest in the attainments of the whole class, these tutor-using middle classes have the secret satisfaction of knowing that their own children are insulated from low standards and low expectations, since any deficiencies can be remedied out of school.

No wonder we have such a catastrophic national record in basic primary school literacy and numeracy. It is always the middle classes who are able to manipulate this supposedly universalist system, and make a mockery of the notion of equality of access. If there is a good church school, it is the middle class parents who will have the time and the wit to do the necessary in the eyes of the Lord to get their children in. If there is a good school in a certain area, it is the middle classes who have the economic throw-weight to move into that catchment area, thereby pushing up house prices and making the place even less attainable for the children of the poor.

CAN THE PRIZES STILL GLITTER?
The Future of British Universities in a Changing World

There is only one advantage that such poorer children might have - and that is that they might be naturally smarter than their middle class contemporaries. They may have parents with less influence, time or money. But they may very well be brainier. And so what do we do, in this supposedly equality-conscious country? We absolutely forbid them from making use of the one advantage they may possess. We allow selection by wealth. We allow selection by religion. We allow selection by geographical catchment area. But we have decided that any kind of academic selection, between schools, would be deeply unfair. We feel good about it; we feel what we are doing is morally generous, while in reality we are allowing a conspiracy by the affluent 70 per cent to protect their children from any challenge from bright children among the poorest 30 per cent.

It may very well be that selection at 11 was too early, and I stress for the absence of doubt that no one is proposing a systematic restitution of the Grammar Schools. That is simply off the political agenda, for the reasons I outline above. But in forbidding any kind of academic selection in most of the maintained sector we are quietly entrenching the dominance and privileges of the middle class, and we are ensuring that this country's educational system now resembles two separate planetary systems, drifting ever further apart. Last year 27.1 per cent of pupils in the independent sector gained three A's at A level, compared with 8 per cent in the maintained sector. At GCSE level, comprehensive schools achieved 54 per cent with 5 or more A*-C grades, while the independent sector had 90 per cent.

No wonder it is such a struggle for these Vice-Chancellors to admit more children from underprivileged backgrounds; no wonder the massive expansion in Higher Education - which has been an overwhelmingly good thing - has been overwhelmingly middle class. And so we bully the universities into trying to remedy, at tertiary level, injustices that have been long ago perpetrated at primary level, and we make them sign access agreements and all the rest of it, and above all, in the run-up to university entrance, we try to conceal the growing attainment gap between the maintained and the Independent/Grammar School sectors.

We do this by splurging ever more A-grades at the cohort of candidates. Forty years ago, in 1966, the proportion of candidates getting an A in A level Mathematics was seven per cent. In 2006 it was 43.5 per cent. Now you do the maths. How much better at maths are today's A-level students, on those figures? It's about 620 per cent. Do you believe that? Neither do I. Even allowing for the possibility that the comparison is unfair, and that the exam may have changed, it is obvious that there is serious grade inflation, and that is the second Great White Lie: that standards are rising all the time, and that our kids are getting brighter and brighter.

The result of this polite fiction is, again, to damage the interests of the poor and the underprivileged. Faced with a load of A grades and a load of candidates who seem equally qualified, employers are once again asking whether or not the applicant went to a good school, and that is deeply socially regressive.

Now it is not electorally profitable for a politician to say all this. You sound like a whinger. You sound like a stick-in-the-mud. You sound like a miserable old right-wing *laudator temporis acti*, and even if people may collectively agree with the logic of your assertions – in the sense that they can see that grade inflation is a reality – each parent is individually making a very different calculation. An audience of middle aged middle class Britons will loudly agree that A levels have become easier, but as they look at the besuited Conservative (it is normally, alas, a Conservative) making these criticisms, they privately grasp that this fellow proposes to make it more difficult for their son or daughter to get an A at A level. Hmmm, they think: it might be more prudent to vote for the other guys, the ones who stand up year after year and announce that sorghum yields in the Donbass region are at an all-time high, comrades, and that more A star to C grade tractors are rolling out of the factories in Novosibirsk.

Parents may collectively deplore grade inflation, but each will individually calculate that their child is better off getting a depreciated A than an inflation-proof B or a C. So the lie goes on for year after year, to the point where the market suddenly and inexorably asserts itself.

Despite all the protestations of ministers, some universities have simply given up on the A level as a utensil of differentiation, and are preparing to set a new pre-U exam. And which type of school will be best placed to pump-prime its children for that exam? The fee-paying schools, and the grammar schools, of course; and so once again the net effect of the Great White Lie – that standards are improving across the system – is to disadvantage the very schools and candidates that are most in need of help.

There are already huge numbers of schools that find it a struggle to provide adequate tuition in the crunchy subjects often required for university entrance. It was a blessed relief the other day when Cambridge announced that some subjects were to be preferred over others, and that on the whole the STEM subjects, Ancient or Modern Languages and History were regarded as a better preparation for a degree at Cambridge than business studies or media studies. It was a relief, because for too long we have all collaborated in Great White Lie number three, namely that all subjects are somehow equally challenging, and that an A in media studies is worth as much as an A in some tough deterministic subject such as physics.

We have connived in this lie because it is part of the great deceitful "polyfilla" we use to conceal the gap between most of the maintained sector on the one hand, and the Grammar Schools and the fee-paying sector on the other. It is partly as a result of this pretence, therefore, that some of these crunchier subjects are all but dying out in some parts of inner city Britain. Look at the numbers doing advanced mathematics in the London Borough of Camden. Look at the numbers doing physics. There is now overwhelming evidence that schools are diverting pupils of medium ability away from more challenging subjects and into the softer options because an A is an A is an A, and the league table system means that schools face chronic and terrible pressure to harvest as many A's as possible, no matter whether that A is in maths or media studies.

Universities therefore find themselves in the ludicrous position of being simultaneously urged by government to widen access, and to accept more candidates to read science; and yet every time they accept a good STEM subject entrant, the chances are that they are admitting someone with an already privileged educational background.

Science is under threat in the maintained sector, finally and most obviously, because there are not enough good science teachers, and one of the reasons why there aren't enough science teachers is that science teachers have tended to be male – and there aren't enough male teachers altogether. That is our educational white lie number four: that male and female teachers are interchangeable, and that the gender of your teachers should make no difference to the performance of adolescent males.

Of course it may be politically expedient to assert this fallacy, especially since the number of male teachers has declined so precipitously; but what rubbish it is, and how convenient for the middle classes. I couldn't say exactly why it is that adolescent males seem to respond more easily to instruction from males. Maybe it is something to do with the competitive way they identify with their intellectual role models, or something on those lines. Never mind the reasons. Just look at the results of the boys' schools with a high proportion of male teachers, and consider how wildly unjust it is that the ruling classes on the whole use schools where male pupils have a high chance of being taught by male teachers – and yet the safe, non-sexist view is that the gender of the teacher is immaterial to outcomes.

The result of this lie, once again, is to entrench the advantages of the middle class, and to entrench the disadvantages of those who are obliged to use the rest of the maintained sector, where female to male teacher ratio in primary schools is now at something like 13 to one. The social problems associated with this imbalance – the absence of male role models in school and at home – go far wider, of course, than university entrance. But as they look at their difficulties with widening access, I bet most Vice-Chancellors would agree that the primary school classroom is where the problems begin.

If there is one thing we can do to create a more equal and fairer society, and to lift people out of poverty, and to widen access to university, it would be to end the savage injustice by which 44 per cent of 11 year olds leave their primary schools either illiterate or innumerate. If people cannot read and write properly, we are not only depriving them of the essential tools they will need to have any hope of entering higher education. If you can't write – if you cannot compose your thoughts sequentially on paper – then in an important respect you cannot think.

It is a scandal that for so long the middle classes have insisted on synthetic phonics (C-A-T) for their own children, and yet been quite content to allow other people's children to muddle through on "recognising the word". At every crucial point in our educational system, we see the affluent middle classes conniving in a self-serving deception. They go along with the fictions that standards are always rising and that all subjects are as challenging as each other, because these fictions mask the gap in attainment between schools and mask the advantages the middle classes are stealthily securing. Above all we actively propagate the nonsense that there is no selection in the British system, when in fact the one group that has no chance of exercising its one natural advantage - native wit - is the bright poor.

There are some obvious things we can do, such as insisting on synthetic phonics and changing the school league table weightings, so that an A in further maths is not exactly commensurate with an A in media studies. We can recruit more science teachers, and boost modern languages, and we can continue to campaign to persuade people from non-traditional backgrounds to see themselves as university material, a campaign in which the government's current lack of success is certainly not for lack good intentions.

Then there are more difficult things. Fifty years after Tony Crosland wrote the "Future of Socialism", the class-based divisions in the British educational system are in some ways as acute as ever. The Grammar Schools have gone, removing the ladder for the poor, but the independent schools power ahead, turbo-charged with the prosperity of the UK housing market and the financial services industry. It is surely time to look at the second part of Crosland's solution, which was more progressive than the abolition of the Grammar Schools, and that is to end the apartheid of the 1944 Butler Act. We have taken a great step forward in higher education, in the sense that the government has been wise and brave enough to introduce a means-tested system of co-payment.

As we have seen, middle-class lefties such as the Blairs are ruthless in using secret co-payment systems, by topping up state education with private tutoring. Is it not time, as a society, that we stopped the absurd insistence that no private money may come into state schools, and vice versa? Is it not time to give more thought to a means-tested voucher system for all secondary schools, and radically open up educational opportunities for families on modest incomes?

I began this piece by noting that all educationalists have a dilemma, in that it is not obvious whether it will be psychologically more effective to be enthusiastic or critical. Looking back, I worry that I may have overdone the criticism, and I certainly don't want this read as another Tory howl of pain about declining standards and dumbing down and so on.

Whatever its shortcomings, British higher education has been an outstanding success story. But the next Tory government will be wholehearted in its determination to widen access and to re-ignite the social mobility that has fizzled under this government. We can't do that unless we are more honest about the current bifurcation in our school system, and the first step to salvation is to stop telling the Great White Lies.

FIRST IN MY FAMILY: WIDENING PARTICIPATION

Bill Rammell

Bill Rammell MP is Minister of State for Lifelong Learning, Further and Higher Education - a position he has held since 2005. He joined the government in 2001 as Parliamentary Private Secretary to Tessa Jowell. In the October 2002 reshuffle he was promoted to Parliamentary Under-Secretary of State at the Foreign Office. He was educated at Burnt Mill comprehensive school in Harlow, and studied French at University College, Cardiff, where he was later president of the Student's Union.

I am immensely proud to have been the first in my family to go to university, one of the landmark events of my life. I am forever grateful to those who helped me achieve that – family, friends and my school, Burnt Mill Comprehensive. It was without question a life-enriching experience. That's what makes me absolutely determined to do what I can to make sure that no one who has the potential and ability is denied the opportunity to benefit from higher education.

I am also immensely proud of the efforts of people working in and around the education system to make sure that our universities are accessible to everyone with the desire and potential to benefit. So that there are many more "firsts in the family". So that it's no longer the exception that a working class kid, such as I, should have his or her potential recognised, nurtured and encouraged to flourish. Regrettably, I don't believe we are at that position yet. Even today with all the huge improvements in our lives since my childhood, we cannot say that we have managed fully to strip away all inequalities and that an individual's life chances are the same no matter what background they are born into. The most basic analysis showing that only 28.2% of young entrants to higher education come from the lowest four socio-economic backgrounds is a stark reminder of that.

Ensuring everyone who has the potential to go to university can do so is both a social and economic imperative. A degree is still the best passport to middle class comfort and security, soon 50% of UK jobs will require graduate level qualifications and we are still behind our competitors in terms of the proportions of young people who enter Higher Education

In my job, I am assailed by not just the enormity of the task in overturning the prejudices and deep-seated misunderstanding of the nature, purpose and value of higher education, but also by the determination of those that see that things are not as fair as they should be. Their commitment to broadening participation in higher education and to securing fair access to the courses and institutions that students deserve based on their achievement and potential is impressive, to say the least.

Raising attainment of under-represented groups is of course the key to widening participation in higher education. What happens in schools is therefore critical. It is where the real progress is to be made – in raising standards, pupil attainment and in inculcating in students the desire for and belief in higher education as a realistic ambition, especially amongst those who would not otherwise see the relevance of higher education, nor its accessibility.

While we know that of those who achieve 2 A levels, around 90% do progress to HE irrespective of their background, that is only a partial picture. We need to think hard about those who don't currently make it as far as A levels or other level 3 qualifications. We have a major challenge to keep people in learning. This is where schools and universities working together to raise aspirations - and thereby improve staying on rates - is so important. Aspirations are closely linked to attainment. Recent research (Goldthorpe et al, 2005, *Primary and Secondary Effects in Class Differentials in Educational Attainment: the Transition to A-Level Courses in England and Wales*) found that 'secondary effects' such as aspirations, rather than prior attainment accounted for up to 25% in the difference in staying on rates at 16 between high and low social classes. If we include the impact that aspirations have on attainment at GCSE, the true secondary effects could be as much as 50%. Therefore developing aspiration is probably the most important thing we can do to expand participation.

Moreover, I am concerned that if our education system excludes some people from higher education who could benefit from it, then society too is the loser: we are wasting talent and holding back its productive potential, which results in lower GDP and fewer of the wider social benefits that higher education can bring otherwise.

In looking for ways to overcome barriers - real or perceived - to students' progression into higher education, my thoughts turn more and more to the relationship that exists between our schools and our universities. What it is and what it can become.

For some, there always has been such a relationship, with some schools keener than others to make the links and forge the partnerships. In the past, these might have been independent schools, but never exclusively so. The difference today is that it is not just schools looking to develop a relationship but universities themselves are increasingly keen to work with and alongside schools, raising aspirations amongst students who otherwise would not give higher education a second thought and helping to increase attainment levels and progression rates particularly by students from deprived backgrounds.

Activities between schools and universities such as mentoring by undergraduates, HE visits and taster days, summer schools, master classes, talks by HE staff and students can all make a difference. These sorts of intervention are often part of a locally designed and delivered *Aimhigher* programme. It shows that often it is simple things that work best. For example, those 17-18 year olds who experienced speaking to staff from a university were 3 times more likely to aspire to HE; those who had attended an *Aimhigher* Roadshow were 1.5 times more likely to aspire to HE (again among the cohort aged 17-18); while those going on residential visits were nearly twice as likely to aspire to HE (the 16-17 year old cohort). The results around attainment are also worth noting: those who were designated within the widening participation cohort in years 10 and 11 were twice as likely to achieve 5 A*-Cs at GCSE and achieved 1.7 points more than similar non-members.

More and more HE institutions are taking their relationships with schools very seriously. They already invest significant time and energy in supporting and collaborating with schools. Most are involved in *Aimhigher* partnerships and a wide variety of outreach activities, an increasing number are connecting over the developing

14-19 curriculum and qualifications reform agenda, while others offer schools support through programmes of continuing professional development for staff. The range of collaborative work between HE institutions and schools is impressive and it is indicative of how much HEIs have to offer schools through partnership working.

I am not convinced that as much is being done as could be, nor that there is not scope for further evolution and strengthening of school-HE partnerships. That would be foolhardy and a constraint on local initiative. I do believe that there are challenges around how to focus these partnerships on tackling the most intractable problems. It's also important that HE institutions reflect carefully on how they go about identifying and working with partner schools. Where the focus of the partnership is raising aspirations amongst under-represented groups, for example, how do the activities reach the target audience within each school? There is some concern (identified by UUK in *From the Margins to the Mainstream: Embedding Widening Participation in Higher Education, 2005*) that HE institutions identify and work with schools in disadvantaged areas as a proxy for socio-economic status. Of itself, this will not ensure that the intended beneficiaries within those schools are identified and supported.

There are many reasons why it is important that schools and HE institutions should work together. Teachers and other school staff are often the front line in advising young people about HE choices and decisions. To do that well they need to understand the HE admissions process, the HE curriculum, the variety of learning methodologies and the increasing availability of part-time and other flexible forms of delivery. They also need to be up to speed on new opportunities in higher education such as Foundation Degrees and the development of new courses. All of this is absolutely essential to help schools to prepare their pupils for the realities of studying at a university or other higher education institution. It is also vital underpinning for high quality, accurate and relevant information, advice and guidance on the options available to potential HE applicants. It is heartbreaking to hear stories about out-dated accounts of university life being passed on to young and impressionable people, misdirecting them as to the real nature of today's higher education offerings and misguiding them as they make one of the most important decisions in their lives to date.

It works the other way too. Higher education staff should make more efforts to understand the school curriculum, how learning is delivered and how pupils are prepared for HE. This helps to achieve a transition into higher education which is as smooth as possible, avoiding gaps in the curriculum or considering how any gaps can best be bridged and students supported. Understanding the ways in which young people have been taught and their receptiveness to different pedagogies will do much to help HE teachers settle their new entrants into the world of study at the new level. HE staff also need to understand the full range of qualifications available at level 3 (it's not just about A levels), why students choose to study them and the implications for applications, entry, and teaching and learning in HE.

I make no bones about my sub-text here. It's the point I mentioned earlier about information, advice and guidance. We continually hear that pupils do not get accurate, up-to-date advice and guidance about HE. The situation is said to be most acute for those on vocational or work-based programmes. We are told that HE staff do not understand the range of level 3 qualifications on offer alongside A levels, which can disadvantage some students in the admissions process. Mainly this is anecdotal feedback but there is also research evidence to support it - eg Helen Connor & Brenda Little: *Vocational ladders or crazy paving? Making your way to higher levels* (LSDA, 2005). It was also raised by the Admissions to Higher Education Steering Group in their 2004 Report: *Fair admissions to higher education: recommendations for good practice*, usually referred to as the Schwartz report.

Staff exchanges can be a good way for teachers from both sectors to improve, develop and bring up to date their knowledge of how the other operates. For example, a few years ago we piloted a scheme to support school or college teachers to spend time in a university carrying out a relevant project. Projects could be designed to help teachers familiarise themselves with specific aspects of university life, practices, policies, provision, or curriculum issues across the transition from school to university. *Aimhigher* partnerships can use some of their funding allocation to develop and support this sort of programme today if they so choose. HE students themselves can also be a valuable link between schools and higher education. The Student Associates Scheme, now in its fourth year, has to date placed around 24,000 HE students into schools. It aims to do two things: to encourage able undergraduates into teaching; and to provide role models for school pupils and encourage them to see higher education as a realistic and viable proposition. Schemes such as these seem to me to be win-win situations – for learners (at school and in HE), for schools and for higher education institutions.

I suggest that school-HE interactions are more important today than ever before. I believe this for a number of reasons. First, there is increasing choice and flexibility about what and where young people study between the ages of 14-19. Alongside that, there is an expanding and changing range and type of higher education – new courses, new forms of delivery. Underpinning that is a progressive financial support package for students to ensure that higher education is affordable. Faced with choices and decisions to make in these areas, potential applicants to higher education will look to their teachers and others involved in the processes for help in plotting their way through. Schools and universities have a clear responsibility for guiding and steering young people so that they can work through the options that appeal to them and can see how their ambitions can be realised. But only by working together will the different parts of the education system be able to meet their own objectives on behalf of the learners that put their faith in them.

An excellent example of the importance and relevance of school - HE collaboration is to be found in the new specialised Diplomas. The Diplomas will be a significant development of the curriculum and qualification landscape. They are being designed by employers and HE institutions as a blend of theoretical and 'applied' learning which will create new opportunities and new ways of learning, and provide a new route into higher education. Staff in schools, colleges and HE will want to work together through the local 14-19 partnerships and the Lifelong Learning Networks so there is clarity about what the changes will mean for Diploma students and their progression. Universities can play a wider role in supporting the development and implementation of Diplomas too – for example by helping those schools and colleges that will deliver them with staff development and materials, identifying the implications for HE admissions and curricula. They might also open up their resources such as libraries to help Diploma students; and could provide work experience opportunities for them.

But we need to be clear: without active engagement in the development of diplomas and recognition of them as an entry route to HE, diplomas will not succeed.

Everything I have said is possible, practicable but above all essential to ensure that young people have the best possible bases from which to identify and start upon the pathways that are right for them. The best chance we have of achieving that is through recognising the importance of building on, strengthening and extending current partnerships so that they become more sustainable and broader, focusing on the needs of the school and its pupils. The issues they could choose to tackle will often be responsive to local needs and circumstances. They might for example choose to concentrate on support for raising standards (eg by arranging access by schools to HE subject specialists or facilities); or on developing specific subjects (Modern Foreign Languages, science); or on aspiration-raising, providing new challenges for gifted & talented pupils, or helping with staff development.

I have explained why I believe that the need for interaction between schools and higher education institutions is greater than ever before. The opportunities for that to happen are also such as they have never been. Some HE institutions are looking to get involved in sponsoring Academies. Others are interested to support the creation of Trust schools to help them manage relationships with one or more partner schools on a longer-term, more sustainable basis. Of the schools that have already expressed interest in acquiring a Trust the most frequently cited preferred partner is a higher education institution. I am heartened by that, both as a sign that schools and universities have recognised the importance of their cooperation and as an indication that they are willing to grasp the nettle and tackle long-standing issues in a new and exciting way.

The funding climate and policy context for university and schools to work together to improve attainment, aspiration and progression has never been better. And this Labour Government is determined to continue to push this agenda forward.

I believe passionately in the power of organisations working together, sharing and spreading their expertise. Together, schools, colleges and higher education institutions hold in their grasp new and exciting opportunities to secure and reinforce a fully collaborative and cooperative education system that puts the needs of the learner at its heart and works tirelessly to demolish unfairness, inequality and needless barriers to progression. More "firsts in the family": that is my vision and ambition.

DO UNIVERSITIES REALLY HAVE TO CHANGE?

David Watson

Professor Sir David Watson is Professor of Higher Education Management at the Institute of Education, University of London, where he is also Course Director for the MBA in Higher Education Management. A historian, he was Vice-Chancellor of the University of Brighton between 1990 and 2005. He has played a key role in the development of Higher Education, sitting on numerous influential boards, committees and review groups. He was knighted in 1998 for services to higher education. He is a trustee of Agora.

Introduction

Universities at the beginning of the twenty-first century are perhaps more in the public gaze than at any stage in their history. In some ways those working inside the system welcome the attention. In other ways it can be more than a little intimidating.

The weight of expectation is, of course, enormous, and it has intensified rather than created some traditional dilemmas for universities. As in previous eras of university history, institutions are required to be:

- both conservative and radical (in their "pure" senses);
- both critical and supportive (of our myriad "stake-holders");
- both autonomous and accountable (especially in relation to our financial support); and hence
- both private and public (in legal and constitutional senses);
- both excellent and equal (in ambition and values);
- both certain and provisional (in our intellectual contributions);
- both traditional and innovative (in approach);
- both ceremonial and iconoclastic (in style); and
- both local and international (in focus) (Watson, 2007).

These pressures operate in two directions: from the "inside-out" and from the "outside-in."

"Inside-out" developments

At the heart of the intrinsic pressures there is a set of *epistemological* challenges, based in the changing ways in which teachers and researchers view the world. Michael Gibbons and his collaborators offer an influential shorthand account of this transformation. They see an inexorable and irreversible shift from 'mode 1' knowledge generation - pure, disciplinary, homogeneous, expert-led, supply-driven, hierarchical, peer-reviewed, and almost exclusively university-based - to 'mode 2' - applied, problem-centred, transdisciplinary, heterogeneous, hybrid, demand-driven, entrepreneurial, network-embedded (Gibbons *et al.* 1994).

One "internal" effect is the tendency to dissolve disciplinary traditions and subject-based hierarchies. Academics are also increasingly likely to have cemented mode 2-style alliances beyond their employers' boundaries.

Meanwhile, several of these developments have implications for the curriculum, not least as they are influenced by the changing interests and values of the student body.

First there is the need to adapt to changing patterns of subject choice (UUK, 2006). Modern students are canny consumers. They need to be, especially as an increasing proportion of new workforce entrants are graduates. Indeed, they are regularly more effective readers of the emerging employment scene than either the providing institutions or external stakeholders such as government and employers. Alison Wolf describes the "rational teenager" and his or her justifiable distrust of narrow, apparently end-stopped vocational qualifications (Wolf, 2002: 79, 87, 177).

Nor are they respecters of traditional disciplinary or professional boundaries. The success of "media studies" in the UK is probably the most graphic cautionary tale. The rapid growth of such courses led initially to popular and political outrage; the graduates are now more likely to be employed in occupations related to their degree studies than those who read law.

What about the internal cultural implications of such apparent instrumentality? John Ahier and his collaborators have tested views of "future lives as employees and citizens" held by final year students at one "old" and one "new" English university (Cambridge and Anglia Polytechnic, now Anglia Ruskin University). Instrumental priorities do not seem to have corroded this generation of students' strong sense of a "social sphere" to which they contribute and of "sociality" more generally.

In other words, while the current generation of British students – like many elsewhere in the world – have to think long and hard about their economic life-chances, it is crude and inaccurate to typecast them as "Thatcher's children". Meanwhile, this stance is not incompatible with the decline of both interest and confidence in traditional political activity (often previously seen as a proxy for student citizenship). Ahier *et al.* describe their interviewees' "desire to retain a sense of themselves as moral actors" as well as "a sense of a civil society beyond the narrowly political that provides the space in which that desire can be lived out" (Ahier *et al.*, 2002: 153).

Is such confidence justified? The Wider Benefits of Learning (WBL) group at the Institute of Education has been tracking the experience of the 1958 National Child Development Study (now aged 42) and the 1970 British Cohort Study (now aged 30). Their findings are dramatic. Despite the considerable expansion of the UK graduate population, significant benefits have been sustained in the "domains of health, the labour market, citizenship and parenthood" (Bynner *et al.*.: 2003: 4). However, it is important also to acknowledge a worm in the apple. Students from poorer backgrounds who start on full-time HE and then drop out fall behind their contemporaries with lower qualifications in almost all of these respects (Ibid: 25; HEFCE, 2002: 37).

Universities also have to respond to the effect of revised preparation and expectations of students, not least as a result of the younger generation's experience of ICT. Jason Frand's seminal essay on "the information-age mindset" presents an expression of this dilemma. Frand identifies "ten attributes reflecting values and behaviors" of the resulting mindset. The driving concept is borrowed from Alan Kay of Xerox: "Technology is anything that isn't around when you are born." Many of the other nine are familiar to the parents and teachers of early twenty first-century teenagers: Internet better than TV; reality no longer real; doing rather than knowing; Nintendo not Logic; multitasking a way of life; typing rather than handwriting; staying connected; zero tolerance for delays; and the blurring of the creator/consumer line in a world of screen-accessible and malleable material (Frand, 2000).

There is a subtle network of influences going on here. Students are not only choosing "different" subjects, but they are also making other choices which affect the shape and content of their studies (notably in how they use IT).

Other lifestyle issues are also relevant. The modern undergraduate in the UK works regularly for money, not only to cope with changing patterns of student support but also to maintain a lifestyle (Pemberton and Winn, 2005). Another phenomenon is the recent revival of a traditional form of student citizenship: that of volunteering.

Next, it is important to consider the teacher's perspective. Cultural and other changes in the student body are matched by shifts in the demography and organisation of the academic profession itself. As it has grown it has become younger and more likely to have experience outside as well as inside the academy. The average age of teaching staff in UK higher education institutions is now 42.7 (HESA, 2004/05). The main message is about the combined effects of generational change and of expansion. As a cohort of academics brought into the profession by an earlier spurt of expansion retires at the same time as the system anticipates a new spurt, turnover will be rapid. In these circumstances "internal" socialisation is likely to weaken and new perspectives to gain greater purchase. One effect is a wider and more generous understanding of "professional" contributions to learning support. In short, there is a potentially "new" definition of the academic role at work here; and new professionals will also require new models of leadership and management.

To take stock so far: the moral system of the university as a community is shifting radically. A new mode of knowledge production and use is being compounded by shifting interests of students and staff. So far, such pressures could be identified as *intrinsic*, requiring response to deep cultural changes embedded within the academic enterprise itself.

"Outside-in" Developments

Simultaneously, the university is subject to *extrinsic* pressures for change.

First, there is the emergence of rival centres of reference to universities and colleges, including corporate universities, commercial accreditation of training courses, and assumption of responsibility for both initial accreditation and continuing professional development by professional and statutory bodies (including in direct competition with higher education institutions). In the UK, both the University for Industry (UfI) and the National Health Service University (NHSU) were examples of officially sponsored entryism. However, such public and private initiatives may find it equally hard to survive and prosper. The UfI has sensibly re-branded itself as an adult advisory service (LearnDirect), the NHSU is no more, and the "for-profit" sector in the USA has, after an initial boom, fallen upon hard times.

Many of the more general external pressures are *social*. Here the major concern, internationally, is socio-economic patterns of participation and their relevance for social polarisation. The gap between those with access to education and resulting skills, to information, and to influence, and those without is widening not narrowing.

Participation can also have an effect on public confidence in the value of higher education. In the UK HE is generally regarded in the popular media with a mixture of envy and contempt. Negative stories – about student behaviour, about novel degrees, about drop-outs and the like – can rapidly become moral panics. The contrast with the United States is instructive, where until recently university and college stories have had an easier ride than they deserve.

There is a powerful demographic base to this divergence. A comfortable majority of American adults (at least 60%) enroll in college of some kind. The UK government's 50% target for full or part-time enrolments of under 30s pales into insignificance alongside this achievement, but even here the inexorable penetration of adult life by those with (largely positive) experience of higher education could be predicted to have the same effect on public attitudes. The WBL studies also point in this direction by identifying the positive influence of graduates on their children's learning (Bynner *et.al.*: 51-54).

Economic questions are significantly about utility. An example is the threat of under-employment, where some employers (led in the UK by the Confederation of British Industry (CBI) query the focus on the production of graduates despite the government's insistence that their 50% target is driven by economic priorities (for example, that 70% of new jobs will require graduate skills by 2010).

Much of the resulting confusion arises from two sources. One is the lack of real information about the skills market, nationally and locally. The second source of confusion is the tendency of employers to use qualifications for different purposes: either directly making use of the "human capital" inherent in higher qualifications, or simply regarding a qualification at a certain level as a screening device or "signal" not necessarily related to employment needs.

Finally from the outside there is *political* controversy. Politicians from the current UK government and its predecessor have been highly ambivalent about higher education, following a public mood where it is not in general positively referenced. They want market forces, but they also want arm's length micro-management. They accuse institutions of supply-side thinking, but intervene with untested supply-side experiments. They listen to employers (who by and large don't pay for mainstream HE,) but not to students (who *are* paying, if only, from 2006, on a deferred basis). They will take credit, but are reluctant to share risk. They want "modern" higher education, and yet they hanker after *Brideshead Revisited.* In contrast to their enthusiasm for health, they are certainly not prepared to pay significantly more for it (Watson and Bowden, 2005).

The UK may not be alone in these pathologies. All over the world there is a struggle between governments wanting greater differentiation between "types" of higher education institutions, and colleges and universities chasing common or similar measures of esteem. One result could be called the "binary trap:" systems without formal stratification think that they are missing something and should have it; systems with it also think they are missing something and should do without it.

To take stock again: the new university community is under pressure from increased competition with other providers, from intensified demands by self-perceived "stakeholders," and from more detailed and specific political management than ever before.

Just how "inside-out" and "outside-in" pressures overlap and intertwine in complex ways in the life of the contemporary university can be illustrated in several ways. I will take three examples.

The Global Challenge

Too much of the current rhetoric (and of the action) seems to be about global higher education as a simple market, and about the bottom line for institutions. Several of the resulting questions are ethical, for example about how we operate responsibly in these changing circumstances.

This avoids having to face up to several things. First there is the damage done by colonial-style intervention which "substitutes" for traditional university functions in developing countries. An example is in research, where a proper domestic capacity is needed to pull through a properly qualified academic workforce. This connects with the need to bring up to date the historical obligation of more advanced systems of higher education to assist less developed systems to progress. A strategy for simply driving out the competition can all too easily deny this rich history.

Meanwhile the development of European and North American models of intellectual property can be seen as a preemptive strike (or, even worse, as asset-stripping).

Simultaneously, there is the danger of a kind of reverse saturation of domestic markets by under-priced and sometimes shoddy goods in the form of e-learning. The General Agreement of Trade in Services (GATS), supported by the World Trade Organisation (WTO) opens up the possibility of enforced access to domestic educational markets in precisely this way.

Finally and, in the long term perhaps most serious, is the failure adequately to address those parts of the modern university curriculum that should lead to responsible global citizenship.

The Challenge of Leadership

The inexorable tendency is for university leaders to overestimate the extrinsic influences and underestimate the intrinsic influences on the development of the university in the knowledge society. Such a conclusion is consonant with theory about the knowledge society itself. In this field as elsewhere (for example in ICT,) the participants outperform (in the sense of being ahead of) the policy-makers in terms of relative influence on the changing shape of the system.

If correct, this thesis has some important consequences for what leaders are trying to do. For example, dealing successfully with external influences, as it were "from above," in the interests of preserving the status quo (i.e. achieving "institutional comfort") may turn out to be a Pyrrhic victory, if the internal pressures for change, as it were "from below," have meanwhile transformed the system (Slowey and Watson, 2003: 159).

The Challenge of Engagement

How does the responsible university cope in these circumstances? What about what the Association of Commonwealth Universities calls "engagement" (Bjarnson and Coldstream, 2003)? There are several vitally important commitments for our universities as communities within the community.

First, we need to follow Marx: we can make our own history, but not necessarily under circumstances of our own choosing. We need to *understand and build on our history*. Around the world, the majority of the well-established universities would not have come into being without serious civic support: examples are the US land-grant colleges, the great Victorian and Edwardian civics in England, and the sandstone universities in Australia.

CAN THE PRIZES STILL GLITTER?
The Future of British Universities in a Changing World

Secondly, we need to be more conscious of the *public interest in universities, and our obligations to maintain and develop it.* This is an inevitable consequence of the 21st century interest in universities, and it lies at the heart of most of the dilemmas with which this chapter began.

Thirdly, universities need to internalise the *principles of working in partnership*, such as understanding when to follow as well as when to lead. Pursuing the "social agenda" means two types of activity on the part of universities, which are themselves sometimes in tension. The first is about developments inside, notably action on admissions and student support, but also about choice of teaching, research and service priorities. The second is significantly outside, where the university recognises that it has an obligation to help to change matters (for example on schooling, or on community capability).

There are apparent risks in this second sphere, which not all universities are prepared to take. For example, the kind of partnerships involved may necessitate taking a junior rather than a senior, determining role (something which powerful institutions like universities do not always find comfortable). Secondly, there are ambiguities about the bottom line, when a general social good (such as better staying-on rates in school) may not directly benefit the university which has made the investment.

Finally, it is no accident that all of these strictures are about the concept of the *sector*. One of the most distinctive features of the development of the UK system of higher education has been its willingness to take academic responsibility for its own enlargement. The UK system is admired around the world for its commitment to systematic peer review. So it is deeply ironic that at home the "quality wars" have threatened to tear the sector apart. Taking the long historical view, the "collaborative" gene was there from the start, for example through London external degrees and the system of "validating universities" (notably the Victoria University of Manchester). External members of university college committees played their part in the late nineteenth and early twentieth centuries, before the two major phases of late twentieth century expansion. These were overseen, in turn, by academic advisory committees for the post-Robbins foundations, and by the Council for National

Academic Awards for what was termed "public sector higher education". But perhaps the most potent symbol is that of the external examiner, a figure of immense moral importance, significantly envied in other systems. There is a danger at present in British higher education of a decline in civility, of over-hyped inter-institutional competition, and of loss of commitment to the controlled reputational range implied by mutual assurance of quality.

Conclusion

To take stock for the third (and final) time, how and why do universities have to change? The answer has surely to do with establishing the balance of continuity and change. Commentators are fond of quoting Guiseppe de Lampedusa's *Leopard*, "If we want things to stay as they are, things will have to change" (the latest is Oxford's Chancellor Chris Patten, on the day that the Congregation votes on governance reforms [MacLeod, 2006]). The encouraging message is that universities have managed in the past to reinvent themselves while holding on to important shared values, and they can do so again.

References

Ahier, J., Beck, J., and Moore, R. (2002) *Graduate Citizens? Issues of citizenship and higher education* London: Routledge Falmer.

Bjarnson, Svava, and Coldstream, Patrick (2003) *The Idea of Engagement: universities in society.* London: Association of Commonwealth Universities.

Bynner, John, Dolton, Peter, Feinstein Leon, Makepiece, Gerry, Malmberg, Lars and Woods, Laura, (2003), *Revisiting the Benefits of Higher Education: a report by the Bedford Group for Lifecourse and Statistical Studies,* Institute of Education. HEFCE: Bristol (April).

Jason L. (2000), The Information Age Mindset; changes in students and implications for higher education, *Educause Review* 35.5 (September/October), 14-24.

Gibbons, M., Limoges, C., Nowotny, H., Schwarzman, S., Scott, P. and Trow, M. (1994), *The New Production of Knowledge: the dynamics of science and research in contemporary societies.* London, Sage.

Higher Education Funding Council for England (HEFCE) (2002), *The Wider Benefits of Higher Education: report by the Institute of Education* Report 01/46 (July).

CAN THE PRIZES STILL GLITTER?
The Future of British Universities in a Changing World

Higher Education Statistics Agency (2004/05), *Reference Volume: resources in higher education.* HESA: London.

MacLeod, D (2006) Down to Business. *Education Guardian* (14 November), 1-2.

Pemberton, S. and Winn, S. (2005) '*The financial situation of students at the University of Brighton: the fourteenth report, 2004/05.*' Health and Social Policy Research Centre, University of Brighton.

Slowey, Maria, and Watson, David (2003) *Higher Education and the Lifecourse.* Maidenhead: SRHE and Open University Press.

Universities UK (UUK) (2006), *Patterns of UK higher education institutions: the sixth report.* London: UUK.

Watson, David (2007) *Managing Civic and Community Engagement.* Maidenhead: Open University Press.

Watson, David and Bowden, Rachel (2005), *The turtle and the fruit fly: New Labour and UK higher education, 2001-2005.* University of Brighton Education Research Centre Occasional Paper. University of Brighton, May.

Wolf, Alison (2002), *Does Education Matter? Myths about education and economic growth.* London: Penguin.

Editors: Hugo de Burgh, Anna Fazackerley, Jeremy Black

Part 2

LOOKING FURTHER AFIELD

THE NEW GLOBAL HIGHER EDUCATION MARKET

Editors: Hugo de Burgh, Anna Fazackerley, Jeremy Black

WHAT IS SCHOLARSHIP IN THE 21ST CENTURY? THE IDEAS OF A UNIVERSITY

Charles Pasternak

Dr Charles Pasternak is the Director of the Oxford International Biomedical Centre. He read chemistry, followed by a DPhil in biochemistry, at Oxford University. He taught biochemistry at Oxford for sixteen years, before moving to St George's Medical School, University of London, to become founder-chairman of biochemistry. Through OIBC he is active in promoting scientific research in developing countries, and in furthering an understanding of science by young people and the lay public.

I have used the word scholarship in my title, as I believe that is what universities largely have been, are, and should be, about.

The identity of the oldest university depends on definition. There were centres of learning in China already in the twenty-third century BCE, long before the evolution of a written script, and certainly after it during the Zhou dynasty,[1] in India by the seventh century BCE, and in Athens a century thereafter. Many attributes of today's universities, like holding a 'chair', 'reading' for a subject, and obtaining a 'degree', as well as academic robes and mortar boards, can be traced back to the madrasas established by the Arabs.[2] The earliest of these, the Jami'at al-Qarawiyyin of Fez, is said to date back to 859, though the first Arab university as such is taken to be that of Al-Azhar in Cairo, established around a century later. The Islamic university of Sangkor in Mali, West Africa, a loose-knit confederation of several independent schools, dates back to the same time. The university of Bologna, founded in 1088, is regarded as the oldest in Europe, but philosophy, mathematics, astronomy and medicine were already being studied in

---

[1] 1052-256 BCE

[2] See William Dalrymple, referring to George Makdisi: The Rise of Colleges: Institutions of Learning in Islam and the West, in the New York Review of Books December 1, 2005

Cordoba centuries earlier. The distinction between religious institutions, like Christian monasteries or Muslim madrasas (even the Athenian Academy had a religious connotation to begin with), and the earliest universities is a subtle one. We should not forget, for example, that Princeton, prior to Woodrow Wilson's presidency in 1902, had been an essentially Presbyterian institution for a hundred and fifty years, or that at Oxford, dissenters were unable to obtain a BA degree until 1858 (and an MA not until 1871).

The Purpose of a University

When Benjamin Franklin was asked by a lady 'What is the use of electricity?', his response was 'Madam, what is the use of a new-born child?' (A similar riposte to this question is attributed to Michael Faraday).[3] I consider the purpose of universities to be two-fold: to teach students to think logically, and to promote scholarship. The first aim can be achieved irrespective of subject. I tried to impart logical argument to Oxford undergraduates in terms of biochemistry; my colleagues were doing it through mathematics and physics, history and politics, philosophy and theology, language and literature. It is more difficult to achieve through subjects like dance, drama and theatre, fashion, jazz, jewellery or photography.[4] Yet the value of *any* taught course is marginal. By and large, students are able to learn the essentials of a subject on their own: well, in the case of the brightest; reasonably, in the case of the average; badly, in the case of the weakest. Teachers merely help to hone the skills that a student is able to acquire on his own: the ability to think logically, that I referred to earlier, is an example. Of course it is necessary to study a trade – be it medicine or mining, publishing or plumbing – through the acquisition of specific knowledge at the hands of qualified practitioners, but this should not be a feature of undergraduate courses.

Engaging in research is what I mean by the pursuit of scholarship. It is carried out by graduates and their seniors, and is an appropriate activity for universities to foster. But it can equally well be exercised in research institutes, in libraries, or in the home (previously those of

---

[3] Walter Gratzer: *Eurekas and Euphorias. The Oxford Book of Scientific Anecdotes.* (Oxford University Press, Oxford, 2002), p 31.

[4] Some of the undergraduate courses offered by Middlesex University today.

the wealthy, now achievable anywhere through electronic information). The quest for new knowledge – satisfying our curiosity - may be the distinguishing feature of the human species,[5] but it does not require a university for its enactment. From what I have said so far, you might conclude that universities – in contrast to schools and hospitals, law courts and centres for the distribution of food - are a desirable, but not a necessary, feature of civilised societies. I would not disagree. Plato's Academy and Aristotle's Lyceum of the fourth century BCE contributed to the richness of life in ancient Athens, but the absence of such institutions within the Roman republic[6] or its subsequent empire did not detract from their effectiveness in fostering art and literature, technology and medicine, across the entire Mediterranean world. The Maya developed astronomy to an amazing degree, but it was not achieved through a university-type of institution.

Academics frequently advise governments on matters of education. Occasionally they join the administration itself – witness US Secretaries of State Henry Kissinger, Madeleine Albright or Condoleezza Rice, all former professors (at Harvard, Georgetown and Stanford, respectively). In this country, where the government is made up of elected politicians, the practice is less frequent: campaigning with devious philosophical argument for an obtuse cause within a university may come as second nature to many an academic, but appealing for the votes of ordinary citizens across the country requires different skills. Two colleagues at Oxford who possessed these come to mind: John Patton (geographer) and Bryan Gould (economist). The first became a not very successful Secretary of State for Education under John Major, the second was instrumental in reforming the Labour Party, but failed to reach expected office: his leader, Neil Kinnock, lost the election of 1992. Students have, of course, long exercised political clout: effective in France in 1968, less so in the USA or UK. But exerting influence beyond its boundaries is not the role of a university. *Plus ratio quam vis (Better the argument than power)*, the motto of the Jagiellan University of Crakow (founded 1363), reminds us of its true purpose.

---

[5] Charles Pasternak: *Quest: The Essence of Humanity* (John Wiley 2003, paperback 2004)

[6] Sulla destroyed the Lyceum during the First Mithridatic War during the early 80s BCE

Structure and Governance

Universities have been transnational, if not global, from the outset. Bishop Stephen of Tournai and Archbishop Heraclus of Tyre, both Frenchmen, studied at Bologna University in the 12th century, and the Greek scholar Manuel Chrysolovas did so in the 14th century. Prior to the eleventh century, it was to Cordoba in Moorish Spain that Christian scholars came for enlightenment. Today the classrooms, libraries and laboratories of universities in Britain – as elsewhere - are filled with students and staff from every continent. So British universities are already global in terms of their members, and they should certainly remain so.

But what of the structure of universities? Should they remain national institutions or should they themselves become global, like pharmaceutical corporations or oil companies? Global universities already exist. There is the Islamic University of Technology, based in Dhaka, Bangladesh. Then there is the United Nations University (UNU), established by the General Assembly of the United Nations in 1973. It is essentially a graduate university, linked from its headquarters in Tokyo to more than a dozen research centres world-wide: the World Institute for Development Economics Research (UNU-WIDER) in Finland, the Maastricht Economic and Social Research and Training Centre on Innovation and Technology (UNU-MERIT) in The Netherlands, the Institute for Natural Resources in Africa (UNU-INRA) in Ghana, the Programme for Biotechnology in Latin America and the Caribbean (UNU-BIOLAC), and the International Leadership Institute (UNU-ILI) in Jordan are some examples. But institutions with fancy acronyms, cleverly distributed across the globe, promoting research in politically correct areas, do not make great universities. The scholars of Paris and Lund, Heidelberg and Geneva, Imperial College and Stanford, continue their studies undisturbed.

Bureaucratic organisations - the United Nations is matched only by the European Union for profligacy and ineffectiveness – have a poor track record of achieving their goals. British universities should be wary of following such global institutions in their management structure. On the one hand, governance by delegations or committees invites failure. Recall Walter Bagehot's warning in the nineteenth

CAN THE PRIZES STILL GLITTER?
The Future of British Universities in a Changing World

century: 'No deliberative assembly can exist with every member wishing to lead, and no one willing to follow. ... Rigorous reasoning would not manage a parish vestry, much less a great nation'.[7] On the other hand, it is equally unwise for universities to become subservient to multinational corporations in order to fund even a part of their expenditure. By all means accept donations in the manner of American universities, where the only attached strings are the benefactors' names on buildings or chairs (in both senses of the word): Harvard raises well in excess of $500 million *per year* in this manner, and other universities are not far behind. Anything else would be worse than the present situation in which government fines universities for attracting the brightest students. This is already forcing several institutions to consider the bold example set by Buckingham in 1976, when it established itself as the first truly independent university in Britain.

To initiate innovative change is to prosper; to follow political trends invites decline. Perhaps the most significant development in our universities over the last half-century has been the increase in graduate students. Although this was triggered partly by the lust for fee-paying students from overseas, the move has been entirely beneficial. The same is true of the increase in foreign students at undergraduate level. Such globalisation, as mentioned above, is entirely consonant with the purpose of a university. Yet graduate students, especially in scientific subjects, require expensive infrastructure. Where successive UK governments have failed, is the pretence that all institutions are of equal merit, all able to deliver high-quality research programmes. We should embrace the example of the State of California.[8] This supports two separate types of university institution. First, campuses like UC Berkeley, UCLA (in Los Angeles) or UCSD (in La Jolla, close to San Diego), that carry out prestigious research and that, with 7 similar establishments, constitute the University of California (UC) system. Second, essentially undergraduate campuses like those in San Francisco, Fullerton or San Diego, that with 20 other campuses form the California State University (CSU) system. The latter provides

---

[7] From *Letters on the French Coup d'Etat*, III, in *Literary Studies* (Everyman) I, 307; quoted by Jacques Barzun: *The House of Intellect* (Secker & Warburg, London, 1959), p 149.
[8] Charles Pasternak: *Curiosity made us great, but it's waning in the West*; in *Times Higher Education Supplement*, 8 August, 2003]

excellent training for undergraduates, the former for graduates (as well as for undergraduates). Many of the recently-established universities in this country, that are based on former polytechnics, would fit easily into the Cal State model, without loss of respect or morale. Moulding the minds of our youngsters through contact with inspired teachers is as worthy an enterprise as research on fruit flies or elementary particles.

Universities must resist the temptation to follow student income by the closure of waning (in terms of number of applicants) departments in favour of new, trendy (and often 'dumbed down') ones. Biochemistry departments sprang up in this country from 1902 (at Liverpool) onwards, not because students clamoured for this topic (the Oxford department was founded in 1921, yet did not teach biochemistry as an undergraduate course until 1949,) but because the study of life in terms of molecules[9] had become possible, and an interesting discipline for study. I appreciate that staff who supervise six graduate students are not as cost-effective as those who lecture to sixty, but financial considerations should not outweigh academic ones. If government is unwilling to support scholarship in subjects like classics or chemistry, British universities will have to try harder to raise their own funds from successful corporate institutions and wealthy individuals. The motto of the Jagiellan University in Cracow, that I quoted earlier, changed during the divisive times in Poland two hundred years after its foundation: it is now *Academy Never Surrenders*.

Resumé

Universities play an important, though not a crucial, part in the life-blood of a nation. Most British ones are already global in terms of students and staff. Moves to alter their structure and governance in a manner detrimental to their independence should be resisted. Their heritage is too precious to be discarded in favour of political expediency.

---

[9] See, for example, Charles Pasternak: *The Molecules Within Us: Our Body in Health and Disease* (Plenum, New York, 1998)

COMPETITION IN INTERNATIONAL EDUCATION: A LOOK AHEAD

Robert Boucher

Professor Bob Boucher CBE has been Vice-Chancellor of the University of Sheffield since 2001. He was previously Vice-Chancellor of the University of Manchester Institute of Science and Technology (UMIST). Professor Boucher is chairman of the International Strategy Group of Universities UK and Treasurer of the Association of Commonwealth Universities. He was awarded a CBE in. 2000 for his services to higher education and the engineering profession, and is a Fellow of the Royal Academy of Engineering. He is Chair of the White Rose University Consortium.

This essay focuses on the international activities that may be expected of higher education institutions in the future from the perspective of UK higher education, though much that is written here will be applicable more broadly.

UK higher education institutions (HEIs) in the future might be expected to display collectively the following characteristics: a greater number of overseas campuses providing for local and third country markets; more engagement in mixed mode distance learning (blended learning is the preferred term today) for undergraduate, postgraduate and research provision; higher proportions of international students on domestic campuses; a high level of overseas mobility of domestic students; wide engagement in franchised, validated and twinned provision; membership of actively collaborating international networks; and a highly international faculty mix. Of course, all of these require a look at the background of increasing international competition in both domestic and overseas locations as well as in the market for the traditional mobile international student.

This is only how the future might look. How realistic is it? What questions arise to challenge this portrayal? What are some of the opportunities and threats for UK HEIs?

Overseas Campuses

As world leaders in higher education, universities like Stanford, Cambridge, and Harvard could sweep up market share – but they protect their brands and their style of provision is costly, so it is unlikely they would want to even enter the overseas undergraduate market, let alone dominate it. However, many universities will enter these markets whether hoping they will achieve additional revenue or positive brand projection.

Will such provision overseas always have to be skewed by having to avoid high cost laboratory-based activity? For example, in the UK, physics and chemistry departments have already been cut back as too costly to maintain.

Could overseas campuses established by research-intensive UK HEIs have a research environment like their domestic campuses? If so, who will fund, in particular, the research environment regarded as so essential for learning and teaching in such institutions? Will overseas governments be willing to increase their competitive research funding or face the political consequences of allowing overseas competition for their existing research funding stream? Singapore, for example, seeks to establish a small number of campuses for about 12,000 students, largely for the non-Singaporean market, with high quality overseas providers. But let us envisage that say 50% of the students (i.e. 6,000) will be undertaking laboratory-based programmes, requiring some 400 faculty to teach them. Who provides and equips and updates the laboratories? Where do the substantial research funds and post-doctoral researchers this implies come from to underpin the research of say 1000 research students? Are science and engineering subjects therefore a no-go area for research-intensive universities or could they really get access to the local university funding streams?

The successful establishment of an overseas campus requires a resident core of staff with experience of the domestic campus. They will play a key role in transferring expected behaviours and aspects of the culture of the UK University – probity, standards, quality, customer care, and so on. Without this, the overseas campus cannot truly be a campus of the UK University, producing like graduates to that of the university.

Will the commercial partner in such ventures, necessary at a minimum to provide capital investment, seek to influence the recruitment of students and apply downward cost pressures on provision? This could be a real threat whenever the joint venture is loss making (almost certain in its early years) or later when new managers take over and the formal contract rather than the spirit of the original players prevails.

Apart from any service fees they might charge, can the UK HEI really repatriate profits? Even if permitted in laws and agreements, what would the effects of local adverse publicity and local politics be on exporting potential profits rather than ploughing them back into the local facilities, especially if the country is a poor one?

There are undoubtedly benefits of brand projection– especially for early-movers - but only if the outcomes (graduates and research) are comparable with the quality at the domestic campus will there be long-term brand enhancement.

Opportunities attract new competitors so others will enter the English language international student market. English language based provision is available in several other European countries already and emerging further afield. Singaporean providers are establishing in China. Competitive offshore campuses of reputable providers from other competitor countries will want their market slice too, not just of students from the overseas campus host country but of those from regional third countries too. The same is true of educational hubs in, for example, Singapore. All this will inevitably bring downward price pressures in the fight for market share, especially if over-supply develops amongst comparable brands.

Mixed Mode Distance Learning

There is general agreement that the pure e-learning model does not work easily, and then only in a small minority of situations. There is a widely held view that this provision is not for the immature undergraduate learner. It may work for mature undergraduate students if such a market exists. It may be appropriate for HEIs to have as a requirement of enrolment to e-learning provision that the student has had a period of work or life experience which demonstrates his or her ability to take responsibility for their own learning. If good regular local tutoring can be established, however, then the young market becomes possible, for which the UK's Open University provides a fine model.

There is a stronger case for e-learning for postgraduate students. They will be mature learners with flexible learning needs, well-suited to an element of e-learning.

E-learning will develop faster when a large depository of material is available to draw upon, complemented by providers' materials and methods. MIT made a good start providing web-based material but much of it provides little more than that available from a modern textbook or course notes. Even animations and hypertext web links can be on CD roms.

UK distance learning providers could benefit from having a UK physical facility in larger overseas markets. This would create efficiencies by allowing shared administration, marketing, equipment, IT, and so on.

High Overseas Mobility of Domestic Students

There is general agreement that this is a desirable goal but as we know from experience there are challenges. Being confident of the quality of partners' provision and curriculum fit, as your number of partners grows, will be a challenge. The need for quality assurance is a good reason for promoting the development of some mutual standards for and recognition of national agencies, though a one-model system would be unwise!

Transferring grades can be challenging. This becomes a quite significant issue, and potential barrier, when the grade contributes to the final degree outcome. One solution would be to arrange the experience in an earlier year of a four-year course but this is usually not a solution in a three-year course.

Because of this, and also the element of the unknown, the better students are sometimes deterred by the risk. We need to work hard to reduce risk and make sure students understand that we are doing so.

Finally we, as recipients of larger and more academically and culturally mixed cohorts of inbound exchange students to various courses, will have to plan and provide better to deal with their academic transition and this will place resource demands on academic staff.

So, besides academic barriers, overseas mobility or exchanges have cost barriers too, not only for the students but the HEIs too.

Franchised, Validated & Twinned Provision

Franchising and validating are common activities but it is notable that in the revised UK quality assurance system collaborative provision has often been the factor receiving the most negative ratings and publicity for institutions. There is a clear reputational risk which has to be balanced against any possible brand benefits in the country and of course the income from service fees.

Twinning is a common arrangement. For most research universities, since they deliver degrees in a research environment, no twinnings are acceptable beyond possibly first year provision. As partner colleges mature, they want to provide more, or even all, of the programme themselves. Conscious of the maintenance of standards, a university can then get forced out by a less concerned peer. A university that delivers its degrees in a research environment should, for the maintenance of their standards, have clear limits on the amount of credit acceptable from a non-research environment (or else alter its mission). Despite this, market pressures have, it seems, occasionally led research-intensive universities to accepting 50% and even 66% of such credit, a change of ethos that appears driven by financial pressure.

Active Collaborating International Network

It is important to be part of an international network if only because we do not yet know exactly how important it may become! As one amongst many, the Worldwide Universities Network (WUN) comprises 18 research-intensive partners - 6 UK, 5 US, 3 other European, 2 Chinese and one each from Australia and Canada. It does not seek to be active at undergraduate level, although it would not necessarily exclude appropriate opportunities, being an international research and graduate school. Others may participate to bring strength to research projects. The WUN group believes that there is increasing research requiring international collaboration on, for example, environment, security, migration, multi-location corporates. Groupings like WUN seek to offer funders a capability that is unmatchable within any single institution. WUN see postgraduate provision benefiting in the same way, especially in emerging areas like nanotechnology. The research experience of research students and post-doctoral assistants is enhanced by video-conferenced seminars and periods in partners' laboratories and libraries.

WUN merely serves as a example of an initiative by it members, driven by both international competition and opportunity, to compete more effectively and win increased recognition internationally, issues no university can afford not to address.

Highly International Faculty Mix

An international faculty mix is not a major goal in itself but rather the result of hiring the best candidates in a global labour marketplace. Internationally competitive HEIs are finding that the proportion of non-UK faculty and research staff appointed in recent years far exceeds the proportion in is existing staff population. In other words, strong growth is taking place. There is a non-EU majority. This is a clear demonstration that ours is a global market for staff. However, it is demanding in terms of providing competitive salaries and facilities. The former is helped (in the UK) by the Royal Society-Wolfson Research Merit Awards that provide salary enhancement for 5 years to attract top international researchers, but this is not a long- term solution. The likely outcome, indeed increasing reality, is that the leading researchers will attract internationally competitive salaries wherever they are. This ensures we maintain and indeed enhance academic and research standards. Overseas recruits can be an important source of new thinking and new ideas, as well as bringing an international perspective to curriculum development. They also can provide market information from their home country and are obvious candidates for spending periods teaching there. Indeed they may be recruited for that very reason. Overseas recruitment is vital in UK shortage areas like engineering and economics.

International Competition in Domestic Market

Domestically, we cannot expect to remain unchallenged by new competition. Undergraduate state funding is currently not available to private providers so the current providers are favoured. Although there is no current threat, future trade development could threaten this position, or at least erode it. The General Agreement on Trade and Services (GATS) seeks to open up international markets by mutual reduction of trade barriers. A number of countries, including the USA, has introduced higher education into the pool of tradable services.

In any case, our higher fees (since 2006) along with international student fees may encourage some international competitors with more efficient models of provision and/or attracting a modest fee premium for their particular brand. It is also the case that more UK students, looking at the total package of fees, living costs and availability of part-time employment, may find other countries increasingly attractive. Current currency exchange rates only emphasise this point. Higher fees thus threaten us in two ways

It is already the case, and will increasingly be, that high fee courses (for example, MBA, LLM in international law, commercial law), will be attractive to strong international brands. How strong the penetration will be is unknown but again high value Sterling adds further attractions. The part-time postgraduate market is readily open to strong competitors. If the cake is big enough, they will seek a slice.

A major barrier to overseas research universities operating in the UK (and vice-versa) is lack of state research funding for them. This too is a GATS issue. A future government would look at the balance of the threat to HEIs and loss of IP from state-funded research against the return of opening up more overseas markets to UK institutions and also of attracting truly outstanding international providers to the UK. This threat may be a long way off but once one government somewhere moves, others may follow.

Incoming International Students

Incoming international students are a vital source of both talent and revenue and it is a common interest that their experience, from first enquiry to successful graduation, is a good one. Government visa policy recently has been unhelpful, not only in giving the misleading impression that the UK is unwelcoming. The visa extension charges are extortionate. The government refers to the principal of 'beneficiary pays'. The DTI understand the importance to business of UK graduates in overseas markets, the FCO acknowledges their contribution to its goals such as reducing corruption, better governance, Britain as partner of first choice, etc and finally the DFES recognise the vital importance to the financial health of our HEIs. In other words, since the UK is the main beneficiary it is the UK that should pay the majority of the costs.

A second common interest reputational issue is the student experience. Students returning home from any HEI with a poor experience will present negative impressions of all UK HEIs. If the problem becomes large, governments and funders will be deterred too. The good news is that surveys indicate that the overall picture is rather good but not without some areas of concern. Just as the universities act in concert over visa charges, this other common interest is one for organised action also, to propagate good practice, detect bad practice through surveys and work with those offending. The international market is far too competitive for those countries or institutions that provide a poor 'customer experience' to succeed.

Conclusions

The likely mix of future activity, and the types of competition likely to emerge, are predictable, although there will be large variations by institution. Competition for overseas students will continue to intensify, although in a growing market. There will be increasing demand for offshore provision with implications for brands and academic standards and quality. The domestic market will probably face increasing overseas competition as fees rise, particularly as the fee cap is eliminated. GATS is not an immediate threat to universities but vigilance is needed lest it become a real one. There is no room for complacency in a turbulent marketplace.

GLOBALISATION AND A TWO-TIER UNIVERSITY SYSTEM

Gordon Graham

Gordon Graham is Henry Luce III Professor of Philosophy and the Arts at Princeton Theological Seminary. Formerly Regius Professor of Moral Philosophy at the University of Aberdeen, he is author of The Institution of Intellectual Values: realism and idealism in higher education (2005). He is a Fellow of the Royal Society of Edinburgh, and currently chair of the Society for Applied Philosophy, and editor of the Journal of Scottish Philosophy.

As with very many 'buzz' words, 'globalisation' is a term widely used but often in ways that leave its precise meaning uncertain.[1] That it refers to a process of some kind is clear, but just *what* process is less clear. I shall take it to mean a process of change that has the effect of making locality and its boundaries increasingly less significant for the activity that is 'globalised'. By illustration consider a (relatively) simple case – the purchase of fresh fruit. This activity was once almost entirely constrained by the locality in which the purchaser lived. Locality confined the choice by climate and season. Markets sold only fruits that would grow in the particular locality, and in accordance with the season prevailing. Methods of preservation added variety to some extent, and local restrictions could be partially overcome by transport. For most people for most of history, however, locality has been a dominant factor in food, and one that partially explains the characteristic diets associated with different parts of the world. This variety was something that travellers discovered, and it contributed to making travel attractive.

After the advent of the railways, the degree to which transport extended fruit markets was greater than before, especially in the United States with its several varied climates. But it is refrigeration and air freight that have had the greatest impact, and in many parts of the world, as a result of rising levels of prosperity in combination with

---

[1] The literature on globalization is now very considerable. A brief account of the most common definition will be found in Manfred B Steiger *Globalization: a very short introduction* (Oxford, OUP, 2003)

changes in international finance and marketing, the restrictions of locality have been lifted almost entirely. The outcome is what we might call the 'strawberries in January' phenomenon. To say that the market in fruit is now globalised, as I am using this term, does not mean that it is dominated by a few large corporations operating world wide (though it may be) but that from the point of view of the consumer, it is no longer of special significance where on the globe a given fruit is grown. One further consequence is that, for large numbers of people, such age old patterns as seed time and harvest, summer and winter, do not matter any more, at least as far as diet is concerned.

Globalisation in this sense is the most important outcome of the internet. The world wide web's distinctive feature as a medium of communication lies in its indifference to national boundaries, time, season, and to some extent language. The web is part of an immense transformation that digital technology has brought about in almost every aspect of life, and a large part of the change relates to 'information technology'. The term is not unproblematic,[2] but it does capture the importance of this transformation for scholarship, for scientific inquiry and for higher education. Though the world of the scientist and scholar has always been international to a degree, the internet, together with other advances in digital technology, has removed almost all the geographical limits which previously prevailed. The issue I am concerned with is the significance of globalisation so characterised for the ideal of a commonwealth of universities with, broadly speaking, equal status.

It is worth remarking that this ideal is for the most part a European one. In the United States, it has long been acknowledged that there is a hierarchy of universities, at the top of which sits the 'Ivy League'. Some universities that are not Ivy League enjoy the same reputation for excellence, but there are also many good institutions with PhD programs, research centres and distinguished faculty members, which are neither regarded nor regard themselves as being on a par with the very best. Nothing much follows from this differentiation, however. Scholars and scientists at these institutions participate in the same

---

[2] I discuss some of the relevant issues surrounding this concept in *The Institution of Intellectual Values: realism and idealism in higher education Essay IV* (Exeter, Imprint Academic 2005)

conferences and publish in the same journals as do those from the Ivy League. Of course, below this again is another level, and another, and so on. With respect to these lower level institutions there is and need be no pretence of equality with Harvard or Princeton; they can do what they do well, even if they do not do anything at Ivy League level.

There is however another important division in the US – between the university and the liberal arts college. In general terms, this division marks the difference between higher level educational institutions that engage in research as well as teaching, and those that do not. It is just such a division that academics in the United Kingdom (and some other parts of Europe) have in mind when they speak of a 'two-tier system'. But between Europe and North America there is this crucial difference. The American liberal arts college is an admirable (and widely admired) institution, though for a variety of reasons (some of which we will return to), it has come under threat in recent decades and now forms a very small part of the higher education sector in the US and Canada. In sharp contrast, 'teaching only' is a status to which European and British universities fear relegation, a second class status within the commonwealth of universities as a whole.

Two questions naturally arise. Is 'teaching only' rightly regarded as second class status for a university? And is this a classification to which globalisation has given powerful impetus? I shall explore these questions in reverse order.

The Significance of 'Teaching Only'

It might be supposed that recent developments in information technology and especially the internet have introduced a new equality between students and teachers at institutions of higher learning. From the first foundation of universities and colleges, and for almost the whole of their history, a crucial distinguishing feature was the size and quality of the library to which members of the university had access. The libraries of Harvard College or the Bodleian in Oxford for example, provided unrivalled resources for research and study. Other ancient universities could claim less valuable collections of books and periodicals, but all of them easily and vastly outshone the libraries of newer and smaller institutions. With extensive programs of digitisation, electronic versions of journals and desktop online access, a great deal of this disparity has become irrelevant. Often it no longer matters if a given book or periodical is not available in the local library, because it is available online. Something of the same point applies in fact to purchase. With the existence of Amazon, abe and the like, the fact that the local bookstore is very unlikely to stock a book, whether new or second hand, has become irrelevant. A still further development lies in distance learning. Formerly a second best, many of its disadvantages can now be overcome, and its advantages exploited. Courses can be offered and enrolled in anywhere in the world. Study materials can be updated with far less effort; teacher-student interaction and response times can match, and even exceed, those that previously required personal contact.

All these innovations are unmistakable effects of globalisation as I have defined it -- the increasing irrelevance of locality. Whether the textbook, the journal, the teacher or the manuscript is near at hand or far away is irrelevant to their availability for educational and research purposes. The value of this new world order can be exaggerated, of course. Online desk top access for staff and students may still require a level of expenditure that exceeds the resources of a small institution, especially in poorer parts of the world. Online subscription to current journals and back issues is not free, and digitised materials can remain controlled. In general though, the position is vastly different to what it was. How is it then that fear of relegation tends to be more marked than before?

It is important to observe that the equalising impact of digital technology is far greater in social sciences and the humanities than in the natural and medical sciences. The difference between scientific laboratories in different localities remains and is not much transcended by the internet. This is partly a function of available equipment, and the presence of the people who comprise a research team. More expensive equipment and the ability to pay highly competitive salaries give wealthy institutions a marked advantage over the less wealthy. The gap between the two is intensified further by the increasing cost of scientific inquiry. Whereas original historical research (say) is relatively cheap and facilitated by internet access to documents, original work in the sciences is now very expensive and possible only for those, however talented, who can find the right milieu.

In such circumstances it is inevitable that institutions which formerly had successful programmes of scientific research should lose them. Moreover, insofar as such institutions call upon the State for financial support, the responsible control of public expenditure will remove funds from research programmes that cannot result in truly significant outcomes. When this happens, it is inevitable that some of the scientists recruited to the institution in question, and possibly the most intellectually fertile, should seek positions elsewhere, and in their turn be sought by institutions which can use that intellectual fertility to enhance their academic status and reputation. Equally inevitably, the scientists left behind must regard themselves as second class, and being confined largely to teaching their subjects, will in all likelihood come to regard teachers as second division scientists. In turn this mindset, and reputation, spills over into other subject areas, where research active academics come to feel that their status would be better served by membership of an institution that is highly regarded overall. So they too seek positions elsewhere, and an institutional 'brain drain' takes place.

This is a plausible scenario, and one that has been realised in many places. But does it have any thing to do with globalisation in particular? The process just described gives causal priority to the rising cost of science, and it is the fact that the globalisation made possible by the internet etc *cannot* offset this, that explains the emergence of a second 'teaching only' division. Yet globalisation does bring a further dimension to the explanation, and that is the context of comparison.

The Context of Comparison

Universities began in Europe and from the start they were 'international' in that they were institutions of Christendom and not of the countries in which they happened to be located. This transnational character is reflected in the fact that they were established on papal authority. Each was a 'university' of 'nations', which is to say colleges that drew their students from different geographical areas, so that national rivalries made their appearance within rather than between universities. All that is a very long time ago, of course, and the intervening centuries have brought about deep change.[3] One of these is the altered status of universities to national institutions whose power to confer degrees (with a few exceptions) was granted and regulated by the nation state. This was the result in large part of political nationalism in the 19th century and the immensely expanded role of government in educational provision, especially since World War I, and one consequence was to make the academic reputations of universities a matter of national pride. The effect of globalisation has been to intensify this competition for status by hugely expanding the context in which it is sought. Whereas it was once enough for a university to seek to be (one of) the best in the country (as it still is for a secondary school), the requirement now is that a university be a world class institution (as no secondary school is required to be). Furthermore, this new context of comparison is made ever present by global communications networks and the internet which play so large a part in contemporary academic inquiry. It is in *this* way that the process of globalisation has fed the tendency to discriminate between first class/second class universities.

In itself, of course, this discrimination need not correspond to the research/teaching division. It does so because the reputation of university academics is almost exclusively judged on research publication. It is this that has contributed in large part to the decline of the US liberal arts college referred to earlier. The archetypal college professors who made up the Faculty at such institutions secured their reputations among their students, and the esteem in which they were held could not extend itself much beyond the generations of students they taught. By contrast academic esteem now must reflect a contribution to the world of scholarship at large and thus extend far beyond the confines of the lecture hall. Esteem *within* the lecture hall, hardly counts at all. One result is that liberal arts colleges have no choice but to recruit new faculty from graduate schools that incline their students to place the greatest value on this alternative mark of esteem, and thus to leave the task of teaching to those who cannot do so.

---

[3] I offer a brief history of universities in *Universities: the recovery of an idea* Chap 1 (Exeter, Imprint Academic), revised and reprinted in *The Institution of Intellectual Values: realism and idealism in higher education.*

CAN THE PRIZES STILL GLITTER?
The Future of British Universities in a Changing World

A similar tendency can be discerned in other contexts. National assessments of research prowess, which several European governments have instigated, have led both to research publication and international standing as being the chief (arguably sole) marks of both personal and institutional academic worth. Combined with the fact that not all individuals or institutions can measure up to this standard equally well, it must come as no surprise that institutions in which teaching is the principal activity should appear to those within and without them as second class, and a move towards this position one of relegation.

Is this inevitable? We can detect and describe something of the process that has led to this position, but the language of inevitability suggests a determinism in the affairs of human beings that we have a deep inclination to resist. 'Men', Marx observes in the *18th Brumaire of Louis Bonaparte* 'make their own history, but they do not make it just as they please; they do not make it under circumstances chosen by themselves',[4] and this middle ground between fatalistic passivity and an absurd over estimation of the power of human agency seems the right position to take. It does not imply, however, that the process just described can be reversed, or even that further moves in this direction can successfully be resisted, which amounts to conceding a measure of inevitability. Where human agency has played its part, and continues to do so is in the choices that academics and academic managers have made under the circumstances the current of the times has presented. Two of these choices seem to me crucial. First, there has been a widespread willingness to seek and accept the position in which the principal paymaster of almost all universities is the State, but an equal unwillingness to admit (or even understand) that this necessarily brings with it a loss of autonomy, and thus a seriously weakened ability to defend and protect academic values when they come under attack. Secondly, there has been a willingness (even eagerness) to accept international research status as the only measure of quality worth taking seriously.

The second concession derives such warrant as it has from the thought that that every country, however small its population or limited its resources, can hope to transform at least one of its

---

[4] *Marx Engels: Selected Works in One Volume*, (London, Lawrence and Wishart, 1968) p. 96

universities (perhaps more) into a world class institution whose scholars and scientists regularly contribute to knowledge and understanding at the academic 'cutting edge'. If (say) Berkeley, Harvard, Princeton, Cambridge or the Sorbonnne are taken as benchmarks, such a hope seems to me to rest upon an absurdity. The disparities of history, finance and population are simply too vast. But more importantly, the pursuit of such an ambition can bring intellectual and cultural impoverishment in its wake.

In illustration of this I cite my own experience as Chair of the international panel charged by the quality assurance agency for the universities of the Netherlands (QANU) with assessing the research excellence of the Dutch philosophy faculties. The criteria laid down for the panel by QANU gave pride of place to international excellence and research leadership in the specified sub-areas of philosophy as reflected mainly (though not exclusively) in publication. In a global context, this effectively means publication in English. On the other hand publication in Dutch is vital both for the purposes of maintaining a scholarly vernacular and so that intellectual inquiry may make a contribution to public discussion and debate (a role of special importance in moral and political philosophy). Given the criteria, however, truly excellent work in Dutch that brought philosophical acumen to local cultural life, could not count as being in the forefront. That this was cause for complaint in some quarters is both understandable and (in my view) justifiable. Yet the criteria laid down for the panel by QANU had been formulated in consultation with a committee comprising the Deans of the Philosophy Faculties, and finalised with their agreement.

Similar distorting effects have resulted from the British Research Assessment Exercise which encourages all the universities of England, Scotland, Wales and Northern Ireland, and all academics within them, to assess the value of their work exclusively against standards which put parity with Harvard or the Sorbonne at the top. In this (mostly) fruitless effort to obtain 'stars' (since overall research finance is not increased thereby) a 'market' in academic reputations has resulted, with extensive and expensive programmes of hiring comparable to those common for a long time in the US. The consequence is that contribution to both institution and community has been significantly eroded, and pedagogical commitment almost wholly discounted.

CAN THE PRIZES STILL GLITTER?
The Future of British Universities in a Changing World

Conversations among academics show these to be both facts of common experience, and of regret. Yet, for all that, no serious academic voice has been raised against them. The Roberts review of the RAE invited extensive academic consultation and resulted in no serious proposals for change. It now seems likely that in future such exercises *will* take a different form – but because of the desire of government to contain their cost, not because of any academic purpose or value that universities have insisted on protecting.

In short, it does seem that the division of universities in Europe into at least two leagues – serious research institutions and 'mere' teaching institutions, will become increasingly apparent, and that in part this is the result of the globalised context in which universities and academics have come to measure themselves. But there is nothing in the process of globalisation as I have defined it that has made this inevitable, and much in the conduct of academics and managers that has hastened it.

Editors: Hugo de Burgh, Anna Fazackerley, Jeremy Black

FUNDING AND FREEDOM: WHERE WE ARE GOING WRONG

Chris Patten*

The Rt Hon Lord Patten of Barnes CH, is Chancellor of the universities of Oxford and Newcastle. Lord Patten was elected as Conservative MP for Bath in 1979, a seat he held until April 1992. From 1992-97 he served as Governor of Hong Kong, overseeing the return of Hong Kong to China. He was Chairman of the Independent Commission on Policing for Northern Ireland set up under the Good Friday Peace Agreement, which reported in 1999. He read Modern History at Balliol College, Oxford.

British universities are more independent than higher education institutions in most European countries. However, it is deeply concerning that they are much less independent on the whole than American universities.

However, before I make any generalisations about American freedom I would like to add a qualification. When you talk about the United States there is a danger of lumping together all different types of institutions – community colleges, state universities and private Ivy League universities – in a way that is unhelpful. There is also a danger of overlooking the extent to which research at some American universities has become politicised in a way that isn't true in this country. The whole furore about creationism and intelligent design, the debate about embryonic stem cell research and the political issues surrounding the Middle East conflict are all impacting severely on researchers. When talking about American independence I am not overlooking these problems. Nonetheless, on the whole, elite institutions in the United States enjoy a level of independence that elite universities here crave but certainly do not have.

In Europe there are a number of countries where the very notion of university autonomy is laughable. In some European countries universities are agents not only of government, but also of the welfare

---

* Chris Patten spoke to Anna Fazackerley.

state. In these places the ability of a university principal to move money from one budget to another, to close a department that is in deficit or to expand a department that is doing well, is strictly limited. In Britain, whatever excessive controls we may have, we are not in that situation.

In the UK the problems universities face are twofold. First, in almost all walks of life there has been excessive centralisation over the last few years and universities have not escaped. This usually means Treasury control. In particular any increase in spending or any new grant is hung about like a Christmas tree with controls and reporting requirements. Universities are not simply given the authority to get on with what they are here to do. They are constantly under pressure to meet government requirements. The two most obvious and damaging constraints are institutions being expected to make up for the deficiencies of secondary education, and the push for social inclusion. Let me be clear about this. I am very strongly in favour of social inclusion as an objective of higher education policy. But I am not in favour of social inclusion at the expense of academic standards. At its crudest the widening participation agenda has been reckless in its impact on standards.

Secondly - and this is the most crucial element - universities here (and indeed in most of Europe,) are left in a No Man's Land, in which they neither get enough funding from the state nor are they allowed to raise money themselves beyond the ridiculously low limits of the tuition fee. Universities today get 1.1 per cent of GDP in this country, compared with America's 2.6 per cent.

This is not something we can simply blame on Labour governments. Until the 1970s, universities were pretty well funded, but the expansion of higher education that we have seen since then has been paid for by squeezing the amount of government money available per student. In the last two decades of the twentieth century we doubled the number of students and halved the amount of money given to them. And resources were squeezed particularly hard in the Conservative years, although this was a trend that was continued in the Blair-Brown early years too. I don't think the Conservatives can look back on their stewardship of universities with any great pride. The problem was that we didn't have the courage of our convictions.

We squeezed public spending on universities, but we didn't then say to universities: "You must go out and raise money yourselves".

There is at the root of all the problems facing universities in the UK and across Europe a resource issue that we cannot go on ducking. If America spends roughly two-and-a-half times what we do on higher education – and moreover if they are spending two-and-a-half times what we do on a limited number of elite universities – we shouldn't be surprised if we fall further and further behind. And while we are resting on our laurels we must remember that China and India are coming up on the outside.

Universities have three main sources of revenue: the taxpayer, private endowments and tuition fees. If you decide the government can't afford to spend any more of the taxpayers' money, and if at the same time you conclude that private endowment requires a major sea-change in public attitudes that will not happen overnight, that only leaves tuition fees.

Top-up fees have become a very emotive issue in this country, but really the answer is very simple. The main determinant of people's lifetime earnings is whether they go to university or not. Therefore it does not seem unreasonable to me for some investment to be made by the students who will benefit. University is a middle class ramp-up after all. It is perfectly crazy that parents are prepared to pay £10,000 or even £12,000 a year for private day school, but then they groan in horror about paying a few thousand pounds for tuition fees.

The most common argument levelled against tuition fees is that they put people from poorer backgrounds off going to university. Yet there is absolutely no evidence at all that this is the case. It hasn't been the case in New Zealand so why should it be so here? If you look at the social composition of the student population over the last fifty years the proportion of children from blue-collar families and the proportion of children from white-collar families have remained static. The proportion was exactly the same at the end of the last century as it was in the 1960s. The huge expansion of higher education simply has not drawn in a higher proportion of kids from working class backgrounds.

CAN THE PRIZES STILL GLITTER?
The Future of British Universities in a Changing World

Yet is there the political appetite to face up to this problem and drive universities forward? Gordon Brown is clearly genuinely interested in higher education. While Mr Blair can take some credit for having been converted to the principle of top-up fees by Roy Jenkins, I don't think he is really very concerned with the university sector. Probably the best thing Tony Blair has done for research was to leave Lord Sainsbury in the science minister's job for as long as he did – David Sainsbury was really good for science. However, while he may be interested, Gordon Brown is dogged by three factors. First is the sort of knee-jerk class war socialism that made such a fool of itself in the very public Laura Spence case at Oxford. There is no question that that was incredibly damaging. Secondly I think Mr Brown is excessively enthusiastic about the management competence of American universities in comparison with ours. True they may achieve a lot, but they are achieving a lot with vastly greater funds. Finally, I think Mr Brown is always inclined to exaggerate how much new money he has actually put into the system.

Sooner or later we will have to face up to the fact that we have to ask students to pay for their higher education. I would like to see universities set their own individual caps on tuition fees. The principal government interest should be in ensuring that universities who raise fees for different subjects – because there is no reason why different subjects should have to cost the same – have in place adequate bursary schemes to ensure that admission is needs blind.

Of course this would put a particular pressure on universities like Oxford and Cambridge to raise a large amount of money through endowment for generous bursary schemes. The battle that has been rumbling in the background at Oxford for years over governance is not irrelevant here. If we can demonstrate to alumni and benefactors that we are interested in their intellectual contribution to what we are trying to do, and that we are open to their advice, then it makes it much easier for us to encourage people to give money. It is extremely difficult if we are effectively saying we don't want your opinions, we just want your cheques. It is frankly offensive to assume that any alumnus of Oxford who might donate has a secret yearning to transform the institution into Asda.

Nonetheless top-up fees are an emotive issue. It is important for the Conservative party to avoid, under pressure, blocking off any options before the General Election. I would be inclined to keep my options open, and then after an election I would want to establish a commission which would explore the issue and look at real evidence.

That said we don't have much time. Top-up fees will be reviewed again in 2009. I think it is very likely that a Brown government will either kick the ball into touch, or make a modest adjustment. Fees of £5,000 would be better than £3,000, but it still would not be enough revenue to support our cash-starved universities. One of the most popular courses at Oxford – engineering and management – could be filled twice over with students, and there are lots of potentially exciting options for expansion, but it costs £15,000 a student to teach and we only get £5,000. We could subsidise it from other courses but where does one stop with such an approach? The problem is the same for physics and management, and chemistry and management, to name just a few.

We can no longer afford to bury our heads in the sand. We must loosen the red tape that binds British universities and allow them to raise the money they need to truly compete.

THE BOLOGNA PROCESS: WHERE IS IT GOING?

Susan Bassnett

Susan Bassnett is Professor in the Centre for Translation and Comparative Cultural Studies at The University of Warwick, which she founded in the 1980s. She was educated in several European countries, which gave her experience of diverse languages and cultures, and began her academic career in Italy, lecturing in universities around the world. She is the author of over twenty books and a regular contributor to national newspapers. She is a trustee of Agora.

All over Europe academics, students and university administrators are talking about *Bologna*. In some countries, such as the Netherlands or Italy, root and branch changes are under way. The curriculum across Europe is being rethought, future plans are being constructed around the Bologna Declaration and, so far-reaching is the likely impact that, in Australia, the University of Melbourne is engaged in reforms that take account of what is perceived as happening on this side of the world. When you visit European universities, it is immediately apparent that Bologna dominates the conversation, though recently I heard a senior UK academic ask in bewildered tones: 'What's all this about Bologna? Why is everyone going on about Bologna all the time? Is there something important I should know about?'

Well, yes. Bologna is important, but the UK academic could be forgiven for his ignorance for, although the rest of Europe may be discussing the impact of what are being termed 'the Bologna reforms', this is not so in Britain, despite the fact that the British government signed up to the agreement, along with 28 other European countries, in 1999. In some institutions, notably those nearer to the English Channel, and those in the Scottish system where four year degrees are the norm, Bologna is not such a mystery, but elsewhere there is little awareness of a future driven by the Bologna agenda.

What is the Bologna Declaration?

The declared aim of the document signed in Bologna just before the new Millenium by Ministers of Education from across the continent was to create a European Higher Education Area by 2010. The purpose of this is to enable students to move freely between universities, regardless of nationality. In the past, there had been considerable difficulty in recognising degrees awarded in other higher education systems, so that the Bologna proposals were welcomed both as a simplification of a very complex situation and as a system that would give students greater flexibility and more choice.

For this plan to come into effect, there needed to be a common university system, hence the signing of the declaration necessarily involved a series of changes to individual universities to bring them into line one with another. Once the common structure was up and running, it was presumed, not only would European students be able to move around freely, but students from other parts of the world would also view the new, flexible European higher education system as highly desirable, which would make it easier to compete with leading universities of the world, many of which are in North America, Australia and Asia.

The idea of pan-European mobility had been current for some time, and schemes, named after historical figures such as Socrates or Erasmus, fostered student exchange at undergraduate level between countries. If the Bologna Declaration were to work perfectly, a student should be able to study wherever he or she chose, be able to transfer credits and be assured of the same quality of education and standards everywhere. In this ideal vision of the future, a student might spend one year in Leiden, then proceed to Lisbon, Liverpool and Lyons, amassing credits along the way. Few would disagree with such a vision, which is premised on the idea that the European citizen of the future should ideally know several languages and feel a sense of belonging in all parts of the continent.

Embarking on Reform

The Sorbonne Declaration had been signed in 1998, setting in train future developments and establishing two cycles of reform, one at undergraduate level and the other at postgraduate level. This, in effect, has constituted the principle set of changes that have begun to be made, and at the same time has also aroused the greatest concerns. For across Europe, the length of a standard degree programme varies enormously. In England, (though not in Scotland) an average undergraduate degree takes three years to achieve, whereas in most countries the average time is four years. In some countries that rose to five years, and in some subjects, such as engineering, architecture or medicine many degree programmes ran for five or even six years. In Italy, as in many other countries, the standard formula for a degree was four years of taught courses, followed by a short dissertation. One point of contention, therefore, was how to assess the achievement of a student who had studied for only three years against that of a student who had studied for four or five years and written a dissertation into the bargain.

Another difficulty that needed to be tackled was the diversity of examination systems operating in different countries. In Britain, course work and the extended essay are standard forms of assessment in most subjects, hence writing competence has been seen as fundamental to the British degree. Elsewhere, oral examinations have been preferred, with the objective of training students in forms of rhetoric and spoken skills, and with little extended writing being done before the final dissertation. The British, uniquely, have an external examiner system that monitors assessment practices and is intended to ensure parity across the system, but the use of external examiners would be inconceivable elsewhere in Europe.

Bologna decided on a model that, to some extent, follows the British. Degrees were to be of three years duration, hence the burden of reforming the curriculum fell on those countries whose degree programmes lasted four or five years. There was little for British universities to do in the first stage of implementing reforms, and the strength of the Quality Assurance Agency, established since 1997 to monitor the quality of education offered in the UK, meant also that systems of quality control that had not been developed so fully in many countries were already well in place in the UK. There is to be a fully-fledged European qualifications framework, and most UK universities have already established a qualifications framework so that their managers consider themselves at an advantage. However, there is still a great deal of work to be done, and consultations on the European Qualifications Framework continue.

Ensuring Quality

Underpinning the implementation of Bologna is the need to ensure comparability across all signatory countries, which increased to 45 after a further meeting in Bergen in 2005, with the addition of Armenia, Azerbaijan, Georgia, Moldova and Ukraine. To this end, a series of European quality assurance agencies have been established with an over-arching European Association for Quality Assurance, known as ENQA. There will be regular cycles of reviews of institutions, and these reviews are increasingly likely to have international panel members. Peer review, rather than some form of inspectorate, is the favoured model, and here again the UK has a great deal to offer in that its quality assurance audit model has been widely accepted by the sector. However, discussions are continuing as to how to apportion responsibility for quality assurance and unsurprisingly, as yet there is no consensus. Quality assurance was established as a priority at the Berlin meeting in 2003, one of the series of ministerial summits that have been held every two years to take the Bologna agenda forward and to assess what progress has been made.

Higher Degrees

The main issue for UK universities is how Bologna principles are likely to be applied to higher degrees. The standard English format is for a three year undergraduate degree to be followed by a one year Masters, with a further three years leading to a doctorate. Funding councils operate within a 'one plus three model' for doctoral candidates and monitor completion rates rigorously with that in mind. Out of Bologna, however, has come a 'three plus two model', so that students would undertake a shortened first degree but then proceed to a two year Masters course. This satisfies the many European academics who are unhappy with the idea of three year degrees which they see as a dilution of standards and a dumbing down of higher education. However, the UK has established a local and international market for one year taught Masters programmes and, although there are some two year programmes, many believe that making two year master courses compulsory would be disadvantageous. The issue has yet to be resolved.

Perhaps even more problematic for the UK system are the current discussions about doctoral qualifications. The British system has traditionally eschewed taught components, requiring a student to produce an original piece of extended writing (the criteria which define originality vary according to the institution) which is then examined *in camera* by two specially appointed examiners. This contrasts with the public examination system that prevails across Europe and with the tradition in many countries of having an oral examination conducted by an examining board rather than by just two specialists. There are also large differences of opinion as to what constitutes a doctorate. In some countries, no PhD programmes existed so they have had to be invented. Some involve amassing credits for taught courses, on the North American model, some have opted for a system of hourly credits, whereby students have to demonstrate that they have attended a certain number of courses and acquired the requisite number of hours. The length of a doctoral dissertation varies not only across university systems, but also between institutions in each system and between disciplines. The only common denominator for determining doctoral quality at present is a statement that the thesis must be of publishable quality, though here again the terms of reference are loose and ambiguous.

One positive step has been the establishment of networks such as Hermes involving individual institutions to provide programmes of training for doctoral candidates. International seminar series for doctoral candidates have proliferated because funding is available and this trend will continue.

Future Implications

Opinion is divided as to the success of the Bologna process so far. Many European academics see the changes to their higher educational systems as happening too fast and without proper consultation; in short that many of the changes are based on political, rather than on intellectual, criteria. Setting the changes in train has involved an enormous amount of work, as there have had to be major modifications to the curriculum, changes in teaching methods and a radical rethinking of what degree programmes are actually for. There is widespread concern about how quality assurance controls will operate in practice and a strong resistance to the idea of an inspectorate, though there is also general recognition that some form of local and international quality assurance system is essential if there is to be genuine parity across the continent. Instituting higher degree programmes has also been a daunting task in some countries, with no precedent upon which to build and very diverse models upon which to draw. There is still a great deal of thinking to be done about master and doctoral qualifications.

In the United Kingdom, the changes have been less drastic so far, and Bologna has not had anything like the same impact that it has had in countries such as Portugal, Spain or the Netherlands. Nevertheless, European-wide mobility for students and for academics is undoubtedly going to bring major shifts of consciousness in all countries before very long.

One aspect of the student exchange schemes that pre-dated Bologna has been the difference in student movement between the UK and the rest of Europe. There have been far more students from other European countries opting to study in the UK than British students choosing to study abroad. This is principally because whereas continental students can follow courses in English, the decline in foreign language learning in UK schools and universities has had a drastic impact on the ability of students to take up opportunities to study in other countries (unless the degree be taught in English). This is a serious problem that will need to be addressed, since UK students are likely to find themselves disadvantaged in future when competing for jobs with students whose degree has been undertaken in two or more languages. Such degrees are among the advantages of the pan-European degrees.

Ideally, if more universities were to offer degree programmes in English, UK students might opt to study abroad, but at present the combination of student debt and poor linguistic skills is an obstacle to British student choice. Financial constraints have also been deterring UK students from undertaking higher degrees, and the possible implementation of a two-year Masters could make this situation worse.

CAN THE PRIZES STILL GLITTER?
The Future of British Universities in a Changing World

The British senior academic who asked in puzzlement what Bologna is all about would do well to reflect on the future implications of a European Higher Education Area, for it is well underway and is unlikely to be reversed. Individual countries will argue for the retention of some of their preferred institutional traditions, but have already shown willingness to jettison others. The principal area of struggle will be, inevitably, between academics and politicians, with the former urging a more cautious approach to change and the latter trying to push reforms through as fast as possible. The issue of how quality assurance agencies are to run is crucial, for academics across the continent are united in insisting upon the autonomy of intellectuals in any monitoring process and there is likely to be strong resistance to increased regulation.

In the UK, it is to be hoped that greater rapprochement with European university networks will regenerate interest in foreign languages and lead also to reforms of the antiquated system of acquiring a doctorate. Both the matter of providing doctor level courses and the way in which doctorates are currently examined are badly in need of modernisation.

The Bologna Declaration is idealistic and has emerged from a vision of Europe with which not every country agrees. The difficulties of ensuring similar quality from the Atlantic shores to the Black Sea, with so many different histories, different attitudes to the role of universities in society and different expectations, are enormous, but the underlying principle is sound. In an increasingly globalised world, with millions of people in transit every day, and in a Europe that sees itself as an economic community with widening borders and diminishing boundaries, ensuring the free movement of students is logical. What remains to be seen is how long and how hard is the road that still needs to be travelled to achieve that goal.

PRIVATE UNIVERSITIES AROUND THE WORLD

James Tooley and James Stanfield

James Tooley is professor of education policy at Newcastle University, where he directs the E.G. West Centre. He has recently completed a three-year research project funded by the John Templeton Foundation exploring low cost private education in developing countries. He is about to become strategic advisor to the $100 million Orient Global Foundation Education Fund aimed at providing investment for low cost private education.

James Stanfield is a PhD student in the E.G. West Centre, Newcastle University. He is co-author of a number of books and articles, including the collection Government Failure: E.G. West on Education.

A few years ago, James Tooley wrote a celebration of 25 years of the University of Buckingham, then, as now, Britain's only truly independent university (Tooley, 2002). In that piece, 'seven straws in the wind' were predicated, identifying likely trends that would impact on the future of British universities. Two of these trends appear as relevant today as they were then: the rise of private universities worldwide and, in particular, the rise of *for-profit* universities. In a world where governments struggle to invest in and maintain universities, and where competition is global, we predict that British universities will find it hard to keep up, particularly with the new breed of lean for-profit universities, hungry for expansion and offering great rewards to investors.

Only two decades ago private universities were either marginal or absent from the majority of countries around the world. Today however these new institutions are capturing a major portion of new enrolments across Eastern and Central Europe, the Middle East, Northern and Sub-Sahara Africa, East and South Asia, and Latin America. Recent data shows in Brazil, for instance, 89 percent of higher education institutions and 71 percent of enrolments in the private sector. In Chile, the figures are 93 percent and 71 percent. In the Philippines 81 percent of higher education institutions are private, while in South Korea it is 87 percent, with enrolments of 76 percent and 78 percent respectively (Levy, 2006).

In these countries, private institutions are currently not necessarily the most prestigious. They may be relatively small, but, importantly, they are often non-selective, catering for those students who have been excluded from access to state higher education. Because these institutions are serving potentially mass markets, the market is likely to start behaving in ways similar to other 'Bottom of the Pyramid' markets – through consolidation, the creation of brand names, with innovation spurred on by competition (Prahalad, 2005). This is particularly the case because of the prevalence of for-profit higher education institutions within these markets – which will be keen to expand market share to increase profits. In Brazil, for instance, around two-thirds of the private higher education institutions are for-profits, while in the Philippines, nearly half of all student enrolments in the for-profit private sector. From Malaysia it is reported that 90 percent of private higher education institutions (that make up 92 percent of total higher education institutions) are for-profit (Kinser and Levy, 2005).

A country where these trends can most clearly be observed is China, where currently it is estimated that 39 percent of higher education institutions and nearly 10 percent of enrolment is in the private sector, but where a revolution in the sector is clearly underway (Levy, 2006). From the mid-1980s onwards the Chinese government began to allow, even encourage, the development of private higher education, resulting in its rapid growth today, especially within its larger cities. Today, there are now over 1,200 private higher education institutions, enrolling up to one and half million students. As these private higher education institutions receive little or no financial assistance from the government, the majority are market driven, competing for students who pay tuition and other fees. An increasing number of private universities are also now looking to take advantage of their private status by attracting investment from financial markets. Most significantly, we can see consolidation and investment in brands already taking place in embryonic form: for China has recently witnessed the growth of a number of large education groups whose operations are focused entirely on education. Examples include Zhjiang Wan Li Education Group, Ningbo Hua

Mao Education Group, Ka Lunhu Education Group, Wuxi Zhong Rui Education Group, Heilongjiang East Asian Education Group and finally Beijing Nan Yang Education Group.

The majority of these private higher education institutions concentrate on courses designed to meet existing market needs, such as business management, marketing, finance and computer science. Some specialise in vocational and technical programmes, providing skilled technicians for local enterprises – something eschewed by their public counterparts. It is the private universities that these particularly helped to cultivate the millions of professional technicians for China's rapidly expanding economy. Currently, British universities are increasingly dependent on fees from overseas students, in particular from China, to supplement government funding. It is our view that as these for-profit higher education companies expand and consolidate in China, they will be seen to be offering a high-quality, low-cost alternative that will undermine current demand for western university places.

All this is about so-called developing countries, which some (although not the current authors) believe may not be so relevant to our situation in Britain. But then we can turn to the American market, and see some extraordinary developments taking place, particularly in for-profit higher education. The latest figures show nearly 60 percent of higher education institutions in America are private, with 23 percent of all enrolment. Importantly, within the private sector, 24 percent of enrolment is in the for-profit sector.

While companies have owned for-profit institutions since the 1930s they were usually owned as subsidiaries of companies that were not principally in the business of education. During the 1980s however a new generation of 'pure play' corporate owners began to emerge whose primary business was education. The chain of for-profit universities, DeVry, made its initial public offering in 1991, and signalled the start of what has been dubbed the '1990s Wall Street Era' (Kinser, 2006). DeVry was the first for-profit institution to go public as a stand alone degree-granting college; it initiated the steady and continuing growth in the number of degree-granting for profit institutions in the US. With the arrival of these new providers from the late 1990s onwards, the competitive environment is now beginning to change. These recent developments have signalled the transformation noted above that is beginning in developing countries, of consolidation of the market of for-profit higher education from the 'small mom and pop organisations' to 'giant shareholder-owned chains that tap into private capital markets to finance their expansion' (Kinser, 2006).

The thirteen Wall Street companies currently active in the for-profit higher education sector in the US are a diverse group. Their size and scope are recorded in Table 1.

Together these 13 publicly traded companies enrol a total of 871,000 students on more than 700 campuses across 44 states. In terms of the number of students, the Apollo Group is currently the largest organisation with a total of 255,600 students enrolled across 82 campuses. According to figures from 2004 these 13 companies have a combined market value of $34 billion, with the wealthiest being Apollo ($14.7 billion), Kaplan Higher Education ($4.9 billion) and Career Education Corporation ($3.1 billion). While the Apollo Group lost over $2 billion in market value during 2005, all thirteen have increased in value since 2000 with the following six at least doubling in value: ITT Educational Services, Career Education, Strayer, Apollo Group, Laureate Education and Education Management Corporation.

As is clear from the table, the 13 'Wall Street' institutions have expanded rapidly since going public. Three major strategies have been employed to move forward this expansion. First, the institutions have simply expanded enrolment in existing locations. Second they have expanded enrolment by opening new branches in new locations – Apollo for instance added 28 campuses between 2000 and 2004, while Corinthian added 89. Third, the companies have acquired competitor institutions. Most of the growth of Apollo and DeVry was the result of branching out into new campuses. Conversely, much of the growth of Corinthian and Kaplan was through the acquisition of competitor institutions.

All of the for-profit higher education institutions in the US focus their activities on delivering educational programmes in career-orientated fields including: personal and culinary services; health professions and clinical sciences, business and computer sciences. However, those that are quoted on Wall Street are more likely to

Table 1: Private for-profit universities quoted on Wall Street

Ownership	Founded	Public	Enrolment		Campuses	
			At IPO	2004	At IPO	2004
Apollo	1973	1994	27,469	255,600	33	82
Career Educ.	1994	1998	13,000	101,5000	18	82
Concorde	1986	1988	n/a	9,323	19	12
Corinthian	1995	1999	16,000	64,810	35	133
DeVry	1931	1991	25,000	55,575	19	75
Education Mgt.	1962	1996	14,000	58,828	13	67
EVCI	1997	1999	n/a	3,900	0	2
ITT	1963	1994	22,000	40,876	54	77
Kaplan	1940	1996	4,300	57,600	14	75
Laureate	1979	1993	n/a	159,250	0	44
Lincoln	1999	2005	16,266		28	28
Strayer	1892	1996	7,500	34,687	8	32
UTI	1965	2003	10,568	13,076	7	8

Source: Kinser, 2006.

concentrate their programmes on computer science, business and health, with over 80 percent offering at least one of these three courses. The 'Wall Street' universities are found to have an even narrower focus than the for-profits in general – offering only 26 specialities compared to 36 programmes in the for-profits in general. Indeed, the Apollo Group awards 75 percent of its qualifications in business, while Corinthian awards 71 percent of its qualifications in health services.

In Britain, one of the early and key innovations of the private University of Buckingham was to move its working year away from what it considered to be the anachronistic one, common in state universities, to allow continuous year-round use of its facilities, with no long summer break. Similar innovations are apparent in the for-profit universities in the United States. Amongst all for-profit institutions, the most popular schedule (48 percent) is the continuous calendar, with no common breaks for holidays, adapting the teaching schedule for the convenience of the learners, rather than to the faculty. A further 20 percent have a four session model, similar to the

Table 2: Most Popular Instructional Programmes

All For-Profit Institutions	Percent of Campuses offering courses
Personal and culinary services	41.6
Health professions and clinical sciences	38.6
Business, management, marketing	30.3
Computer and information sciences	29.3
Engineering technologies	15
Legal professions and studies	12.3
Wall Street	
Computer and information sciences	60.4
Business, management, marketing	58.7
Health professions and clinical sciences	51.2
Education	38.7
Engineering technologies	32.9
Legal professions and studies	15.3
Visual and performing arts	14.4

Source: Kinser, 2006.

University of Buckingham. Key players in the 'Wall Street' group offering non-traditional academic calendars include Apollo, Concorde, Corinthian, Kaplan and UTI.

One way of making economies for the for-profit model in higher education is the extensive use of part-time faculty, paid to teach specific courses over a particular time period, rather than employed year round for teaching and research as in traditional universities. In general, about 65 percent of faculty in the for-profit sector is employed on such a part-time basis. However, this bias towards part-time faculty is most strongly supported in those higher education companies quoted on Wall Street: where 75 percent of institutions rely on part time faculty, compared with 52 percent of the non-quoted for-profit institutions. (However, these figures may be slightly misleading, because Apollo alone accounts for two thirds of all part-time faculty employed by the 13 Wall Street institutions, with 99 percent of Apollo's faculty employed part time), (Kinser, 2006)

Important lessons can be learned from the US experience, especially from the successful growth strategies employed in recent years by the for-profit players. Significantly, new growth potential in the US may be limited, and these chains will be looking for expansion in the rest of the world. Careful readers of the *Times Higher Education Supplement* back pages, for instance, will have noted Kaplan's recent acquisition of campuses in London, and their aggressive marketing for top personnel to move their vision forward in the UK.

Private higher education is becoming hugely important around the world. In many countries, including the important example of China, it serves students otherwise excluded from state education, and thus has access to potentially huge markets. For profit private higher education is also growing at an extraordinary rate, with large brands seeking to become global players. No-one in British universities can afford to ignore these trends. Perhaps we could even sit up and think about the possibility of increasing private investment here too.

References:

Kinser, Kevin (forthcoming) Dimensions of Corporate Ownership in For-Profit Higher Education, *Review of Higher Education*

Kinser, Kevin and Levy, Daniel C. (2005), *The For-Profit Sector: US Patterns and International Echoes in Higher Education*, PROPHE Working Paper #5, February. Program for Research on Private Higher Education, Educational Administration & Policy Studies, University at Albany, State University of New York

Levy, Daniel C (2006) The Unanticipated Explosion: Private Higher Education's Surge, *Comparative Education Review*, vol. 50, no.2.

Prahalad, C.K. (2005), *The Fortune at the Bottom of the Pyramid: Eradicating Poverty through Profits*, Wharton School Publishing, Upper Saddle River, NJ.

Tooley, James (2002) The Future of Higher Education: Seven Straws in the Wind, in Tooley, James (ed.), *Buckingham at 25: the future of higher education*, London, Institute of Economic Affairs.

SCIENCE: THE EMERGENCE OF THE INTERVERSITY

Peter Atkins

Peter Atkins is professor of chemistry in the University of Oxford, and fellow of Lincoln College. He was educated at the University of Leicester. After his PhD (in electron spin resonance) he went to the University of California as a Harkness fellow. His principal activity is writing textbooks on chemistry, which have a global market, and books on science for the general public. He is a trustee of Agora.

Science is pre-eminently a global pursuit, for it deals with objective truth, which is the same regardless of one's cultural conditioning. Science is transnational and transcultural and, despite what sociologists of science claim, it is independent of the cultural milieu. Of course it has fashions, and waves of activity roll across its landscape, biotechnology today, nanotechnology tomorrow, and so on; but that tidal flow is a reflection of a scientist's interest in exploring new niches, new fields of endeavour, and bringing to bear new techniques. Yes, theories are typically, but not invariably, ephemeral, with what seem like revolutions displacing the cherished; but almost always the replacement of one theory by another is evidence of maturation, not the sudden realisation that a whole intellectual community had goofed. And, yes, when applied to complex issues science has not always been right, but it has always been better than guesswork in alliance with sentiment.

Science is not only global but also increasingly expensive. The further one travels from the obvious, the greater the cost of the journey. That is true whether one is burrowing into the underworld of matter, unravelling a genotype, formulating a better treatment for a disease, travelling to the Moon, or determining the composition of a distant star. Ignorance, though, is more expensive. Ignorance leads to mistakes, ignorance results in disaster, and ignorance leaves a nation economically disadvantaged.

Knowledge, too, can be expensive. Lives prolonged well beyond their conventional span consume the resources of nations and Icaric aspirations can stretch mankind beyond the perimeters of safety. Warfare enhanced by science is more destructive than victory typically warrants: far better that two kings slog it out on a beach than a nation's infrastructure is pulverised to achieve the same end. Aspiration fuelled by a technology that consumes ever more energy could be the ultimate in expense.

Science is not only high-investment, high-return but no-investment, negative-return. Economies that fail to make the investment are left stranded as the tide of industrial and commercial activity ebbs from their shores, and as the young minds from which innovation springs float off in it to more supportive regimes. They know that their skills in science are of universal applicability, and have no difficulty in transplanting their function into other nations. Globalisation is not just an elaboration of commerce and manufacture and a universalisation of knowledge: it is fluidity of employment and the migration of innovative skills.

* * *

Because pessimism stultifies and optimism encourages, I shall adopt the view that science achieves more good than bad, and that its furtherance in a global effort is fundamentally right for the planet and its inhabitants. That good ranges from tangible achievements in medicine and technology, to the deepening of our understanding of our nature and the fabric of reality.

The universities have always been central to the furtherance of fundamental science. They have not been alone, for notable and in some cases cosmically significant advances have also stemmed from enlightened industrial laboratories (the discovery of the cosmic microwave background, which is central to our understanding of the origin of the universe, was achieved at Bell Telephone Laboratories) and of institutes allied closely to universities (the Medical Research Council's Laboratory of Molecular Biology in Cambridge is an outstanding example). Institutes that constitute a thread parallel to universities but which have been detached from most teaching activities, such as those on the Max Planck Institutes in Germany and the similar institutes built on the old Soviet model and now represented by the Russian and Chinese Academies of science, have also made seriously important contributions, as their staffs, largely unencumbered by the obligations of teaching, can focus on research.

CAN THE PRIZES STILL GLITTER?
The Future of British Universities in a Changing World

Universities must remain at the forefront of globally significant research. Research that lacks global significance is second-rate at best, and attractive only to second-rate brains. Second-rate brains fail to inspire their students, who turn to more vibrant pursuits or, if they stay in science, are less likely to achieve their potential. Any government must accept that one of its principal duties is to facilitate the pursuit of globally significant research in all branches of science.

That means money, but not only money. Money, of course, is the easy answer, for it allows a university to fulfil is aspirations by buying faculty on the global market, establishing their laboratories with the finest equipment, supplying them with an army of students, providing a welcoming and attractive environment for post-doctoral workers, and relieving them of whatever duties they find irksome. The Royal Society Research Professorships come reasonably close to this model, and have been resoundingly successful. But for the most part, universities simply cannot afford to buy on the global market either in terms of salaries or infrastructure. It is doubtful that any government would have the guts to raid the national larder to fund a significant number of such posts, although it could do so easily if it ceased waging wars and re-equipping the country with weapons systems that in practice are unusable. Half a dozen MRC-like, Princeton-like institutes of advanced research spanning the sciences and embedded in the milieu of our two or three most respected universities would do the trick and pay for themselves within a decade or two.

"Embedded in respected universities" is the key phrase here. It is essential for the intellectual vibrancy of both research and teaching that there be a seamless interaction between these two components of a university. Undergraduates need to sense that they are in an institution of world-class standing in the pursuit of knowledge as well as its retailing, for that encourages them to achieve their own potential. There need to be permeable walls between the two components of an institution so that a researcher fired with enthusiasm can easily find a way to transmit it to the young without the impediment of thwarting bureaucracy. And where these institutes should be planted is in universities that already have a global presence. It will seem like special pleading, for I am at one obvious candidate, but the honest truth is that when viewed from a global perspective, the United Kingdom has only two universities that are perceived as truly world class, premier league. Any government who wanted to build on strength and invest in quality would have to swallow its prejudices and acknowledge that the only sensible way forward to build a globally respected environment for science would be to invest most of its funds in Oxford and Cambridge. Any other approach, except for the inclusion of our principal science-only institution, Imperial College, would be an inappropriate dilution of funds that would represent a failure to do what canny investors do, which is to build on strength and, in this instance, global perception.

Yes, a handful of other universities provide a brilliant corona to these two-and-a-half institutions, but bullets need to be bit. Other universities have departments of undoubted importance (where would the world be without DNA fingerprinting, which emerged from Leicester?) But I say once again, bullets must be bit. The only sensible way to use limited funds is to invest not only in actual quality but, from a marketing point of view, perceived quality.

* * *

There are, as always, other ways forward, and other models. There are little things that can be done to make life in a British university more enjoyable and therefore, it is reasonable to suppose, more attractive when appointment boards are fishing in global waters. Fishing there is absolutely essential in a globalised science world, for the best talent emerges anywhere, and it is essential for a conventional university (in contrast to the variety I discuss below) to land the big fish wherever they are found. Stipends are, of course, a major bait whatever people say, but a close second lie the infrastructure of support and the quality of the ambience. Support includes the tangibles of laboratory life, the equipment, the students, and the staff; the ambience includes both the tangibles of family life, including education and healthcare, and the intangibles, such as the cultural milieu.

The infrastructure of support includes the readiness of funds and the absence of irksome intrusion. In short, the infrastructure should be welcoming, funding generous to those a university has identified as worth investing in, and the bureaucratic superstructure minimal. There is little doubt that the intrusive bureaucracy of the modern trustless society must be diminished so as to liberate free-ranging minds from the annoyances of irksome paperwork. For excellence to be achieved on a global stage, scientists need to be free to act untrammelled by the petty intrusions of national bean-counting procedures, at least to the extent that these intrusions are less than in the other countries that are competing for their favours. This might sound like special pleading. It is. Because science is intrinsically international and the exploitation of its technological and economic fruits likewise international, more so than any other academic activity, special pleading on its behalf is wholly justified.

I have spoken of the conventional university, one of the traditional island-like universities that are sprinkled largely independently through a country. There are other models. In a truly global scientific world there would be no identifiable institutions and no discrete membership of a particular institution. In the extreme, there would be only a single university in the world and a single unified scientific endeavour. This model, which is built on the Internet, is already emerging as scientists establish collaborations that span the world. It is a natural extension of what is already becoming established to extrapolate it to a global activity that is not just peripheral to the activities of a few universities but has absorbed all universities into a single global entity, an interversity.

The emergence of an interversity might be driven by a variety of factors. The carrot will be the establishment of Internet facilities that provide ever greater personal presence. Expensive systems are already available that enable the equivalent of boardroom discussions; it is easy to extrapolate these systems to the point where scientists seem to be present in person with their colleagues wherever they are in the world and that discussions take place with as much casual ease as those that currently take place over coffee. Already expensive apparatus is available to scientists unable to be present in person (the Hubble Space Telescope is an obvious example). The emergence of reliable computer simulation rather than actual experiment diminishes further the role of being present in a particular location. The development of manipulative techniques that are already used in the nuclear industry and in surgery will further reduce the need to be actually present. The stick that will drive this distance-science is the cost of travel that is sure to increase dramatically over the next decades and the rise in the irksomeness of travel that we are all already encountering. The travel-overhead is becoming so great that virtual meetings and interactions are inevitable. Universities that want to be in the forefront of globalisation should already be starting to develop relationships that are directed at the uniting of their research activities, just as some are already establishing relationships for the exchange of undergraduates, and doing so by anticipating the role of the Internet in the facilitation of easy interaction.

* * *

Any discussion of the globalisation of the scientific endeavour of universities cannot ignore the interaction of industry, both with the role of spin-off companies and the interaction with already globalised industries! .

It would be irresponsible, but perhaps highly effective, to suggest that academic salaries should be kept low in order to encourage scientists to set up spin-off companies to augment their incomes. However, it is certainly the case that a significant number of academics have hit the jackpot and that universities see spin-off companies as a hybrid of milch cow and golden goose. The pressure to spin research into cash will undoubtedly continue and will increase as successful examples show what can be obtained for both individual and institution.

How these golden milch cows will thrive in a globalised university system is hard to predict, not least because different universities have different rules about the commercialisation of intellectual property. At its simplest, the research group responsible for setting up the company will be exploiting its own ideas and there will be a clear trail of ownership consisting of the host university and the scientists, whatever their nationality and affiliation. At its most complex, the research group will not be owned by a single university and the intellectual property will be distributed over institutions with different rules and indeed adopt aggressive postures of ownership between the institutions themselves. There will be solutions, as there always are when cash is at stake, but these conflicts must be foreseen. Everyone involved will have to perceive themselves as forming a team and adopt the long-term view that it is better to encourage further lucrative collaborations than to strangle future innovation by internecine strife.

The opposite facet of this enterprise is the sponsorship of research by globalised industry. Now it is commonplace for industry to support targeted research, and some blue-sky research, in localised universities, one project here and another there. In a jointly globalised emporium, the global industry will sponsor distributed research in the countries in which it operates, and thus act as a marriage broker between dispersed institutions. Thus, the globalisation of industry, already so far advanced, will drive that of the universities that interact with it in research.

* * *

Globalised research might bring in its train a globalised Research Assessment Exercise (RAE), a procedure already distorting the pursuance of long-term research and consuming the energies of researchers throughout the United Kingdom, not to mention sharpening the wiles of vice-chancellors throughout the land. Heaven forbid that the RAE also becomes globalised, perhaps as a function of UNESCO, an organisation deplorably and increasingly disinterested in science, and likewise distort the system but now on a global scale.

But if research money is to be applied globally, not perhaps from a common purse but in a scheme involving matching funds from domestic sources, then a globally acceptable assessment procedure must be in place. That will be a dangerous time for science, for 'international' in the past has always been virtually synonymous with 'heavy-handed and bureaucratic'; and obligations to treat contributing countries equally has meant that political necessity has displaced real talent. The consequent danger is that mediocre, safe science will be encouraged at the expense of brilliant individual innovation. Ways will have to be found to allow global science to flourish with the minimum of international fuss. The history of international collaboration, except for a few brilliant exceptions (CERN comes to mind), inspires nothing but pessimism.

The future direction of science is reasonably easy to identify in general terms and its recognition should underlie all our planning. There are two emerging directions of science: one is towards simplicity and the other is towards complexity. The simplicity strand is represented almost solely by the exploration of the fabric of reality, the identification of ever more fundamental components of the universe and with it a deepening of our understanding of our origin and future. The exploration of complexity epitomises almost all the rest of the scientific and technological endeavour. Thus, it epitomises molecular biology and its ramifications into genetic engineering. But it is not biology alone: complexity is found in the creation of new materials and the current fashion—a highly important fashion despite the glitz—of nanotechnology. Complexity is all about the remarkable and sometimes unpredictable properties that emerge from congeries of interacting simplicities. Smart structures, be they natural, synthetic, or a combination of the two, will be the principal objects of study and the principal tool, apart from chemists' ability to synthesise and modify them, will be computation. That computation will be the dominant manner of investigation—for simulation, analysis, and portrayal— makes the distribution of scientific research over the collaborative network of the interversity a highly practical proposition.

* * *

Science will falter if new blood does not continue to flow through its arteries. It is essential for the progress of humanity that young minds are encouraged to come into the core subjects, namely mathematics, physics, chemistry, and biology. It would be wrong to say that these subjects are currently in a critical state (and certainly not true of self-confident countries like China and India), but their decline in the UK and elsewhere is alarming. These concerns are now commonplace and serious efforts are being made worldwide to restore the enthusiasm for the sciences among the young. The problem we need to address in the current context is the effect of globalisation on the composition, quality, and abundance of the incoming stream of science students.

Globalisation could tilt the problem in either direction. The pessimistic tilt is that globalisation will provide opportunities for our own young minds to disperse into what they perceive to be more welcoming and rewarding environments, a reprise of the brain drain of yesteryear, but at a younger level. To counteract that drift it will be essential for the universities, with the enthusiastic involvement and support of the government, to market the sciences and the overwhelming importance of a secure grounding in the hard sciences (which these days includes biology). The Japanese experience seems to have been that the award recently of Nobel Prizes to them has stimulated a surge in applications for science; but that kind of motivation is hard to organise, except by hopeful, long-term investment. It is a sign, though, that in a global market internationally respected and media-attractive prizes for research can stimulate interest in joining an educational stream. There should be a worry among those whose interest is in this kind of intellectual trickle-down effect that the United Kingdom is starting to lag behind in the Nobel stakes, and more locally a worry that so great a university as Oxford currently (mid 2007) has not a single Nobel Laureate on its staff. The government must take on board the essential demands of pulling in the new stream of students by ensuring that facilities provided for research are of the highest quality and the demands of pushing on those students by encouragement from below.

In a global market, global marketing must be a core activity even simply to ensure that we retain our home-growth of students. Here, though, lies the opportunity that globalisation offers. Provided the quality of our undergraduate courses survives the attrition of under-funding and the nibbling away of intellectual commitment in our high-schools by the introduction of pusillanimous curricula, we can draw from the international well of talent. This drawing of course already takes place; it has been marginally enhanced by our membership of the EU and has been effectuated to some extent by the establishment of overseas simulations of our universities. However, although there are tangible benefits of importing actual bodies and exporting brick-and-mortar simulacrums of our campuses, the future will lie in distance learning. Universities should already be considering how to extend their individual campus experience to penetrate markets overseas and to consider how the interversity can effectuate instruction as well as collaboration for research.

* * *

In short, the Internet is the opportunity for science in our universities. It enhances the reach of the human mind by providing a cheap and readily accessible mode of collaboration, with connected, collaborating brains greater than the sum of the parts. The scientific endeavour, increasingly reliant on computation, is ideally suited to the distribution of effort over a global interversity, and the sense of global effort should stimulate the young to become part of this remarkable human endeavour.

THE UNIVERSITY AS CRUCIBLE OF ENTERPRISE: THE MIT/STANFORD MODEL

Henry Etzkowitz

Henry Etzkowitz is Professor of Management of Innovation at the University of Newcastle. He served for many years as Director of the Science Policy Institute at the State University of New York. Henry is author of Triple Helix: A New Model of Innovation, and MIT and the Rise of Entrepreneurial Science. He is co-founder of the Triple Helix international conference series on university-industry-government relations.

Two prototypical academic entrepreneurs, Vannevar Bush of MIT and Frederick Terman of Stanford University are exemplars of the university as crucible of enterprise through their technology transfer and firm-formation activities in the early 20th century. During the 1930's depression Terman developed a close relationship with the R&D laboratory of a large corporation, negotiating agreements, preparing disclosures and tracking the revenues returned. Terman's objective in creating a licensing program, based on his inventions in radio and electronics, was to return funds to his university lab to support graduate student research.

The start-up process, from the late 19th century, became the primary mode of technology transfer from MIT. Vannevar Bush, at MIT developed a consulting relationship with various firms during the 1920's, following the model of his professors, the consulting engineers who had been recruited into professorships at MIT to jump-start the development of research at what had essentially been an engineering teaching college until the advent of the 20th century. When his employer did not take up a proposed solution that Bush believed possessed general utility with broad commercial potential, he resorted to the establishment of a new firm to realise its value.

The potential of high-tech firm-formation for regional economic development was also perceived by MIT administrators as early as the 1930's. How to institutionalise and generalise the start-up process became the focus of a regional economic development strategy that led to the invention of the venture capital firm in the early post-war (Etzkowitz, 2002). The emergence of the entrepreneurial university with a "third mission" of contributing to economic and social development incorporated the first and second missions of the teaching and Research University. The Humboldtian and Land Grant academic models, with their strong links to government, are synthesised into a complementary format in which each mission enhances and supports the other, despite persisting tensions.

Sources of the Entrepreneurial University Model

There has been considerable interaction between MIT and Stanford; Silicon Valley and Route 128, with innovations in technology transfer and venture capital moving in both directions. At different stages in his career Terman expanded upon developments at MIT (Etzkowitz 2003). Upon retirement in the mid 1960's he diffused these ideas as a consultant to Texas, India and South Korea, where they were taken up and to Northern New Jersey and New York City where they were not. Despite much "learning from the other" both universities and their regions can be seen as representing distinctive "Brownfield" and "Greenfield" types, in part, due to the circumstances of their origins and development.

Universities have been key to growth of these regions as high tech centres from the mid-19th century. MIT, for instance, was founded as a technological university, a variant of the European polytechnic model but with a founding orientation to encompass long term research aims as well as short term goals. Its specific remit was to contribute to the enhancement of the industrial base of its region, the U.S's earliest center of technological industry.

Northern California has been transformed from a Greenfield agricultural site to a high tech region. Boston's history has been more complex, a high tech region in the early 19th century declined to a Brownfield site due to loss of industry, with low tech remnants. However, from at least the 1920's, new firms based on new technologies were established that have restored the region's status as a high tech industrial centre.

In the late 19th century, when Stanford was founded, the surrounding region was agricultural in nature, with technological development based on transferring and utilising the new electrical technologies. Stanford Engineering School provided trained persons for this purpose, although many graduates had to leave the region since the technological base was not strong enough to employ all its graduates.

MIT's relationship to industry was similarly shaped by the nature of its regional base which underwent considerable transformation over time. During its organising stage in the 1840's its founder's intention was to contribute new technologies as well as graduates to support the region's position as the centre of U.S. technological industry. However, by the late 19th century, several decades after its founding in the 1860's the limited development of the school kept its contribution at the level of providing trained graduates. By the 1920's with local industry declining but with MIT gaining a strong research focus, new firms could be spun off from this base.

The Founding of MIT: Triple Helix Interactions

The concept for MIT was developed in the mid-19th century, through the leadership of William Barton Rogers, a professor of geology at the University of Virginia. Rogers envisioned a university that would contribute to the enhancement of industrial technology, through the conduct of research, strongly holding that fundamental or basic research could make an important contribution to that objective. To encourage interaction between university and industry, the new university should be located in an industrial region. At the time, the Boston area was the major industrial centre of the US so Rogers moved to Boston, at the suggestion of his brother, a businessperson in the region, who helped him introduce the concept to business and political leaders.

MIT was founded in 1862, with contributions from local businesspersons and one/third of Massachusetts share of the federal land grant to establish universities that would play a role in economic development; MIT was the only land grant university at the time focused on industry; all the rest had as their main mission improving the agricultural specialties of their state. Although Rogers' vision was large, the available means limited MIT to perform as a teaching college for most of the first half century of its existence. However, by the turn of the century MIT began to initiate research by hiring in as professors consulting engineers, who advised industry on new products and processes and conducted research, as necessary in support of this task. As university professors, they taught students, carried out research but also continued their previous business careers as consultants.

Their fellow professors viewed their activities form the perspective of MIT as it had actually evolved, as a teaching college, rather than from the perspective of Rogers' original vision. They called for the new "consulting" professors to drop their external activities and focus on education. Their new colleagues, replied not by justifying their activities in its own terms but rather on the ground that it made them better teachers since they could bring real world examples from their consulting activities into the classroom. A committee was established to adjudicate this controversial issue. By the time a final report was made disallowing consulting, the consulting professors students, like Vannevar Bush, had risen to high positions in the Institute.

Indeed, Bush as Dean received the report and replied that this was not the terms under which I was hired at MIT. Nevertheless, traditional views were taken into account and a compromise was made. Consulting allowed on a regulated basis, one day per week, a substantial but not unlimited time. The so-called one-fifth rule spread throughout US academia. Subsequent discussion debated whether one day per week included or excluded week-ends and holidays but basically the rule was taken to mean a that while consulting was legitimate; it should not take so much time as to interfere with teaching and research.

The legitimisation of consultation, from which firm-formation, also emanated, when sponsors did not put into practice the consultants suggestions and the decision was made, by Vannevar Bush and other professors to establish a firm themselves. MIT was the first entrepreneurial university. The unity of theory and practice was part of its founders' vision; the one-fifth rule established a clear path for interaction with industry. Other universities followed more slowly. At Stanford, considered by many to be a highly entrepreneurial university, it was only in the mid 1990's that firm formation became accepted. According to a close observer, the University's Director of Technology Licensing, There has been a "...culture change at Stanford since early 90's Previously entrepreneurship was tolerated; Now it is encouraged." (Ku, 2005).

Stanford's Path to the Entrepreneurial University Model[1]

Stanford's originated as a general purpose liberal arts university with a full range of relatively equal disciplinary departments, although it included an engineering school and practical implications in its founders intentions, and thus took a different path toward becoming an entrepreneurial university than MIT, an institution specialised in science and technology but nevertheless with subsidiary humanities elements from its outset, included to broaden the education of its students, to encourage them to become broad scale technology managers.

These paths toward the entrepreneurial university, directly at MIT and indirectly at Stanford, are exemplified by the activities of each school's prototypical entrepreneurial academics, Vannevar Bush at MIT and Frederick Terman at Stanford. These two electrical engineers were well known to each other. Indeed, Terman was Bush's PhD student at MIT and was invited to continue his career there as a member of the faculty but returned to Stanford, due to illness that constrained the early years of his career.

The differences between Bush and Terman, MIT and Stanford, can be seen in their respective views of intellectual property. Bush became discouraged about patents, as a young Assistant Professor, when he found no takers for a patent he had taken out and paid for. Henceforth, Bush pursued a consulting path, solving problems for firms and then taking theoretical issues back to the university to work on with his students.

---

[1] Recent data from Stanford is based on the author's participant observation in OTL, Feb-August 2005, including interviews with faculty members, administrators and OTL staff.

When an employer did not take up an idea that Bush thought had significant commercial value, he organised a start-up firm, Raytheon, with capital from college friends at Tufts. As Terman's academic career progressed; he faced difficulties in providing support for graduate students. Indeed the famous duo of Hewlett and Packard, almost did not occur when one was forced to go east to gain employment, later being invited back to Stanford with the offer of a graduate fellowship.

The intellectual property that Terman generated from his research became a source of fellowship funds. Through an agreement with a former student who had become director of Research at ITT (International Telephone and Telegraph) on Broad Street in New York City's financial district, but also home to R&D facilities, including Bell labs during the pre-war era, Terman forwarded disclosures and received payments that he used to support graduate students. Terman also received inquiries from abroad for his improvements in radio technology and offered similar terms when they did not interfere with his primary relationship to ITT (Terman Papers, Stanford Archives).

In effect, Terman operated a technology licensing office from his faculty office, with a disclosure numbering system and dockets of individual inventions. This occurred more than 30 years before Niels Riemers established a licensing office as an administrative arm of the university. Terman was also active in firm formation, encouraging Hewlett and Packard to form their firm and Bush participated in technology licensing, making regular appearances before MIT's faculty patent committee both as an inventor and as an advisor with suggestions on how to improve other peoples inventions (Etzkowitz, 1995). Nevertheless, Terman and Bush may be taken to exemplify two different, yet complementary, pathways of university industry relations: providing technology to existing firms and using university originated technology as the base for new firms.

University Technology Transfer

The "marketing model" of university technology transfer has superceded an earlier more legalistic approach in which the primary goal was to gain legal protection, primarily in the form of a patent, for technology. The marketing model represents a more activist approach of seeking out firms to utilise technology, invented at university, in which the university has taken an interest. The marketing format of technology transfer was invented by Niels Reimers, the founding director of Stanford University's Office of Technology Licensing (OTL) and then passed on to MIT where it replaced an attempt by the university to act as a venture capitalist, selecting technologies to invest in. This early attempt at university venture capital was built on a faculty committee system of managing intellectual property that had been established in the early 20th century, rather than a professional venture capital arm as in current practice.

When the university investment approach was judged to be a failure, MIT called in Stanford's Director of Technology Licensing to re-organise MIT's operation. Starting form scratch in the late 1970's when technology transfer was a minor responsibility of the University's Office of Contracts and Grants, an administrative unit primarily responsible for dealing with faculty research grants from the federal government, Reimer's, who was then a member of that staff proposed to set up an independent office to actively promote the university's technology to industry. This effort may be seen as a logical extension of the so—called linear model—going from scientific research in the university, typically funded by government since the 2nd World War, to industry for product development.

Nevertheless, the linear model has rarely worked as an automatic "hands off" process (Etzkowitz 2006a). Rare is the technology so self apparently useful and fully realised as it comes out of a university laboratory that it can simply be taken up by an industrial firm and immediately be utilised. Perhaps ironically, such a technology, the Cohen Boyer patent was such an exceptional case, one that provided an ideological model for university technology transfer in recent decades that has been difficult to realise in practice except for a few exceptional cases. Nevertheless, university tech transfer, although still controversial to some academic economists who believe that it will divert faculty members' attention from basic research. Nevertheless, it has been shown that those professors who patent the most also publish the most, a not surprising finding (Blumenthal et al 1986; Van Looy et al 2004).

Publication and patenting have become an overlay, a sequence of activities that although apparently at odds, that can be made compatible. An astute faculty member at Stanford has worked out an arrangement with OTL, allowing a direct relationship with a patent attorney who advises on patentability of an idea even before the invention is made. The process of intellectual property protection moves forward informally even before a disclosure statement is filed or indeed before the invention itself is fully realised. Indeed the discussion typically starts with an idea that is then moved through the research process in the faculty members group simultaneously with IP considerations taken into account.

This shift from transfer to firm formation is propelled by the early stage nature of most academic originated technology. Technology transfer is expected to be the movement of technology between organisations and, in the particular case of university tech transfer, between different types of organisations. However, due to the early stage nature of most academic originated technology, transfer typically takes place to a new firm that the university often plays a key role in founding.

The Google Case

Google exemplifies the shift from transfer to incubation due to the vastly greater amount of funds that can be earned from a successful start-up. OTL had the opportunity as a result of its marketing process to license the Google search technology to an existing firm. The state of the art of the technology was not a barrier. A search industry existed with the capability to recognise the potential uses of the Google algorithms. OTL, based on the criteria of realising the full financial worth of Google search opted to encourage the formation of a new firm.

After the Google IPO which earned the university more than 200 million form its ownership of 2-3 % of the equity in the firm; the Stanford Management Corporation evaluated this apparent success as a relative failure. The IPO had realised billions but the university had gained only a very small part of the earnings. In addition to the percentage that the university received for its "incubation" assistance the Management Corporation proposed that in the future that the university make an investment in each new firm that OTL licenses a university originated technology. By acting as venture capitalist, the university would receive an additional 2-3% of equity in a firm.

Conclusion

An academic transformation from teaching to research to entrepreneurial university can be identified, with different types of regional relationships identified at other universities, beginning with Stanford. The start-up model, typically with the academic as a consultant to the successful start-up, became the norm at MIT. Universities recently involved in technology transfer may be expected to take more explicit measures than schools that are located in successful high tech regions.

Due to its presence in Silicon Valley, the world's leading technology conurbation, Stanford University is expected to have a visible manifestation of technology transfer such as an incubator facility. As the University's director of technology transfer put it, "Visitors expect to see explicit actions." Such actions can be identified in the university's and regions' development. Once success was achieved, a less explicit model could be relied upon, in response to objections to academic entrepreneurship, even if it did not tap the university's full potential.

Although Stanford is one of the most successful universities in generating returns from its intellectual property only a relatively small proportion of its faculty is actively involved with the university's Office of Technology Licensing (OTL), even in research areas with recognised commercial potential. There are two obvious explanations (1) is that a highly entrepreneurial faculty is working directly with industry, transferring its technology through consulting arrangements rather than through the patenting licensing mechanism. (2) many faculty are not highly entrepreneurially oriented.

Lacking explicit mechanisms to assist transfer, they are not interested in engaging in the start-up process through the available informal routes which require a high degree of entrepreneurial interest and involvement on the part of the inventor. Thus, students may take their technology out through the traditional route of becoming firm employees even when offered the opportunity to become an entrepreneur. Growth of ecosystem based on wanting to see impact of ideas is broader than firm formation but provides a context for it.

University technology transfer increasingly focuses on creating new firms based upon academic research. Despite its title, the reality is that the tech transfer office is often less involved in negotiating across established boundaries and more in creating a new boundary around a technology, through helping establish a new firm. MIT and Stanford/ Silicon Valley and Boston have been the exemplars of entrepreneurial universities and successful technology regions. Specific individuals and initiatives can be identified as the sources of these developments that are replicated and translated into other universities and regions world-wide (Etzkowitz, 2006b).

References

Blumenthal D M Gluck, KS Louis, MA Stoto, and D Wise. 1986. "University-industry research relationships in biotechnology: implications for the university" *Science* 13 June: Vol 232 no 4756, pp. 1361 – 1366.

Etzkowitz, Henry. 1994. *"Knowledge as Property: The Massachusetts Institute of Technology and the Debate over Academic Patent Policy"* Minerva Winter.

2002 *MIT and the Rise of Entrepreneurial Science*. London: Routledge 2003. Research Groups as 'Quasi-Firms': the invention of the entrepreneurial university. Research Policy, Feb.

2006 a The new visible hand: an assisted linear model of science and innovation policy *Science and Public Policy* Vol 33, Number 5, 1 June, pp 310-320(11).

2006 b The 'Triple Helix' of the Hadrian's Valley Economy *Parliamentary Monitor*, July/August.

Ku, Katherine, 2005, Director of Stanford OTL, Interview with the author.

Terman Papers, Stanford University Archives.

Van Looy, Bart; Ranga, Marina; Callaert, Julie; Debackere, Koenraad Zimmermann, Edwin. (2004) Combining entrepreneurial and scientific performance in academia: towards a compounded and reciprocal Matthew-effect?" *Research Policy* 33: 3 (April) 425-441.

Editors: Hugo de Burgh, Anna Fazackerley, Jeremy Black

Part 3

CASE STUDIES

HOW ARE UNIVERSITIES CHANGING TO FIT THE NEW MARKET?

Editors: Hugo de Burgh, Anna Fazackerley, Jeremy Black

SUSTAINING OXFORD AS WORLD CLASS

David Palfreyman

David Palfreyman is Bursar and Fellow of New College Oxford. He is also the Director of Oxford Centre for Higher Education Policy Studies (OXCHEPS, www.oxcheps.new.ox.ac.uk). David is a co-editor of the 15-volume Open University series, "Managing Colleges and Universities" and of the forthcoming 12 volume Routledge/Taylor Francis series "Comparative International Higher Education". He is a member of Agora's Advisory Council.

Introduction

I have been told to be stimulating and provocative, perhaps even (uncharacteristically) polemical and opinionated, in discussing how an elite world-class university functions within the national and international higher education markets. Let's be forthright, then, in acknowledging the mini-herd of elephants now ensconced inside the Oxford University Senior Common Room, one in each corner and one wallowing by the sherry decanters in the middle of this elegant room. The five are labelled: 'Remaining World-Class', 'Raising Tuition Fees', 'Protecting Tutorial Teaching', 'Widening Participation', and 'Defending Academic Self-Governance' (the last being sub-titled: 'Keeping the Lunatics in charge of the Asylum').

There is, of course, some overlap amongst these five themes, and much of what is said here about Oxford applies also to Cambridge, the other UK 'Top Ten' global player[1] as an institution similar to Oxford in terms of intensive and expensive undergraduate teaching (via 'supervisions' rather than 'tutorials',) costly research activity (even more 'Big Science' than Oxford,) and the socio-economic background of the students (posh). In varying degrees parts of this essay relate to other elites such as University College London, Imperial College

---

[1] The two world-rankings tables each place Oxford and Cambridge high; firmly up there in the top-ten or even top-five with the US elites such as Harvard, Yale, Princeton, MIT, Berkeley and Stanford: see the *Times Higher* (6 October 2006 and immediately following weeks). See also www.topuniversities.com and the Shanghai Jiao Tong University website www.sjtu.edu.cn/english/index.

London, London School of Economics, Manchester University and Edinburgh University.

Put simply, if we want to maintain the lucrative export industry that is UK HE plc (worth some £3 billion per annum to GDP on top of UK HE's c£40b general contribution within the economy,) these flagship universities must be adequately funded. The whole national higher education brand depends on the continued success of these elite sub-brands. Hence the presence of the elephants in the SCR needs to be honestly addressed if we are to avoid the mediocre and moribund nature of HE systems in other major European countries.[2]

Remaining First Class

In 2004 The Oxford Centre for Higher Education Policy Studies (OxCHEPS) and The Ulanov Partnership costed Oxford[3] using the methodology developed in the US for the National Association of College and University Business Officers (NACUBO) 'Cost of College Project' and hence allowing a direct comparison of metrics with Harvard, Princeton and Berkeley. The essence of the OxCHEPS message was that Oxford needs another £150m a year on top of its £500m budget if it is to remain globally competitive. In the context of a halving of the taxpayer-funded 'unit of resource' within UK HE for undergraduate teaching over some twenty years, the 2006 increase in tuition fees to £3,000 is too little, too late for either Oxford or universities generally. Government is putting in more money for research, but Parliament at the 2009/2010 review of HE funding must not dodge the lifting of the cap on fees to a realistic level of at least £10,000. [4]   Such additional monies, along with Oxford's own

---

[2]   See Richard Lambert & Nick Butler, *The future of European universities: Renaissance or decay?* (2006, Centre for European Reform): their answer is certainly not a 'Eurotopian' entity created by Brussels bureaucratic intervention!

[3]   'Sustaining Oxford' as Item 13 at the Papers page of the OxCHEPS website, and as 'Costing, funding and sustaining higher education: a case-study of Oxford University' (2004) *Higher Education Review* 37(1) 3-31. Roughly, Oxford & Cambridge each have endowment of c£125K per student; Harvard & Yale have c£575K, Stanford £375K, and Princeton (at only 6500 students) a massive £825K! <u>And</u> they have control of their fee income on top of the annual yield from this endowment that is also steadily being topped up from strong alumni-giving...

[4]   For general background (mainly UK, US, EU) see David Palfreyman, *The Economics of Higher Education: Affordability and Access; Costing, Pricing and*

determined efforts at fundraising from alumni and its exploitation of intellectual property, could mean it keeps pace with its US rivals that currently have three or four times its spending power. It is astonishing that Oxford continues to punch so far above its financial weight, reflecting a combination of praiseworthy academic productivity from underpaid and overworked dons, compared with their US colleagues, and a worrying risk that in living off past investment it is now on borrowed time...

Our report warned: 'The gap is widening as the top US universities operate without tuition fee caps and charge the most able to pay what they are able to pay...' The US deploys c2.5% of GDP on HE, twice the OECD average and with the additional funding coming largely from the private input via tuition fees from students and their families. We spelt out the grim message: 'As higher education becomes ever more globalised, many of the best students will go to the US... Many of the best dons will go there as well, where salary and support across the board are far greater. Eventually the best dons will attract the best students and so on; those remaining in the UK will encounter a weakened higher education... top-tier universities will increasingly resort to cost-cutting with hidden impact on the quality of education... [5] The dilution of resources, already acute, will rapidly

---

Accountability (2004, OxCHEPS) – also available on-line as Item 10 at the Papers page of the OxCHEPS website, where it is updated by down-loadable 'Supplementary Notes'. On the legal status of the £3000 fees cap in relation to universities in England and Wales as private charitable corporations and not a branch of government, see David Palfreyman, 'Does OFFA have teeth?' (2004), as Item 16 at the Papers page of the OxCHEPS website; and also Section J ('Fair Access and OFFA') of Chapter 3 in Dennis Farrington & David Palfreyman, *The Law of Higher Education* (2006, Oxford University Press). The taxpayer retreat from the full funding of expanding HE provision is simply an element in the slow process of a shift away from the comprehensive post-War Welfare State towards a public-private welfare mix appropriate for twenty-first century social democracies in a global economy; see for example, J Lewis & R Surrender (eds, *Welfare State Change: Towards a Third Way* (2004)

[5] HEPI Report 26, *The Prosperity of English Universities: Income Growth and the Prospects for New Investment* (2006), at www.hepi.ac.uk, suggests that any spare cash might best be used to improve the staff-student teaching ratio that has declined to above 1:20 in some universities: see also Note 10 below on quality control and consumerism in HE. The HEPI Report No. 27 (October 2006) on 'The Academic Experience of Students in English Universities' is '... a complete analysis of student workload by subject and institution' and comments: 'The extent of the differences is remarkable and raises important policy questions... it is remarkable how consistently

challenge Oxford's eminence among global institutions of higher education.'

And we concluded starkly: 'Ultimately, the resource gap must lead to a reappraisal of Oxford's and other top-tier UK research universities' ambition. This is an issue not merely for the universities themselves, but for the UK broadly: higher education inspires succeeding generations and provides the knowledge and intellectual skills that drive the economy.' The answer lies in the deregulation and liberalisation of HE as the last of the nationalised industries, the creation of a true free market that provides Oxford and others with greater resources based on what the consumers – students (and parents) and knowledge users (commerce and industry) – believe they are worth free of price caps.

Raising Tuition Fees

Any talk of raising tuition fees immediately unites the cunning self-interest of the wealthy middle-classes with the naïve residual socialism of Old Labour backbenchers. Hence the furore around the 2004 Higher Education Bill that proposed fees of £3000 and that Prime Minister Blair got through by a mere 5 votes despite a theoretical Commons majority of some 150. Lord Desai, an academic economist Labour peer, has commented: 'For 35 years I have heard the same argument: if we charge anything, the poor will not get access. The middle classes are clever; they always use the poor to justify their own subsidies... What is happening now is that by charging a single [low] price we have to ration. Such rationing results in bad education... Who gets such bad education? People from lower income

---

those universities [Oxford and Cambridge] appear to require more effort of their students than other universities...'. In terms of the possible use of the extra money generated by higher tuition fees students 'gave much the highest priority to measures which would improve the quality of teaching' (hence HEPI Reports 26 & 27 link together). Here note the Union of Students campaign for more teaching at one well-rated university; and a student writing from a Russell Group elite university (*Daily Telegraph* Letters, 31/1/07) who commented on 'pitiful levels of contact with, or feedback from, our over-worked tutors', and feared that 'a few years hence, such ill-funded degrees will essentially have become residential correspondence courses!'At another Russell Group university the proposed reduction in teaching contact hours to just two (sic!) a week in the final hear of the History course has been fiercely opposed by students.

classes and ethnic minorities... The problem is that people around the country, and especially in another place [the Commons], mistake uniformity for equity... The higher education system in this country has been the biggest robbery the middle classes have perpetrated on the welfare state'.[6]

Similarly, another economist, Nick Barr of the LSE, has long and consistently argued for evidence-based policy making that would increase tuition fees and reduce the taxpayer subsidy of student loans (and of the deferral of the payment of the fees) for the middle classes.[7] Meanwhile the comprehensive comparative analysis by Usher & Cervenan demonstrates that high(ish) fees combined with generous grants and loans carefully targeted at students from the lower socio-economic groups create an HE system that is far more socially equitable than the supposedly fair free public good systems.[8] On

---

[6] Quoted in Robert Stevens, *University to Uni: The Politics of Higher Education in England since 1944* (2004 & 2005, Politico's).

[7] Nicholas Barr & Iain Crawford, *Financing Higher Education: Answers from the UK* (2005, Taylor&Francis). On whether the degree is worth the higher financial private investment by student/family, see Phillip Brown & Anthony Hesketh, *The Mismanagement of Talent: Employability and Jobs in the Knowledge Economy* (2004, Oxford University Press): 'the top vocational jobs go to the graduates from the elite universities'. On whether in economic terms (as opposed to social/cultural benefits) the expansion of HE is really worth the public investment by the taxpayer, see Elhanan Helpman, *The Mystery of Economic Growth* (2004, Harvard University Press) and Alison Wolf, *Does Education Matter? – myths about education and growth* (2002, Penguin): human capital theory is far from being the key factor in achieving economic growth, compared with the rule of law, the avoidance of excessive Government regulation, and (as something that universities can also contribute towards) research and intellectual property exploitation/technology transfer – and even the view that HE contributes substantially to the Economy via IP/IT is challenged as a simplistic exaggeration by D. Egerton, *The Shock of the Old: Technology and Global History since 1900* (2007, Profile Books). It may be that wealthy countries have more university places because they can afford to keep their young in education to 22/23, as opposed to assuming that more graduates of any kind/quality automatically means increased economic growth.

[8] Usher & Cervenan, *Global Higher Education Report: Affordability and Accessibility in Comparative Perspective* (2005, Educational Policy Institute), at www.educationalpolicy.org. The most affordable systems are in continental Europe (UK and US are ranked, respectively, at 14 and 13), but the five most accessible systems in terms of social equity are (in ascending order) Netherlands, Finland, UK, US, Canada and Australia. Do you want fair access for all socio-economic groups in an HE system that is also affordable for lower socio-economic groups, or a less fair system that diverts taxpayer money into heavily subsidising middle class students who

grounds of both social equity and also good business sense Oxford should be charging annual undergraduate tuition fees of c£10,000 to those students and their families that can afford to pay (and many of them will anyway have been paying private school fees of around that amount or even higher).

In charging such fees Oxford must, of course, be utterly needs-blind in selecting students; operating a rigorously fair and methodologically robust student financial aid system of grants/loans so that no applicant is unable to take up a place for financial reasons. At the same time annual increases in fees clearly need to be kept within reasonable bounds (unlike the runaway hikes characterising UK independent school fees and US private universities) by applying firm cost-control, [9] maximising alumni-giving, utilising corporate

---

anyway colonise the best bits of it paying artificially low fees? HEPI in its December 2006 submission to the House of Commons Select Committee on Education and Skills, for its Review of the Future Sustainability of the Higher Education Sector, made the same point: the 2006 tuition fee arrangements are 'among the most progressive in the world... they are logical... they ensure that higher education is truly affordable... they provide positive incentives for students form poor backgrounds... public money is being used to gear private money...'. Building on this state of affairs, HEPI calls for the fee cap of £3000 to be raised so that our universities can remain competitive with key players in the USA.A study for the UUK of the impact upon applications from the introduction of the higher tuition fees in 20006/2007 shows no negative effects for access; see Ramsden & Brown Variable *Tuition Fees in England – assessing the impact on students and higher education I institutions* (UK, February 2007) at www.universitiesuk.ac.uk. Another UUK February 2007 'Research Report on the economic benefits of a degree' confirms that its 'significant economic benefits' at c£160K over a working lifetime compared with those finishing education with A-levels.with no erosion of the supply of graduates.

[9] See the discussion of cost-control/cost-containment in Item 29 at the Papers page of the OxCHEPS website: David Palfreyman, 'Markets, Models and Metrics in Higher Education' (2006). The lack of cost-control and the growing political backlash against fee increases at US Ivy League institutions is noted, as represented by the 'Spellings Report' on the efficiency and effectiveness of US HE. Indeed, as the ever-increasing political sensitivity about the ever-increasing cost of 'Going to College' as part of the American Dream is ratcheted up by this 2006 Federal Report ('A Test of Leadership: Charting the Future of US Higher Education' at www.ed.gov/about/bdscomm/list/hied/future/index) so critical of US HE, see also the Association of Governing Boards of Universities and Colleges response ('The Cost Project') at www.agb.org/cost, calling for more Board involvement in and commitment to cost-containment. Similarly, on Canadian HE see a critical 2006/07 report from the Canadian Council on Learning ('Canadian Post-secondary Education: A Positive Record – An Uncertain Future) at www.ccl-cca.ca: it calls for a national plan to overcome the inherent weakness of a provincial jurisdiction for HE, citing the

bond cheap debt, achieving full economic cost recovery of overheads on research projects, managing endowment investment with flair, and generally earning income wherever possible from conferences and tourism etc.

The freedom to set uncapped tuition fees should not be taken by Oxford as a licence to print money, but as one element of efficient management that need not threaten the widening-participation agenda and that might help protect the tutorial teaching system (both issues as next discussed). It should also reduce the University's temptation to dump uneconomic UK/EU undergraduate places in favour of either more foreign undergraduates paying already high fees or students on taught-masters courses paying market-level fees – a process encouraged by the perverse incentives within the proposed resource allocation model ('JRAM') out for consultation during 2006/07. Incidentally, charging £10K pa as 'the sticker price' (many students will be means-tested to pay less) would still recover only around half of the cost of undergraduate education identified in the OxCHEPS report.[10] We are a long way from making a profit! Moreover, higher fees at other English universities ought not only to be used to improve undergraduate teaching, but 'the empowered student consumer' should absolutely demand that they be utilised in this way![11]

US Spelling Report and its call for a US national strategy. On student financial aid systems, see the forthcoming OxCHEPS report comparing US & UK experience at the Papers page of the website.

[10] See 3 above.

[11] See footnote 5 and consumerism in UK and US HE is explored in Chapter 14 ('The Student as Consumer?') of Dennis Farrington & David Palfreyman, *The Law of Higher Education* (2006, Oxford University Press). On quality control in HE and the appalling waste of taxpayer money by the QAA quango that does not in fact monitor quality at the chalk-face, see Item 25 at the Papers page of the OxCHEPS website: David Palfreyman, 'Quality Assurance & Accreditation in UK HE (and beyond)' (2006). Note that the US Spelling Report (see Note 9 above) calls for much greater comparative information to be made available to US HE 'consumers' (students and their parents, the latter often effectively paying for it): 'Colleges and universities must become more transparent about cost, price, and student success outcomes... provide consumers and policymakers [with] an accessible, understandable way to measure the relative effectiveness of different colleges and universities... we recommend the creation of a consumer-friendly information database on higher education... coupled with a search engine to enable students, parents, policymakers and others to weigh and rank comparative institutional performance' (exactly what this author proposed for UK HE in OxCHEPS Paper 25 referred to above!).

Protecting Tutorial Teaching

Oxford & Cambridge, unlike many elite universities in the UK and USA, still take undergraduate teaching seriously. Notably, the Oxbridge colleges as teaching machines, countering the weight of the academic departments as primarily research operations, protect the institutional commitment to education, in contrast to other elites where teaching has been short-changed to free resources to pursue 'the Kash & Kudos of Research'. That said, tutorial teaching is under pressure in Oxford. It is an expensive commodity with tutor to student ratios at 1:2 rather than the 1:12 or 15 seminars the norm elsewhere. It is dependent on both tutor and tutee making the best of it. The Oxford Tutorial has an almost mystic, cult status; it is Oxford's USP. But is it also an anachronism, a sacred cow to which Oxford pays mere lip-service as it quietly shifts to 'small-group teaching'? Or is it to be preserved at all costs as a pedagogical gem, the jewel in Oxford's crown as the best way to challenge, stimulate and truly educate young minds in the crucial 'lifelong-learning' skill of a Liberal Education, sound analysis and critical thinking, to the wider benefit of society and the economy? Is the added-value of demanding from students far more written work than their counterparts at other universities get the opportunity to turn in, and then putting them on the spot frequently and regularly to discuss the work in a way that now rarely happens even at other elites, worth the expense and duly appreciated by the students and by their future employers? A proper market in tuition fees may answer at least the question of whether the student or his/her family is really interested in intensive undergraduate education.

In *The Oxford Tutorial* a collection of essays brings together the experience of veteran tutors from most subject areas, analysis of the tutorial as a pedagogical process, and research on the reaction of its student participants. [12] It seems that crusty dons can admit to enjoyment in teaching, that the process does develop 'higher learning' or 'deep learning', and that the punters value their tutorials. As Suzanne Shale writes: 'A sceptical, inquiring stance lies right at the very heart of tutorial teaching. No beliefs are unquestionable, no statement is safe from scrutiny, no evidence is incontrovertible, and no

---

[12] See the discussion in Chapter 1 of David Palfreyman, *The Oxford Tutorial* (2001, OxCHEPS); also available online as Item 1 at the Papers page of the OxCHEPS website.

conclusion is inescapable.' The University and the colleges should not fail future students by providing them with a watered down version of what earlier students surveyed so valued: being worked hard and consistently in the intensive tutorial system, and engaging in an intellectual dialogue with their tutors as together they 'read' the subject.

Widening Participation

The woeful lack of a dependable model to inform evidence-based policy making with respect to 'widening participation' is exposed by two items on the HEFCE website,[13] and the picture painted for the UK is broadly the same in many countries.[14] It is very clear that there is no simple causal link between higher tuition fees and reduced participation. As Watson notes, 'the big message' in the recent Gorard Report is that 'we don't really know what we think we know', and the debate is characterised by 'an almost pathetic search for the single-issue intervention that will improve the situation' rather than accepting that it is an inevitably complex and long-term process to improve schools and to raise parental expectations and the level of support. Gorard comments on 'a lack of clear knowledge' and criticises the 'poor quality' of much of the so-called research, as well as noting 'a danger that the widening participation debate is being hijacked by fees and finance issues' rather than appreciating that 'patterns of participation in higher education are highly influenced by family background and early experiences' which leave some on

---

[13] David Watson, 'How to think about widening participation in UK higher education' (July, 2006); and Steve Gorard, 'Review of widening participation research: addressing the barriers to participation in higher education' (July, 2006).

[14] For comparative material, see Ted Tapper & David Palfreyman (eds), *Understanding Mass Higher Education: Comparative perspectives on access* (2005, Routledge/Taylor&Francis). On social inequality in US HE, see William G. Bowen et al, *Equity and Excellence in American Higher Education* (2005, University of Virginia Press); and Michael S. McPherson & Morton Owen Shapiro (eds), *College Access: Opportunity or Privilege?* (2006, College Board). The causes of and the potential solutions to socio-economic under-representation in HE appear to be much the same in the UK and US, except that at least the UK elites are virtuous in relation to 'the preferences of privilege' and the 'legacy' admission of the children of alumni/donors explored in Daniel Golden, *The Price of Admission: How America's Ruling Class Buys Its Way into Elite Colleges – and Who Gets Left Outside the Gates* (2006, Crown).

'learning trajectories' that bring them as 'marginal learners' nowhere near HE (let alone Oxford). Fiddling with HE admissions is too little too late.

Oxford admissions is a fair process. Oxford dons are very much the result of the meritocratic social mobility of 1950s-1970s Britain; they do not want to revert to being the tutor, Samgrass, patronised by his socially elite tutees in *Brideshead Revisited*. The Oxford interview will always be vulnerable to human frailty and will always end up rejecting good candidates – because all the candidates are, on paper, good! The interview is the only way to sift the best from the very good, and better the dons do it than a central admissions administrator or computer. Oxford cannot correct for the multi-deprivation and social exclusion afflicting some youngsters from birth: blaming Oxford, and other elites, is attacking symptoms, not causes. And capping tuition fees, or even abolishing them, will not in itself do anything to widen participation.

Defending Academic Self-Governance

The world-class US private universities have governance sovereignty residing in a lay board of trustees. UK universities are controlled by lay-dominated councils or boards of governors. But Oxford and Cambridge are sui generis in that sovereignty lies with the academic community coming together in the dons' parliament, Congregation (Regent House at the other place). They are also sui generis as collegiate universities, each being a federal structure of a central university core of research focused academic departments surrounded by 35-40 legally autonomous colleges as teaching machines attracting huge loyalty from their 'Old Members' (who are also University alumni). Would Oxford or Cambridge be even more world-class if the academic lunatics ceased to be in charge of these rather successful asylums and instead their councils became lay-dominated? As explained, the challenge in remaining world-class is a lack of money. The current fuss in Oxford is over governance reforms that would effectively end 800 years of academic self-government and are an irrelevant sideshow (and one that, sensibly and robustly, Cambridge has not distracted itself with by supinely frightening itself with nonsense that the Charity Commission or HEFCE or some other bogeyman expects change to the sector norm or else...).

CAN THE PRIZES STILL GLITTER?
The Future of British Universities in a Changing World

Until an Oxford governance working party came up with its ill-considered and internally inconsistent package there had been a consensus stretching from the 1923 Royal Commission through the 1966 Franks Report to the late-1990s North Report that sovereignty should lie with the academics – a consensus echoed in Cambridge in its 1989 Wass review of governance, which would have no truck with the managerialism and corporatism that now pervades so many UK universities.[15] That it not to say that there is no role for the valuable expertise of outsiders: most colleges have long called upon the experience and energy of committed and competent Old Members in generously giving time to serve on their endowment, investment and fundraising committees. The working party's proposals, duly voted on in Congregation during Michaelmas Term 2006, went too far and were, as an Editorial in the *Oxford Magazine* (No. 256, Second Week, Michaelmas Term 2006) commented, 'unnecessary, unjustified and

---

[15] Ted Tapper & David Palfreyman, *Oxford and the Decline of the Collegiate Tradition* (2000, Taylor&Francis). Note that the scandals and governance crises of UK HE have involved institutions where lay members have failed miserably to check the excesses of an overbearing and/or incompetent Vice-Chancellor/Chief Executive and his Senior Management Team of ciphers, as detailed in David Warner & David Palfreyman (eds), *Managing Crisis* (2003, Open University Press/McGraw-Hill *Managing Universities and Colleges* series). Michael Shattock makes much the same point in his volume in that series - *Managing Good Governance in Higher Education* (2006, Open University Press) - and also comments that 'simply because the governance structures at Oxford and Cambridge are different does not mean that their academic performance would be improved by bringing them into line with civic university or even HEC constitutions' (p 153). Moreover, and worryingly, it appears that HEFCE has never met as the 'public body' to properly discuss and carefully determine with adequate information its alleged policy on Oxford & Cambridge as an anomaly in governance terms, and instead has left its officers to divine its 'policy' on Oxford & Cambridge by extrapolating from the general to the particular. Hence, one may question whether HEFCE, as an entity subject to public law, has not itself got governance problems and may indeed by unlawful in applying pressure for governance reform at Oxford. The Select Committee Review, referred to in Note 8 above, will be considering the governance anomaly of Oxford & Cambridge: it is to be hoped that it will do that job with more intellectual rigour than HEFCE so far has been capable of mustering! For more on the damage done to collegiality and shared-values by corporatism and managerialism, see also Ian McNay & Jennifer Bone, *Higher Education and the Human Good* (2006, Open University Press). On the wider purposes and values of 'the university' see David Watson, *Managing Civic and Community Engagement* (forthcoming, Open University Press/McGraw Hill *Managing Universities and Colleges* Series).

without a convincing rationale'. Similarly, an opponent characterised the proposals as 'a governance structure based on autocracy, secrecy, patronage...' (Donald Fraser, *Oxford Magazine*, No. 257, Fourth Week, Michaelmas Term 2006, p. 13). That issue also contained a letter signed by some 40 Cambridge academics calling upon Oxford to think very hard about voting for proposed reforms that threaten 'the survival of our universities as self-governing institutions' and hence their 'atmosphere of unparalleled freedom and autonomy in which scholarship of all kinds has flourished' – a set of reforms, in fact, the like of which Cambridge had itself sensibly rejected in 2003!

The governance debate took place in Congregation on 14th November and 28th November, 2006. At the first meeting an odd amendment was passed that effectively contradicted a significant element of the reforming party's (by now known as 'the Hoodies' after the Vice-Chancellor, Dr Hood) argument for radical change. They argued that HEFCE expected there to be a lay majority on council; yet the Morris/Butler amendment said there need not be and we can decide again in 5 years. The University press office promptly issued a press release prematurely crowing about victory for the reformers; a row led to its withdrawal as an example of spin that has no place in Oxford University. Then at the next meeting to debate the governance proposals, as now amended, the Hoodies were humiliated by gaining less than 40% of the vote, not least because their speakers came across as so bossy and strident (and thereby reinforcing the view that 'reform' meant a shift from democracy to a not very pleasant oligarchy – and one particularly represented by some Hoodies both new to and fairly ignorant of the University, but whose arrogance meant they assumed their managerial recipe could be applied willy-nilly).

A postal vote of all c3750 members of congregation was then called for by more than 50 of the extremist Hoodies signing a petition and that vote (after a week of intensive e-mail activity as misinformation about charity law, and alleged external pressure for governance change, was countered by a rational analysis of the position) led to the announcement on 19th December of the 'reforms' being rejected by some 60% to 40%. One reason for the in person defeat on 28th November and for the postal vote's decisive rejection was, as Alan Ryan, Warden of New College, commented in the *Times Higher* (8/12/06): 'The senior management alienated the workforce by playing fast and loose with the case for change... the [28th November] vote was a rebuke to the amateurishness of the institutional design on offer and to the misguided belief of the central administration that the way to run Oxford is to turn discussion of institutional design into a battle of wills... the [proposed governance] legislation was a clunker...'

It is a great shame that the emotional energy expended in Oxford over these naïve proposals concerning governance could not have been devoted to improving mundane and routine management, and also to facing up to the elephants in the SCR by way of Oxford controlling its own destiny rather than cravenly trying to second-guess what might please third-parties supposedly bothered by the existing governance structure. Appeasement is bad enough, but anticipatory or pre-emptive capitulation is truly pathetic! It is to be hoped that Oxford can now move on from what the *Financial Times* leader (21/12/06) summed up as Dr Hood's 'politically maladroit' handling of the governance saga, including renewed effort to 'find a way of involving outsiders in the university's governance'.

The creation of an entirely lay and truly powerful audit and scrutiny committee is the obvious route that would be welcome to many, including this opponent of the governance 'reforms' to date. A scrutiny committee that must be both a reality-check for Congregation's dondom lest they become utterly disconnected from the real world, and also a balancing force against a potentially over-wheening (but not necessarily competent) Vice-Chancellor and Senior Management Team. A scrutiny committee that would report directly to Congregation not only on Council's performance but also on the role of Congregation itself in setting and implementing and reviewing Oxford's strategy. In addition, Council should have a lay-chair ('the Pro-Chancellor') and its all-important finance committee should also have a lay-chair ('the Treasurer') – thereby creating two new powerful lay University officers, and helping to reassure the world that Oxford is not self-absorbed and inward-looking, while serving as a check on the Executive and importing valuable external wisdom to University decision-making.

Conclusion

The UK is a world-leader in financial services (the City of London) and in HE (Oxford and Cambridge). The former was saved from oblivion by major deregulation in the 1980s (the Big Bang); the latter now needs to be liberalised by way of a much higher fees cap (if not uncapped fees) from 2010 onwards. Along with other sources of increased income, enhanced tuition fees will enable Oxford to keep up with its global competitors – to the benefit of both 'UK plc' and 'UK HE plc' – and to do so without either compromising the widening-participation agenda or short-changing tutorial teaching. It would be a bonus to do all that while remaining a self-governing academic community; and it might anyway be wasted effort if Oxford were to damage itself by becoming corporatist and managerialist. It would be a pity if Oxford's exceptionalism is not allowed to thrive at time when Germany is, at last, beginning to reform its HE system by granting greater autonomy to institutions, introducing tuition fees, and funding ten of its universities as elites to compete with Oxford, Cambridge and the US Ivy League. Life in the top echelon of globalised HE is not going to get any less competitive (not least as China's universities develop) and the best chance of survival lies in being as free as possible from the dead-hand of Government interference in pricing the product – a freedom, however, that, rightly, demands in return Oxford remains an open and accessible academic meritocracy.

(For more on Oxford, on HE governance and management generally, and on comparative international HE material is listed below.)[16]

---

[16] On Oxford... Chapter 2 ('The Ancient Collegiate Universities: Oxford and Cambridge') in David Warner & David Palfreyman (eds), *The State of UK Higher Education: Managing Change and Diversity* (2001, Open University Press). Also the text cited in Note 15 above. On HE management... David Warner & David Palfreyman (eds), *Higher Education Management: The Key Elements* (1996, Open University Press), and its spin-off 15 volume series, *Managing Universities and Colleges* (1999-2007, Open University Press/McGraw-Hill) as detailed at the Resources page of the OxCHEPS website. Specifically on governance, see Michael Shattock, *Managing Good Governance in Higher Education* (2006), within the series (as already cited in Note 15 above); and for the legal framework see Chapter 5 ('Governance Structures') in Dennis Farrington & David Palfreyman, *The Law of Higher Education* (2006, Oxford University Press) – especially para. 5.02, footnote 3 which is expanded online at the Law Updates page of the OxCHEPS website where an HE Law Casebook also supports this 2006 text. On comparative HE, see the

CAN THE PRIZES STILL GLITTER?
The Future of British Universities in a Changing World

projected 12 volumes of *International Higher Education* (2008 onwards, Routledge/Taylor&Francis), a series edited by Palfreyman/Scott/Tapper and as detailed on the Series page at the OxCHEPS website: the first volume will be on elites within HE systems (Tapper & Palfreyman); later volumes will consider governance at both system level and also at local HEI level.

Editors: Hugo de Burgh, Anna Fazackerley, Jeremy Black

EXETER AS A CASE STUDY FOR A CHANGING HIGHER EDUCTION MARKETPLACE

Steve Smith

Professor Steve Smith has been the Vice-Chancellor of the University of Exeter since 2002, having previously been Senior Pro Vice-Chancellor (Academic Affairs) and Professor of International Politics at the University of Wales, Aberystwyth. In 2001 he became only the second UK academic to be elected President of the International Studies Association in the USA. He was also the recipient of the Susan Strange Award of the International Studies Association in 1999 for the person who has most challenged the received wisdom I the profession. He is chair of the 1994 Group of smaller research intensive universities.

In November 2004, the senior management of the University of Exeter announced that they were planning a major restructuring. The plans, based on an analysis contained in a document called 'Imagining the Future', called for the closure of the Music, Italian and Chemistry departments, as well as significant staff reductions in virtually all the other areas of the university that had achieved rankings of 4 in the 2001 Research Assessment Exercise (RAE). There followed a considerable public debate about the restructuring plans, including some 95 national news stories in the following six weeks, an Enquiry and then a Report from of the House of Commons Science and Technology Committee, and very vocal campaigns by many of the students (and their parents) in the subjects affected, and by societies such as the Royal Society of Chemistry. This chapter seeks to explain the thinking behind the restructuring, because it was part of a clear strategy to respond to fundamental changes underway in British higher education. I will do this first by outlining the main developments in the higher education (HE) environment, and then link Exeter's restructuring to these changes.

When I took up the post of Vice-Chancellor, in 2002, I remember very vividly an early meeting with the then HEFCE Chief Executive Howard Newby who talked to me about the danger of universities getting stuck in the 'squeezed middle.' If you were a post-1992 university, then your teaching and access led mission was pretty clear. If you were a top 20 research led university then your mission was also obvious. But, what if you were neither of those two things? The stark truth is that, without the restructuring, I candidly think that the university would by now have been part of the 'squeezed middle'. It is my firm belief that the restructuring has placed Exeter in a position whereby it can take advantage of the opportunities offered by the new HE market.

Let me turn first to this emerging HE market. Broadly speaking there are two main trends at work.

Research Concentration.

Put simply, over the last decade the percentage of funding council and research council income going to 25 institutions has increased. Now 75% of the QR income distributed by the results of the RAE goes to 25 universities, and 84% of Research Council income goes to 25 universities. Within QR, whereas 81% went to 5*/5 units in 2001, today it is over 86%.

The most important development since 2001 has been the steep increase in the funding gradient applied to the RAE outcomes. Thus whereas in 2001 the funding ratio allocated to 4/5/5* grades was 2.25/3.375/4.05, in 2003 that changed to 1/2.793/3.362. By 2006, this gradient had increased to 1/3.12/3.95. Thus whereas in 2001 a 5* grade got roughly 1.8 more than a 4 grade, by 2006 that ration had become 3.95, that is to say, it had more than doubled. The result of this change meant that whereas in 2001 a submitted member of staff in, say, a 4 ranking Chemistry department was funded at £28.7k, by 2004 this had declined by 42% to £16.6k. By way of contrast, the figures per submitted member of staff in a Physics department that improved from a 4 to a 5 in the 2001 RAE exercise, saw the amount they received increase by 86% between 2001 and 2004. In other words, the concentration of funding resulting from the 2001 RAE led to a massive cliff-edge effect, whereby the funding of 4 ranking activity was significantly reduced. Indeed, the then Secretary of State, Charles Clarke, explicitly spoke of stopping all funding for 4 ranking departments after the 2001 RAE results were published, and it was only a major rearguard action by HEFCE that kept some, albeit reduced, funding for them.

These decisions result in five institutions in England getting over 60% of the total HEFCE (Research and Teaching) Funding for research; another 25 institutions get over 25%, 8 pre-1992 universities get between 13% and 25%, and all the post-1992 universities get under 10%, with 8 getting over 5% and 15 getting under 2%. This is a very concentrated research environment. The Russell Group of traditional research universities and the 1994 Group of smaller research intensive universities have approximately 16 times the QR income of the post-1992 universities.

The Emerging Market for UK and International Students

The 2004 Higher Education Act increased the level of fees for English students. Although the fee debt was deferred until after graduation (and when the student was earning over £15k a year), and although the poorest students would get maintenance grants of £2,700 a year, this policy undoubtedly altered the nature of the relationship between student and university. Students began to think of themselves more as consumers, and thus paid far more attention to the 'value' of the education they received. The introduction of the National Student Survey in 2005 gave hitherto unavailable ratings from (potentially) all third year students on the quality of their course. Students also started to look very carefully at the level of services they received, the quality of academic and student accommodation, and issues such as the number of contact hours they had on their course. All of these factors will become even more significant if, as expected, the cap on fees gets lifted after the 2009 general election.

The Labour Government has not only committed itself to increasing the participation rate to 50%, but it also strongly pushed the need to get a much wider than hitherto social mix into British universities. The key point about this move was that it led the government to introduce a variety of means of achieving this end, mainly through the introduction of foundation degrees, increasing support for part-time students, and encouraging deeper links between Further Education and HE. This meant that part of the sector could pursue this goal and could really flourish as very strong performers on the Widening Participation (WP) agenda in a way that had not been possible before. In this sense, the WP agenda defined the core mission for a group of post-1992 universities. At the same time, all universities were required to develop significant bursary schemes in order to be able to charge up to the new fee level of £3000. Thus even those institutions which did not see themselves as in the access and WP market were required to be in a market of trying to attract more and more good students from lower socio-economic backgrounds. As they were only introduced for the 2006 entry, this is likely to be a major issue in HE as the various bursary arrangements become better known, with universities competing in terms of their bursary provisions.

These trends were explicitly discussed in the government's 2003 White Paper on Higher Education, which raised for the first time the possibility of universities following distinctly different missions, with some concentrating on research and others focussing on teaching. This was a sea-change from the assumption of a 'level playing field' that accompanied the decision in 1992 to abolish the binary line and transform the Polytechnics into Universities. These trends also lay behind HEFCE's proposals in 2003 for a core-plus model of funding, whereby all universities would undertake four core activities, teaching, research, WP and business outreach, but some institutions would define their missions as being excellent in any one or more of these. Together the White Paper and HEFCE's proposals indicated that the sector was to be far more diverse in institutional mission than had been the case until then. Crucially, the implication was that universities could succeed in a variety of different missions; they did not all have to do the same things. But the implication of such a differentiated market was that market failure was also possible, and that prospect can only increase as the market becomes more mature, and as research concentration increases, and as the fees cap comes off.

Exeter

What about Exeter? Well, the basic facts can be stated briefly. Exeter is a medium-sized English university. Currently, it has about 13,900 students, and 2,800 staff. It has a turnover of around £140m, with activity based in three campuses (Streatham and St Lukes in Exeter, and the Cornwall campus near Falmouth). The university has always enjoyed a strong reputation as a very popular undergraduate destination for students from the south of England. In the 1960s it was common to talk of the university as one of the main destinations for students who did not go to Oxbridge; accordingly it has an enormously successful and loyal set of alumni. But Exeter's popularity as an undergraduate destination (currently it ranks 13th in the UK on applications per place) probably meant that by the late 1990s it had not felt it had to work as hard as other institutions on its research, its graduate recruitment and its international student market. Thus the amount of its non residential/catering income that came from sources other than the state was some 7% lower than the average for the 1994 Group, as a result of much lower international and graduate student recruitment than its competitors, In the 1996 RAE the institution fell from 14th to 47th in The Times Higher league table, by 2001 it had fought its way back up to 31st, but even this recovery masked structural problems. Whereas about 63% of staff in the Humanities and Social Sciences were in 5/5* units of assessment, only 27% of staff in the sciences were in 5/5* units. Indeed, in the institution as a whole, 43% of staff were in units graded below 5/5* (compare this to a national average of 45%, including both pre- and post-1992 institutions).

As mentioned above, I arrived as Vice-Chancellor in 2002, to be followed by the appointment of David Allen as Registrar and Secretary in 2003. Both of us were attracted to the potential of Exeter, but each of us realised that it was an institution that had to change or else it would not succeed as a research-led university. I had noted in my interviews that Exeter was going to struggle to survive as a research-led university unless it underwent considerable re-structuring. I felt that the HE world was moving much more quickly towards the creation of a much smaller research-led part of the sector than many of the 62 pre-1992 universities realised. I said that my goal would be to get Exeter into the 'top 20' by 2010. The slogan became 'top 20 by 2010'. By 2004 David Allen and I had undertaken the analysis of what needed to be done, and crucially had built a strong core team of DVCs, Deans and senior administrations who together shared a common analysis of both the developing HE scene and, crucially, Exeter's place within that scene - what Burton Clark sees as the 'strengthened steering core' necessary for an entrepreneurial university.[1]

'Imagining the Future' summed up our analysis of the key problems as follows:

3. The public policy landscape is now much clearer than when I took office in 2002. The Higher Education Act is now on the Statute Book and barring a political earthquake at the next General Election, variable tuition fees will be introduced for full-time home/EU undergraduates in 2006. I would expect the £3,000 cap on tuition fees to be lifted in the next but one Parliament as the costs of higher education continue to rise more quickly than revenues. There is an international trend to introduce more private contributions to tuition and I would expect that to continue, with the strongest brands, as in any market, attracting premium prices for a premium product.

4. In research the story is one of ever-greater concentration of resources, particularly in science, medicine and engineering but also in the humanities and social sciences. Over 75% of public research funding in the UK is channelled into 25 universities. The JIF and SRIF processes are concentrating major capital investment into fewer universities and the grants and contracts tend to follow these investments, creating large, powerful, well-found research groups whose sustainability is attractive to research sponsors and students. The move to full economic costing will intensify this trend, since there will be less but better funded research in fewer places.

5. Alongside the OST drive to concentrate research funding is the increasing selectivity of HEFCE QR funding, based upon RAE outcomes. Biology and Chemistry in Exeter for example (rated 4) attracts £20.9k per FTE academic staff member when the figure for 5 rated Physics is £46.2k. Biological and Chemical Sciences has over twice the number of academic staff that Physics has and yet earns less QR

---

[1] Clark, Burton R. (1998) Creating Entrepreneurial Universities: Organizational Pathways of Transformation. Higher Education journal. Springer Netherlands.

(£913k cf £970k).   While there has been talk of some protection being provided for subjects of national importance in challenging markets eg Physical Sciences, Modern Languages, Arabic and Middle Eastern Studies, it is clear that any protection will apply only to 5/5* units.

6.   In the 2001 RAE only 2% of our submission (German) was 5*, 55% was rated 5 and 41% 4. By contrast, York, a university of very similar size and shape as Exeter recorded 18% 5*, 66% 5 and only 8% 4. It may well be that after the 2008 RAE (which is likely to be the last) only work of international standard ie in the 3*, 4* range will be funded. This would make it impossible for the equivalent of 4s to find matching funds to meet full economic costs and would lead to further cross subsidy of the 5s to the 4s, thus damaging the competitiveness of the former.

7.   Against this background the University has a mountain to climb and limited time to do it. We have to catch up and overhaul competitors who are far from standing still. We will only be able to do so if we eliminate cross subsidy as soon as possible and invest in our strengths wisely and selectively. Focusing on our strengths has been University policy for some years. It now needs to accelerate with resolution.

8.   As a matter of urgency we need to examine the size and shape of the University. A high priority for the DVCs is to agree stretching but achievable targets for diverse income generation in Schools that are "must-gets".   Our new Resource Allocation Model incentivises Schools to win income and control costs. Cross subsidy will be phased out in favour of strategic investment.   Schools that fail to meet targets will therefore inevitably suffer disinvestment.

9.   With a turnover of £113 million and 13,000 students we are too small and stretched over too many subjects in a world where critical mass is increasingly important. We need to grow, particularly in unregulated markets such as postgraduate, international, Continuing Professional Development and industrial research contracts. A university such as Warwick might be the model for investment led

growth, entrepreneurially managed. Growth has the added advantage of helping to spread central overheads over more activity.

10. Our growth needs to be selective. We are currently spreading our jam too thinly and cannot sustain or achieve international excellence over the 37 subjects we submitted to the 2001 RAE. [Imagining the Future, November 2004, pp 2-3]

The document went on to outline our proposals, which were to cease entry to single honours Chemistry, Music and Italian with immediate effect. We would of course teach out the students currently on the programmes. In addition we planned significant staff cuts in all 4 ranking areas, and also in the School of Education and Lifelong Learning, which although a 5 ranking unit in 2001, was a 5C, meaning that it had only submitted between 60% and 79% of staff. The assumption that underlay our thinking was that with our resources spread so thinly (submitting to 37 units, compared to the 1994 Group average of 23 subject areas) we could not afford the investment to build up all our 4 (and 5C) units to what would count as internationally competitive and sustainable research units after the next RAE exercise in 2008. Put very simply, Exeter had been subsidising loss-making activity for decades, and the way of doing this had been to use the surpluses created by its most successful subjects, For example, Chemistry had cumulative deficits of £3.527m (measured as actual deficits plus the amounts it was unable to provide towards central costs). In a world of increasing research concentration, such a policy could only result in the decline of our most successful subjects, since they were starved of investment in order to prop up deficit subjects.

This analysis developed out of the Vice-Chancellor's Executive Group (VCEG) residential held on 28-30 September 2004. We took our thinking to a special meeting of the Senior Management Group (SMG) on 18 November, and then planned to announce the proposals on 22 November, the day before they were formally tabled at the key university committee (Strategy, Performance and Resources Committee - SPARC). Our plan was for me to go and meet all staff in the affected areas, and then to hold meetings on 24 November with the students in each area. Unfortunately one colleague leaked the plans, despite an agreement at SMG that we would respect confidentiality so that staff could hear the news first from me in face-to-face meetings, and then students could be informed immediately thereafter. The Royal Society of Chemistry was informed of the plans on 19 November, and contacted the press that afternoon. From that moment onwards we were reacting to events not shaping them, and my main regret over the entire process is that our staff and students found out about some of our plans via the media.

On the other hand, the proposals were accepted without amendment by SPARC on 23 November. They then went to Senate on 1 December, and on to Council on 20 December. Both bodies overwhelmingly passed the proposals (though by then the senior management had modified the proposals to close Italian (instead we proposed closing only single honours Italian), because of its role in joint honours provision. In Senate the key vote was 38-10, and in Council it was 28-2 (with the two being mandated student representatives). We tried to be completely transparent, and thus made available all our planning material and financial analysis to anyone who requested it. We held regular liaison meetings with both the campus trade unions and the Student Guild, and provided the media, and the government, with all the details they asked us for. That does not mean that people agreed with us, but ultimately we won the arguments because we based our decisions on hard, transparent data and on clear analysis. Interestingly, many opponents told us that we in fact had a further (hidden) agenda, that the 2004 restructuring was only the first phase of a 'master plan'. The truth is that there was no such follow-on phase, and we really did give out all the information that we had.

The entire senior management team spent the period between 22 November and 20 December dealing on the one hand with the incredible press and public attention that the proposals generated, and on the other with understandably worried and upset staff and students. Over 2,000 students demonstrated on campus on 25 November, and BBC TV news ran the outcome of the Senate vote as its third item on both the main 6pm and 10pm national news broadcasts on 1 December. On 14 December 2004 I gave evidence in a closed, informal, meeting of the House of Commons Select Committee on Science and Technology, and on 9 March 2005 I appeared in a formal session of the Committee to answer their questions about the closure of Chemistry. As I explained, the key reasons for our decisions were to do with ensuring that Exeter's portfolio contained only subjects that were sustainable as international quality research and teaching units. In the sciences, this meant that subjects had to satisfy three conditions: first, they had to be 5 ranking in RAE terms (or be clearly on their way to achieving that grade in the new 2008 currency); second they had to have a record in research council grant getting that indicated that they were internationally competitive; thirdly, they had to be able to attract sufficient numbers of high quality students to cover their teaching costs. Chemistry at Exeter met none of these conditions, whereas, by way of contrast Biosciences did. Chemistry was losing £188k a year on its teaching and some £605k on its research, and its research grant income was down 36% since 2001/02. Biosciences made a small surplus on its teaching (£12k), had an increase in research income of 76% since 2001/02, and was clearly on a strong upward trajectory with its RAE performance. Taken together, whereas Chemistry had a combined deficit of £3.527m from 1997/98 to 2004/04, Biosciences had a surplus of £526k.

The outcome of the proposed restructuring was that the subjects did stop recruiting as from the 2005 intake. We negotiated the transfer of 124 undergraduate and 15 postgraduate Chemistry students, mainly either to other programmes at Exeter or to one of two South-West universities, Bristol and Bath. Each student was given £2000 in compensation, and automatic progression to Bath or Bristol as long as they passed the relevant year-end examinations. A small number of Chemistry students completed their degrees at Exeter, whilst the final year of Music students complete this summer. In total, we negotiated voluntary severance with 149 staff - 77 academic and 72 support staff. This is not the place to discuss in any detail the reasons why we think that the restructuring has been a significant success, since the proof of the wisdom of our decisions can truly only be known after a few more years.

However, the initial signs are extremely encouraging. First, our provisional analysis of our research strength indicates that we should be able to submit over 90% of our staff to the 2008 RAE at a threshold of at least 2* performance (which compares roughly to the borderline for a 5 rating in the 2001 exercise, where we only had 57% of staff so graded). Second, Exeter has come in the top ten in the National Student Survey for each of the two years in which it has run. Third, our admissions figures seem to have leapt ahead (after a small drop for

2006 admission of 8.6% (on a like-for-like basis), currently applications are over 20% up on the same date last year. Fourth, research grant income has grown significantly, with the 2005/06 figure being some 21% over the 2003/04 figure, and initial figures for 2006/07 showing a similar rate of increase over the 2005/06 total). Fifthly, we (as in the Peninsula Medical School, run by Exeter along with the University of Plymouth) succeeded in being awarded the only new dental school in the UK for 40 years, as well as receiving one third of all the new medical numbers allocated. Finally we have been able to recruit absolutely outstanding staff at all levels and in virtually every subject area. Conversely we have seen very few staff leave Exeter, far below what we would expect as the normal churn of staff movement. These and other factors have contributed to the University achieving 18th place in the Sunday Times league table, its highest ever position in any league table. We know that there are further improvements to come in the data for future league tables, but to repeat: the key tests will come as the market develops further.

Our objective, as noted above, is to make sure that Exeter is a top 20 university by 2010. To make sure that we can do everything in our power to make that happen, we have had to will the ends as well as willing the means. At Exeter, we compare our performance in mission critical areas against 15 other universities. The comparator group is based on universities that are competing for top 20 places. We think that half of the top 20 fills itself - institutions like Oxford, Cambridge and Imperial are unlikely to be displaced! The other half is less settled. Why are we so obsessed with top 20? This is because the noises emerging from Whitehall suggest that the trend will be to reduce the number of research-led universities. We think it will be less than the current number and perhaps as few as 20. This is the likely endgame for the research concentration process that has occurred over the past few years. Interestingly, researchers themselves are beginning to make career decisions based on this information. When we interview people for top academic positions we are increasingly questioned as to the future direction of the institution as a whole. This is markedly different from the past when researchers were mainly interested only in their department, their research group or themselves. Over the last year we have recruited around 100 new academics to areas of research strength. There has also been a noticeable movement of good staff away from universities that they think might not make the cut.

So we know not only how Exeter compares with its peers, but also where we are ahead of the game, on a par with the rest, or have some way to go to catch up. And, crucially, where improvement is necessary we know by how much we have to improve. Our corporate plan falls out of this process with separate strategies covering areas such as student satisfaction, teaching and learning, research, the provision of information services, improving the estate, employability, science and so on. All investment decisions are made on the basis of whether or not they serve the top 20 agenda. So, for example, we have excellent science but to be top 20 we need bigger research teams. Therefore, we have developed a science strategy with costed investment plans to develop four key themes of research.

The Future

So what other issues are influencing our planning at the present time? I will deal briefly with the two main areas that I argued above are forming the emerging market in higher education: the student experience and research concentration.

Firstly, the student experience. It has been obvious for some time that students are increasingly thinking like customers. This is mainly a symptom of having to pay higher tuition fees. Performing well in the National Student Survey becomes more important in this sort of environment and our academic departments have taken this on board. Departments that did less well in the first survey have studied the data and made improvements based on that information. This has resulted in a much more even performance for the university in the second survey, although we do have our stars such as our School of Business and Economics who came top in the UK, or near the top, in all the subjects they teach. So there remain learning opportunities for our other departments. Improvement is always possible. A related aspect of investing in the student experience involves improvements to the university estate. Our biggest campus is the result of more than 80 years of growth on one site. We are currently developing an ambitious plan to make the centre of the campus much more student-focused and ban motor vehicles to the fringes. Other investment decisions have focused on revamping our main student areas over the last two years.

However, the important message about students as customers is that expectations will continue to rise and keeping up with that will be a challenge particularly if in the future the cap on student fees is raised or removed. This raises important questions about the strength of individual universities' brands and what fee they should be charging. If this happens we will have travelled a long way from the days of 'free' higher education. Our thinking about how best to serve our students will have been transformed.

On research concentration, in 2002 Exeter was among 20-30 universities in danger of falling into the 'squeezed middle'. Our research performance wasn't strong enough to make us top 20, yet we were a long way from becoming teaching and access-led. Time was running out fast. The 2008 Research Assessment Exercise represented (and still does!) a last chance to get into that top 20. The post-2008 landscape of increasingly metrics-based research allocation models and the likelihood of selective research competitions for top projects will set the research landscape for years to come. In this light, I suspect that the research-led part of the sector will shrink, as the concentration of research becomes even more marked.

We can see how universities are lining up in different market segments already. The 20 universities in the Russell Group and the 19 universities in the 1994 Group (which I chair) can, I believe, justifiably claim to be the research-led sector of the marketplace. Thirty post-1992 universities are represented through their own lobby group, Campaigning for Mainstream Universities, and a mixture of 17 pre- and post- 1992 universities are members of the new Alliance of Non-Aligned Universities. This still leaves some 15 pre-1992 universities that are not members of any of the missions groups. Critically, institutions can succeed in any part of the emerging market, as long as they know which part of the market they are competing in. Thus, one can be a very successful or a very unsuccessful member of any of the main mission groups, but the real problem occurs when an institution is neither aware of where it actually lies on all the key performance measures nor is able to define its mission. In this light there are a series of 'squeezed middles', that is to say parts of the HE market where some institutions are caught between competing missions and imperatives. The most worrying are those pre-1992 universities that claim to be research-led, and indeed explicitly do not see themselves as either access or primarily teaching institutions, while the performance indicators do not support such an assertion about research intensity. I suspect that this particular pressure will become even more intense following the 2008 RAE and the movement towards a more metric dominated research world.

For all of these reasons, Exeter's 2004/05 restructuring was undertaken to secure its place as a research-led institution. In 2007, Exeter has not yet reached all of its goals, but it has travelled a long way. We are confident it will be among the strongest research-led universities when the 2008 research assessment exercise is completed, and that it will strengthen its position as one of the most popular destinations for students. Without the restructuring exercise, we could not have looked to this future, since our financial resources were going into supporting departments that we candidly felt were unsustainable, rather than investing in the future success of the institutions. Time will tell if we made the right decisions, but we are certain that we have re-positioned Exeter, and to do that required the radical, painful, but necessary re-focussing of 2004/05.

Editors: Hugo de Burgh, Anna Fazackerley, Jeremy Black

THE UNIVERSITY OF SALFORD: A NEW APPROACH

Michael Harloe

Professor Michael Harloe became Vice-Chancellor of the University of Salford in October 1997. He was formerly Dean of Social Sciences and Pro-Vice-Chancellor Research at the University of Essex. A social scientist, Michael was the founder editor of the International Journal of Urban and Regional Research and has co-authored several books on social policy. He serves on a number of national and local committees including the Manchester: Knowledge Capital Board and Universities UK's Employability, Business and Industry Policy Committee.

In the 1830s Oxford rejected a proposal that it should teach mathematics. That decision provoked the following response:

'Bigotry and prejudice have doubtless had their share [in defeating the proposal]...but indolence and incapacity exercise even a wider and more pernicious influence...'

The start of university reform occurred in 1828 with the founding of University College by the Benthamites. However, it wasn't until the latter part of the nineteenth century, with the formation of the great civic universities, that the dominance of the university in the discovery of new knowledge and its transmission was finally established. Only then did the constitution of universities as self-governing, largely autonomous bodies – free to research and teach as they willed - come to be seen as an essential foundation for their mission and ethos. That mission centred on the pursuit of academic excellence.

Over the last century this late nineteenth century model of what a university is and how it is organised has developed and mutated. Changes such as the vast increase in participation in higher education, the enormous rise in state funding and tutelage, the growth of big (and very expensive) science, and the emergence of new disciplinary areas have all had their impact. But to a surprising extent, the way in which we organise and manage our universities didn't change all that much before perhaps the last two decades – despite the fact the pressures for change intensified over time.

By and large, the new universities that developed from the 1960s onwards were created and organised in ways that were similar to their longer established counterparts. There were good reasons for not attempting anything more radical - even if that had been thought about. However, now there are new pressures for change that can no longer be ignored.

We now live in and are increasingly dependent for economic and social progress on the knowledge economy. The performance of national higher education systems is crucially linked to success in this emergent economy. However in the UK and internationally, this knowledge increasingly brings in its wake a series of concerns about fitness for purpose. There are worries about, for example, the lack of global competitiveness of the European university system, the sustainability of university research funding, and questions of autonomy and professionalism and management - especially the degree to which universities are able to adapt and cope with endemic change.

But while those looking in from outside are concerned about universities' capacity for change, those on the inside frequently have a different view. There is a good deal of (academic) literature which sees the changes now taking place in the constitution of universities as threatening their very existence. The title of one recent American book in this genre, for example, is *The University in Ruins*.

Others see higher education surviving (surely a safe bet) but universities as we know them all but disappearing. For example, one German writer suggests that instead of universities there will be a series of mono-disciplinary expert centres linked together electronically for inter-disciplinary collaboration. Such centres could group together and call themselves a university if they wanted to. One nice touch is that laboratory teaching might be done by robots not humans. What we have here is some sort of Fordist reorganisation of higher education so it becomes rather like a car production line.

The problem of such visionary stuff is that it is based on little more than an over-excited and superficial reaction to the impact of new technology, marketisation and globalisation of higher education, sometimes allied to a conservative and dystopic pessimism.

The University of Salford was founded in 1967, yet it has a rich heritage dating back to the nineteenth century. It traces its origins back to the growing demand for skilled scientific and technical workers in Victorian Manchester, the world's first industrial metropolis. This reminds us that the relationship of universities to the knowledge economy is, in fact, no new development, however much its modalities have changed with time. Nor is the University of Salford a stranger to change. It nearly died in 1981 when its Government grant was almost halved overnight. It survived by reasserting and renewing its historic links with business, industry and the community.

Fifteen years later in 1996 the university reinvented itself by means of what was then the largest higher education merger ever attempted (and, unlike more recent and better publicised ones, without an extra penny of public funding to assist it).

Overnight, a small university specialising in science and engineering more than doubled, adding the major and dynamically expanding new disciplines of health and social care and the creative arts. Today, about 30% of its students are in the Faculty of Health & Social Care; 25% each in the Faculties of Arts Media & Social Sciences and Business, Law & the Built Environment; and just under 20% in the Faculty of Science, Engineering & Environment.

But the 1996 merger was just the first in a continuing series of changes which have sought to shape this amalgamated university into something that was more than the sum of its merged parts and that is fit for purpose at the start of the 21st century. First we replaced 38 mono-disciplinary departments and eight faculties with four stronger faculties and a very much smaller number of cross-disciplinary schools. Our research activity had already been reorganised in a series of multi-disciplinary research institutes, a change that resulted in an improving performance in each of the last three Research Assessment Exercises.

Though it has taken time to achieve we are now reshaping an unduly fragmented set of support services too and instituting a much wider series of changes in how the university is organised and managed. This includes plans to radically modernise its constitution – its Charter and Statutes – and to find innovative ways of giving new meaning and purpose to collegiality and staff engagement in shaping its future. It is remarkable just how little innovation (at least, until recently) there has been in how our universities are organised and managed. That can no longer continue.

However, all these changes are but means to an end. There is a fundamental decision that every university has to consciously address in a diversifying system: what position in that system does it seek to occupy? After its 1996 merger, despite its traditional links with business and the community, Salford was a university uncertain of its identity and future direction. In many ways the merger had transformed it into something of a hybrid institution, with strong research-led areas (mainly deriving from the 'old' pre-merger university) alongside dynamic areas of professional education that in the main lacked much of a research tradition (deriving from the two pre-existing colleges). It simply did not, and does not, fit into any simplistic division between teaching-led and research-led institutions.

Our search for a compelling identity and mission led us to reformulate and reinterpret what Salford has always been good at – namely, its wider social and economic mission. This has been embodied in a mission to become an enterprising university - attuned to business and community needs, fulfilling a socially responsive remit and achieving excellence judged by global external standards. This mission builds crucially on innovation, enterprise and research excellence across all its faculties and schools.

In the late 1990s, before the Higher Education Funding Council for England began its support for 'third stream' activities, Salford began its own third stream of academic work through the formation of Academic Enterprise – which exists alongside teaching and research. Salford's work in this area has attracted growing national and international recognition. Put simply, the objective of Academic Enterprise is to 'develop academic opportunities beyond means currently employed' and beyond those normally funnelled through the mainstream activities of teaching and research. A central team (which has grown from five in 1996 to over 30 today) works across the University to stimulate the imagination of our staff to create real improvements both for our partners and ourselves. Over the past six years the income these ideas have generated has grown year by year from a modest £1/2m to around £14m – representing almost 10% of our annual turnover.

Academic Enterprise has not only satisfied real world demands but also enriched university life. It means we know how to help all our partners succeed in business. But we also know how to develop enterprise projects that lead to socially inclusive wealth creation and to work with our partners for mutual benefit.

The remit of Academic Enterprise goes well beyond support for business, spin-out companies and so forth (though it also includes these). The university also has a vital and deepening engagement with its locality and its population on every level.

It is now recognised by the public authorities as a key partner in the social and economic regeneration of central Salford, a process which is accelerating rapidly. Not only does the university contribute its knowledge and skills to these developments but it in turn benefits from them.

For example, the proposed relocation of significant BBC production facilities to Salford Quays, close by the University, opens up major opportunities for the university faculties of Arts, Media & Social Sciences and Science, Engineering & Environment. And the physical changes in its locale will help to transform the image of the university to potential students and staff.

The university is, of course, a major employer of local people and is strengthening these links through a very active community volunteering programme and a highly successful initiative called Salford Young People's University. The latter is held in the summer months and every year inspires young people who would never have considered higher education to do so. All this puts the university at the heart of its local community, and is compatible with its wider aspirations to national and international excellence – contrary perhaps to the more elitist perceptions prevalent elsewhere.

So our mission is focused on enterprise outreach to business, industry and the community. We are also, according to official benchmarks, one of the most effective universities in the country at widening participation in higher education – and the best in the North West. Add to that the fact that over half of our research-active staff rated in the two highest rankings in our last national Research Assessment Exercise, and it's clear to see that Salford is not a university that can easily be pigeonholed according to conventional wisdom about types of university.

The fact is, there are symbiotic and mutually reinforcing relationships between our research excellence, our academic enterprise and our strongly vocational teaching. And there are a significant number of other universities that in their distinctive ways don't fit easily into the over-simplistic divisions that current higher education policy seeks to impose. Both the Funding Council and the government have paid lip service to diversity of mission. But the reality of policy and funding is often very different.

The role of universities in the knowledge economy is indeed a vital one. Paradoxically, however, academics rarely apply their own disciplinary and analytical skills to the current circumstances and future prospects of the institutions that employ them. And when they do it is remarkable how often dispassionate analysis is substituted by special pleading or by a mere desire to oppose or deny change.

It is perhaps little wonder then, that assertions about the significance of, for example, 'world class' universities (and what such a type of university consists of) are so infrequently grounded in adequate understanding of just how higher education influences social and economic development.

But Salford's example suggests that there is much more to this relationship than is currently encompassed in higher education policies and politics, either in the UK or elsewhere. Many outside the universities now feel that decisions about their future are simply too important to be left to the universities themselves. My hope is that, in an increasingly divergent sector, the narrow pursuit of sectional interests will not make the necessary renegotiation of the relations between the universities and society a one-way process.

Editors: Hugo de Burgh, Anna Fazackerley, Jeremy Black

THE MANCHESTER MERGER: STRETCHING THE GOLDEN TRIANGLE

Alan Gilbert

Professor Alan Gilbert came to Manchester in 2004 as President and Vice-Chancellor-elect, to plan for the launch of the new single University of Manchester. Prior to this he served as Vice-Chancellor of The University of Melbourne from 1996. During his term at Melbourne, he initiated Universitas 21, an association of international universities from ten countries. Before joining Melbourne, he was Vice-Chancellor of the University of Tasmania, where he oversaw a merger with the Tasmanian State Institute of Technology.

At midnight on 30 September 2004, the Victoria University of Manchester and the University of Manchester Institute of Science and Technology (UMIST) were constitutionally dissolved and – as the clock ticked over to 1 October 2004 – a new University was established by Royal Charter to inherit all their assets, obligations and liabilities, and their intertwined legacies of scholarly reputation and achievement built up over almost two centuries. The creation of this new University of Manchester, the largest in the UK, was seen by many as one of the boldest experiments in UK higher education history.

Loosely called the "Manchester merger", the experiment actually had little to do with mere aggregation. Scale in a university is at once a strength and a weakness. Many of the great universities of the world are relatively small, generously endowed centres of supreme scholarly excellence. On the other hand, institutions such as Michigan, Berkeley, Toronto and Tokyo, to name but a few, demonstrate that it is also possible for very large universities to operate at the highest level of scholarly virtuosity and research performance. Their success reflects a realistic "fit", maintained over long periods, between size, mission and financial capability of the institution, on the one hand, and the range and focus of the activities in which it seeks to be world-leading, on the other. In small elite institutions everything can be superbly funded; large institutions cannot match the unit-of-resource of well-endowed smaller institutions, but they do in principle have greater opportunities for diverting resources on a very considerable scale into key academic priorities. But to succeed they need that rarest of qualities in higher education: informed, consistent strategic development maintained over a long period.

The Manchester "merger" was the product of strategic thinking and driving ambition. The two legacy institutions were both successful, research-led universities. Both had reasons to be confident about the future, and the merger was not in any sense a last resort for either. It was strategic opportunity, not survival that shaped the thinking behind the creation of the new University. The defining metaphor was "step change". Those driving the merger process saw within their grasp an opportunity not just to create a single institution emphatically greater than the sum of the component parts, but to build in Manchester an academic powerhouse whose international recognition and academic performance would place it unambiguously among the world's greatest and most influential universities.

That powerful vision of major "step change" has not only informed the strategic direction of the new university, but, intriguingly, also facilitated the operational management of the merger. Mergers commonly fail, not necessarily in the sense of ending in total organisational collapse, but by producing a merged entity that is actually less productive than the combined productivity of the partners prior to the merger. Private sector experience suggests that this is true of perhaps three out of four mergers. The challenge in Manchester was to create outcomes at school, faculty and university levels in which the new whole far exceeded the sum of the legacy parts. Anything less than "step change" improvement would have betrayed the *raison d'etre* of the new university.

The result has been a transformational agenda dedicated to elevating The University of Manchester to the first rank of international research-led universities by 2015. Such agendas are common, but rarely truly transformational; rhetorically satisfying, they are often completely irrelevant operationally. Conversely, the *Manchester 2015 Agenda* has been conceived and developed as a practical roadmap for "step change" over the next decade. Its strategic objectives are informed by a clear sense of what it would mean to be a global "Top 25" university in 2015; the annual and quinquennial targets that drive it are based on a detailed analysis of the type and pace of change required to reach each target; the Key Performance Indicators (KPIs) that are used to measure success and/or failure year-on-year demand, wherever possible, quantifiable evidence of performance against plan. Budgets in the university are not only based on the objectives, targets and priorities identified in the *Manchester 2015 Agenda*, but are structured around financial incentives rewarding demonstrable "step change" progress towards the 2015 objectives.

Managing operational issues and expectations associated with the merger has become a secondary issue in such circumstances, albeit one of immense importance. But the power of the "step change" commitment at the heart of the merger has meant that, even before the inauguration of the new University in October 2004 – and certainly since then - retrospective and potentially divisive preoccupations with the efficacy and/or fairness of the merger itself have been overwhelmed by a prospective preoccupation, at once daunting and exhilarating, with the challenges and opportunities raised by the *2015 Agenda*. The management principle here seems to be that while a merger that is an end in itself may become pathologically fixated on legacy issues, a merger mobilising the new organisation around a powerfully transformational agenda has an excellent chance of moving readily through the merger phase.

A clear, widely-embraced strategic agenda is not in itself a guarantee of success in any merger. A merger also has to be well executed. The Manchester merger was a carefully designed process. Much thought, for example, went into the transitional arrangements put in place in 2004. The decision to allow me to take-up my appointment as President and Vice-Chancellor (designate) in February 2004, some eight months before the formal inauguration of the new University, was important in many ways. Professor Sir Martin Harris and Professor John Garside, the Vice-Chancellors of the two predecessor institutions, remained in post until 1st October, ensuring that the two existing universities continued to function normally but also facilitating the kind of planning for the inauguration of the new University vital to enable the transition to occur without loss of direction, morale or momentum in either of the two scholarly communities. Meanwhile, I had several months free from the burden of day-to-day operational management in which to build a senior leadership team, develop the "step change" agenda in consultation with colleagues across the merging institutions, and design the kinds of the governance and management structures that the embryonic institution would need to facilitate its ambitions.

The external environment was also critical to the success of the Manchester merger. The sheer scale and ambition of what was being attempted generated interest, excitement and support well beyond the borders of higher education. Leaders in the City of Manchester and the wider North West region needed no persuading that this experiment had profound implications for the international economic competitiveness and stature of the Manchester city region and the whole of England's North West. Unwavering political and moral support from city authorities, business leaders and the wider community in and beyond Greater Manchester, and much-needed financial investment from the North West Regional Development Agency were all vital to the merger.

High level national interest and support were also important. In higher education, as in other matters, there is a potentially dangerous concentration of resources, infrastructure and expertise in South East England, and specifically in higher education's "Golden Triangle" of Oxford, London and Cambridge. What became the University's *Manchester 2015 Agenda* thus resonated with a widespread belief that the long-term dynamism of the UK economy as a whole will depend on the emergence of one or more globally significant sub-economies outside London and the South East. No comparable economy anywhere in the world is as dependent on the performance of a single city region as the UK economy continues to be. In Greater Manchester, the West Midlands and West Yorkshire, long decades of industrial decline have given way recently to impressive post-industrial regeneration, but current economic trends suggest that even the most dynamic provincial city region has far to go if a genuinely multi-nodal national economy is to emerge in the UK.

Greater Manchester stands out as the city region with perhaps the greatest potential to emerge as a globally significant sub-economy. There is an impressive confidence and willingness to collaborate among the city's political, business and professional leaders. Years of consistent strategic development have blessed it with large scale infrastructure such as Manchester's impressive international airport, and nurtured rich cultural institutions to match the sporting reputation and international visibility that it derives from Manchester United. Yet all such successes are likely to come to nought in an emerging knowledge economy without the presence of a wide spectrum of higher education and advanced training institutions able to provide cutting-edge industries with access to a modern, sophisticated workforce. Support for the merger reflected an accompanying conviction that within the crucial education and training mix, Manchester needs a world renowned research-led university capable of underpinning and driving the City's research, technical and knowledge base.

The merger succeeded, in short, because the internal and external environments were both conducive to success. Regionally and nationally, the idea of the merger fired the imaginations of the policy-makers, politicians and business leaders; locally, it had widespread community support. But without wise, careful, deliberate internal planning and execution throughout the process, and without the powerful reality of shared vision and ambition, a propitious external environment would have meant little.

The same formula - detailed planning and careful implementation, on the one hand, and soaring vision and ambition, on the other - was as vital *after* the new University had been established as it had been in getting the two predecessor institutions to "Inauguration Day". The initial version of *Towards Manchester 2015* was published in September 2004, translating the vision of Manchester as one of the world's leading institutions of higher learning into nine major objectives, and an array of cognate targets, measurable annually, and Key Performance Indicators. From Day One, in short, the new University had a clear sense of common purpose and a planning and accountability framework that promised to turn strategic aspiration into disciplined operational endeavour.

The idea of "step change" and institutional transformation extended to the day-to-day routines and practices of university life. All existing committees were disestablished, and replaced by just three University-level committees: the Board of Governors, the Academic Senate and a new Policy and Resources Committee, chaired by the President and Vice-Chancellor and responsible to the Board for high level planning, budgeting, financial management and performance evaluation. Academically, the new university decided to operate through four powerful Faculties, the Deans of which were also Vice-Presidents of the University, and 23 large Schools. Ambitiously, it determined not to retain any policy, procedure or process from either legacy institution merely by default. It also decided to replace major IT systems across the board. It is dangerous to try to do too much, too soon. The commitment to systematic transformation, not merely incremental change, did create frustrating difficulties during the first few months of the new institution, but incremental change would have meant missing the once-in-an-institutional-lifetime opportunity to radically re-think traditional approaches to the day-to-day business of running a university.

Two years on, the Manchester experiment looks more likely than ever to succeed. Indeed, the merger *per se* is over. Merger-related issues have ceased to be significant conversation pieces in the new institution. More importantly, pre-merger practices and paradigms have ceased to provide frames of reference in contemporary discussions, probably because the "step change" agenda is already bearing fruit. Indicators of success emerged quickly. Research among external stakeholders carried out within months of the merger indicated that the new Manchester brand had been accepted and valued with remarkable speed, a reality confirmed by unbroken growth in student applications despite the loss of the two legacy brands. Manchester scholars were not poached by other institutions wishing to capitalise on the uncertainties created by the merger; on the contrary, the ambition and confidence of the new institution made it remarkably easy to recruit outstanding researchers and research teams from elsewhere. For the first time in more than half a century, Manchester now has, in Joseph Stiglitz, a Nobel Laureate on staff. Similarly, the part-time appointment of Robert Putnam, a distinguished social scientist from Harvard who has been described as "the most influential academic in the world," and the establishment of a formal Harvard University-University of Manchester research collaboration in key areas of the social sciences, is evidence that the drive for excellence that dominates the internal culture of the new university has not gone unnoticed nationally and internationally. Further iconic appointments are anticipated in the near future, some of them on a full-time basis. Such appointments are not seen as ends in themselves, but rather as powerful expressions of intent designed to make the new university a beacon attracting virtuoso scholars at all levels of career development.

The idea is to concentrate virtuosity on a scale at which the clustering of world class people and world class performance reaches "critical mass" – the point at which it become not just world class but *world leading*: one of the two or three places in the world to which brilliant people and ideas in a particular field of research are drawn, irrespective of career stage. Such world leading places, properly nurtured, become self-sustaining foci for research virtuosity. Manchester is seeking to create five or six such concentrations of virtuosity by 2015, and some are already emerging. One is the Brooks World Poverty Institute (BWPI), a multidisciplinary centre that is developing new approaches to poverty research, poverty reduction, inequality and growth. It builds on a long tradition of pioneering research in the international development field at the Victoria University of Manchester and is led by Professor Joseph Stiglitz. We have also created, in partnership with Cancer Research UK and the Christie Hospital, the Manchester Cancer Research Centre, which at launch was already the largest concentration of cancer research in Europe. Research Institutes have also been established in neuroscience, photon science and nuclear science, with the latter area, in particular, showing every sign of meeting the criteria, foreshadowed above, of being world leading.

Monitoring the target of becoming one of the top 25 universities in the world by 2015 may by then involve less impressionistic judgements than it did in 2004. The university's total identifiable research expenditure (an audited figure) has risen year-on-year to £348m in 2005-06. Total research council and trust income grew from £116 million in 2003-04 to £147 million in 2005-06, an increase of 26.7 per cent that, if continued, will see the university significantly exceed its 2015 research target for competitive research income. The respected Shanghai Jao Tong annual ranking of the world's leading universities (perhaps the only reputable international ranking of universities), shows Manchester moving from 78th place in 2004 to 50th place in 2006, and from 12th to 9th in Europe and 6th to 5th in the UK. Compared with such more systematic analysis, the selection of The University of Manchester as the *Times Higher Education Supplement's* "Higher Education Institution of the Year" in 2005, and the *Sunday Times* "University of the Year" in 2006, seem rather ephemeral. But these lesser indicators do confirm a general external appreciation that the Manchester experiment has been a major success.

Research virtuosity is only part of the idea of a great 21st Century university. More than ever in today's dangerous world, universities need to embrace the momentous responsibility of trying to ensure that their graduates will not only be world class professionals, but also informed, humane, committed citizens able to bring genuinely global perspectives to bear on the challenge of building just, humane, sustainable human communities in an increasingly dangerous planet. While all educational activities should have that as one of their ends, The Manchester Leadership Programme (MLP) has been one of a range of distinctive responses in the new university to the profound "third mission" responsibilities that higher education institutions cannot afford to ignore. Through a credit-rated "Leadership in Action" unit and a requirement of 60 hours community work, the MLP gives students the opportunity to confront issues of personal and social values, to reflect on the moral dimensions of professional and civic life and to develop a portfolio of generic leadership skills designed to boost their citizenship qualities as well as their employability. Hundreds of students are already taking the MLP annually, and the reservoir of community work so created is being used systematically to advance a variety of "third mission" activities, most of them associated with the University's major commitment to widening participation and social inclusion.

Paying for virtuosity will remain the great enabling challenge for the *Manchester 2015 Agenda*. The *Agenda* accepts the blunt reality that the resources required to run a world leading university will not come wholly (or perhaps even largely) from Government. We also accept that there *is* no "Mancunian discount". Being serious about matching the best universities in the world means becoming ever more efficient and finding ways to generate the recurrent, discretionary income required for investment in excellence at all levels. It follows that a successful university must develop a competitive, businesslike institutional culture accepting of the need to engage in overtly income-generating activities, including the fee-based educational services delivery on an international scale, effective fund-raising activities, the licensing and and/or pre-commercial development of intellectual property, the encouragement of innovation and the creation of spin-out companies – to name but a few. The *Manchester 2015 Agenda* must be as concerned with progress in these enabling activities as it is in building excellence in relation to its core educational, research and "third mission" priorities.

Implementing such strategies is still at an early stage, and early successes can be misleading. But in the end our greatest strength may turn out to have been a characteristically Mancunian quality - a healthy lack of illusions. For in international higher education as in the global knowledge economy, the world is not a handicap race in which superior institutions carry lead in their saddlebags to prevent them from outstripping otherwise inferior competitors. Like Manchester United in the fiercely competitive world of premiership football, the new University of Manchester will succeed at the highest level only by being able genuinely to match the finest universities in the world in the respect it commands for the quality of its research and the impact of its scholarship. That, ultimately, is the measure of the ambition driving the Manchester merger.

GLOBAL WESTMINSTER

Geoffrey Copland

Geoffrey Copland has been the Vice-Chancellor and Rector of the University of Westminster since January 1996. He studied Physics at Oxford University and has a doctorate in Solid State Physics. He spent eleven years researching and lecturing in physics at Queen Mary College and Queen Elizabeth College, University of London. In 1981 he was appointed Dean of Studies at Goldsmiths' College and in 1987 he became Deputy Rector at the University of Westminster (then known as the Polytechnic of Central London). He has twice been elected Chairman of the England and Northern Ireland Council of Universities UK and was Chairman of the Universities and Colleges Employers Association from 2002-06.

The University Of Westminster's response to the challenges of globalisation has been to develop a global presence, through a range of mechanisms to suit differing circumstances. The challenges posed by globalisation require an integrated university response. It is simply not sufficient to assume that globalisation only affects the international aspects of our work, although I shall concentrate in this chapter largely on the more international or transnational aspects of our response. But underlying that is a recognition that all the markets in which we operate will undergo change. We are developing an overall new Strategic Plan to respond to these challenges. This will include the need to recognise the increasing strength of the users of university services as customers who will have increased choice to meet their needs whether these be research, consultancy, undergraduate, postgraduate or post-experience teaching and learning.

There will be new competitors, often backed by large private resources who will aggressively attack areas where the competition to date has been from institutions like ourselves. These new competitors are likely to make decisions much more rapidly than existing university structures allow. This requires us to adapt our highly structured democratic processes to permit rapid decisions where necessary. They are also far less constrained by the heavy burden of regulation that is imposed on institutions that are in receipt of public funding. There clearly does need to be accountability for the use of public funds but all UK universities are now subject to systems of regulation and reporting that are excessive. Recent moves should relieve this to some extent, but do not go far enough. Of particular concern, which is effectively out of the hands of government is the role of the professional bodies. It is important to have some form of professional regulation and licensing but the overlapping and at times conflicting demands from these bodies hamper responses to changing circumstances and needs arising from the increased impact of globalisation.

The University has established a strong position in the international higher education market through a number of initiatives arising from its International Strategy, as recognised in 2000 and 2005 by the award for two consecutive periods of the Queen's Award for Enterprise: International Trade as well as The Higher Award 2005 for outstanding support for international students.

It has taken the view for some years that whilst the flow of international students into London is important for cultural and economic reasons, continued growth is unlikely to be sustainable in the light of increased global activity from other countries. Indeed a response to environmental sustainability pressures could be to reduce significantly the numbers of students flying around the world for study purposes. Thus our longer term strategy must be to work outside the UK to help to develop capacity where it is most needed and to form mutually beneficial partnerships with leading universities with missions of a similar nature to Westminster in key areas of the world. I shall summarise these areas of activity.

International Recruitment into London

The University has had a long tradition of welcoming students from around the world to study in its campuses in London. In 2005/6 there were some 4000 students from outside the UK studying in the University from 160 different countries. They study at undergraduate and postgraduate levels, with particularly rapid growth of taught postgraduate and research students.   The taught postgraduate programmes have been developed to respond to the clear trend that we identified some years ago for students who have already completed undergraduate programmes in their home countries to need to gain higher level knowledge and skills. We have thus designed a range of specialist taught masters programmes to address the needs of the international market with a particular emphasis on areas of direct relevance to developing countries.

Underpinning this approach to international recruitment has been a clear belief that all students, UK and international, will gain substantial benefit from studying and living together. In that way we can help to develop graduates at all levels who have a stronger appreciation of diversity of international perspectives, cultures, faiths and approaches to thinking about problems. It is as important for our largely London based UK students to gain a real understanding of these issues as it is for our international students. Our London graduates are most likely to find employment in London based organisations which themselves will be dealing with not only cosmopolitan London but international business. Thus the UK students benefit from the presence of a strong international student body.

The government has expressed its desire for universities to be subject to market pressures and there is no more competitive market than the international student market, whether it be competition from other UK universities or from an increasingly large number of countries who seek to build their numbers of international students. To respond to these pressures we have to ensure that international students are exposed to high value courses and have a good experience whilst studying with us.

International Scholarships

The University recognises that offering courses alone is not sufficient to meet the needs, particularly of students who come from economically poorer countries and we wish to extend our tradition of widening participation to the international student market. We have established an international student scholarship fund, valued at over £2million, supported by donations and other gifts from a wide range of people and organisations. The competition for these funds is strong and we are able to help, in various ways, a significant number of international students. A key requirement for the award of these scholarships, over and above that of high academic quality, is that the students can articulate a strong case that the programme to be studied will provide expertise that the holders will take back and use for the benefit of their home communities. In that way we can make a contribution to building capacity in their countries. The strength of that scholarship scheme was recognised in 2005 by the award of the first The Times Higher Award for outstanding support of international students.

International Capacity Building

The University believes that importing students into the UK to study is simply not enough to address the real demands of globalisation, no matter how much students gain from this experience. There are large parts of the world that for a variety of reasons there is a dearth of good quality higher education. The only sustainable way to help to support such countries, which are generally the economically most disadvantaged, is to help to build local university provision which can not only match international standards, but provide locally a more highly skilled professional workforce. Such capacity building can take the form of development projects to improve existing resources, build new institutions including developing staff and relevant curricula which are then entirely locally managed or to build off shore campuses of the University where whilst programmes are delivered locally they are quality assured by the University of Westminster and gain its qualifications.

There is a clear need in many parts of the world to modernise resources, curricula and methods of delivery in order to meet the challenges of the 21st century and global competition. The University has an active programme of staff development for international universities which is supported by work both in London and in the home country. We have found that offering staff development in design and delivery of programmes, research and in institutional management and quality assurance systems can help institutions to make clear advances. This is often conducted partly by in-country work by members of Westminster staff together with intensive programmes for staff from overseas institutions coming to study in London, often for short bursts of activity.

A second form of development work that we undertake is to help to design and build institutions. The best example was a project in Delta State in Nigeria where the state government identified that it had a need to create four new vocationally based higher education institutions. The University established a team to design, project manage and develop these institutions. The state government wanted our expertise to ensure that these would be completed on budget and time to a satisfactory standard. This required a University team to work in Nigeria for some years. In addition to the physical design and building, the government also wanted our academic expertise to design curricula and develop the staff to deliver it. On satisfactory completion of this project, working institutions were handed over to Delta State and our staff who had been involved had themselves gained great insights into the challenges of operating in different environments.

Projects of this nature help to build the overall international reputation of the University as an institution that has not only traditional academic expertise but which is responsive to international requirements.

Another strand of capacity development is that of not only building physical capacity but also having a long-term commitment to a country or region. A particular example has been the establishment of Westminster International University in Tashkent in Uzbekistan.

This project was initiated by the Uzbek government who were seeking a new way of delivering higher education in Uzbekistan with a view to establishing a regional centre for Central Asia. The requirement was to establish a new style of University with English as the language for teaching and operation, a western style and quality of curriculum which would produce graduates who were versed in western methods who would hold degrees that would have international currency. It also needed to be able to operate independently of the state and with a different ethos from the established universities in that country. Uzbekistan had previously sent its brightest students under their government scholarship scheme to study in the UK and USA. This was posing problems of outflow of hard currency and on occasions, a lack of willingness of these scholars to return to use their skills and education in Uzbekistan. The development project was put out to competition brokered by the

British Council with the selection being made by representatives from Uzbekistan. The University of Westminster was invited as a result of that competition to establish this new university. We already had a track record of development of staff for Uzbekistan and other emerging Central Asian countries through the Diplomatic Academy of London which is an integral part of the University. This Academy is focused on the education and development of diplomats and had delivered intensive training courses in diplomacy for these countries as they became independent following the collapse of the Soviet Union in the early 1990s. It has also run specialist development programmes for a wide range of other countries.

The Westminster International University in Tashkent is now firmly established and the first groups of students have graduated. These graduates are proving to be highly employable locally as they not only have highly developed English language skills but internationally recognised degrees of the University of Westminster. They are thus well equipped to help with the development of the region and its relations with the western countries.

International Partnerships

The globalisation of higher education provides a range of opportunities and challenges to existing universities. The challenges derive from much increased competition, not only from existing universities but from new institutions, usually developed by the private sector, which has identified higher education as a long term sustainable area for investment. This can lead to a range of new institutions which are much more market responsive than the traditional university. The University of Westminster is responding to the potential and actual challenges posed by the competition, new and old, by asserting its own values which have stood it in good stead for 170 years. These values include being responsive to the needs of individuals and of the communities in which it operates. Apart from the international development projects for discrete new developments as described briefly here, the university continues to seek partners with similar values and ethos with whom to work. This is work that has been in progress for a number of years and is not something that we have suddenly developed in response to the global challenge, but it is being pursued with new vigour as the competition develops. Some of these partnerships are bilateral for the mutual exchange of students, staff and research opportunities. Others are multilateral but for similar purposes. In some cases we have developed programmes in which we recognise qualifications or intermediate stages from our partners to allow student transfer to complete degrees in London at both undergraduate and postgraduate levels. Other examples are based on research and knowledge transfer collaboration. The China Media Centre of the University has been established quite specifically to develop strong links with the Chinese media, partly directly in partnership with Chinese universities. The Max Lock Centre has been developed to support sustainable city developments in developing countries, and was able to respond rapidly to the Tsunami crisis in South East Asia through its established development networks.

The University is a founder member of a new network of universities of similar nature and ethos in world cities. This is being established to form multilateral partnerships for the development of research projects related to world cities and for international curriculum developments to enable our students to gain wider opportunities through shared programmes.

Benefits and Risks to the University

I have described briefly some of the recent projects undertaken by the university to respond to some of the key challenges of globalisation. These are only some of the wide range of international activities that the university undertakes to support its mission to respond to global challenges.

They form a part of a much broader strategy by the university to ensure its continuing international competitiveness. This started decades ago with the first development work to establish new higher education institutions in Africa and Singapore from which established universities have developed. The growth of international students in the university has been enhanced by the development of a genuinely international curriculum taught in London which is attractive to UK and international students alike. The international scholarship scheme has been developed to support students who could not otherwise afford to study in London. Our global reach is strengthened by the commitment to developing new, and supporting existing, higher education resources in countries where there is a need. The lessons learned from working with overseas partners feed back into our London activities.

Not every venture is successful, for a variety of reasons. We were invited to assist with the development of a science based college in the Middle East a few years ago but withdrew from this when it became clear that the partner institution did not have the same emphasis on the need for delivery of programmes of international standard. We will not compromise on standards because in the long term this would be damaging to the holders of our qualifications. We are equally clear that any partners must conduct their affairs in accordance with high ethical and financial standards. Failure to meet these standards would damage the reputation of the university and would not fulfil what we regard as the contract with the students to prepare them not only technically but also ethically for their roles in the global society.

Any partnership venture or offshore operation will carry with it an element of risk in terms of finance, quality and standards. Before entering any partnership or other arrangement where the university has a stake requires a due diligence exercise and thoughtful risk assessment. It is also essential to have an exit strategy for the university in the event of the partnership breaking down. A key element of such a strategy has to be the protection of students to ensure that they are not disadvantaged by the premature closure of an arrangement. Given the political instability in many parts of the world, particularly some developing areas, there also has to be a strategy to protect the interests of any university staff working offshore. A further important consideration is that in any venture, we have to ensure that no UK government money is used. These activities must be separately accounted and accountable. This requires careful planning and management structures.

Summary

The UW recognises the relevance of globalisation first of all in its teaching curricula. These need to be relevant for a 'globalising' world. This international dimension is reflected in the university's staff body (60+ nationalities) and student body (160+ nationalities). Historically all research has had a strong international dimension but the UW plans to go further by linking its transnational education strategy to the reality of globalisation of knowledge transfer activities. Thus local strength is linked to international strength, creating a real potential for synergy.

The university's involvement in transnational education, and in fact all international activities, assumes that there will be substantial academic benefit, social benefit and sustainability of operations. Partnerships are the preferred operational mode, whether through university networks, through academic partnerships or through public-public or public-private partnerships. When operating in a market environment, rather than HE system, risks associated with operations are to be recognised and one needs to be prepared for worse case scenarios.

Editors: Hugo de Burgh, Anna Fazackerley, Jeremy Black

THE UNIVERSITY OF BUCKINGHAM: INDEPENDENCE IS THE WAY FORWARD IN HIGHER EDUCATION

Terence Kealey

Terence Kealey is the Vice Chancellor of the University of Buckingham, the only private university in the UK. Dr Kealey received his doctorate from Oxford University in 1982 and worked as the Wellcome Senior Research Fellow in Clinical Science at the Nuffield Department of Clinical Biochemistry, University of Oxford. He then moved to Cambridge University to become a lecturer in the Department of Clinical Biochemistry.

The Medieval Period

If we are to understand how best to run universities, we first have to know what they are. Fortunately, we can define the university – at any rate the western university - by its history.

The western university tradition is some 900 years old, the first institution having been founded in Bologna around 1100. By 1100 trade in Italy had recovered from the collapse of the Roman Empire, and in the absence of statutory commercial law a voluntary legal code, the *lex mercatoria*, had evolved.[1] Certain merchants had begun to specialise as advocates in the commercial courts, and the Bologna *collegium* was established by young men wishing to enter the renascent profession. Soon afterwards, similar foundations were created at Padua, Montpelier and other Mediterranean cities as student initiatives.[2] The students themselves actually ran those early universities, and they appointed the staff. We see an occasional survival of the student origins of universities – and of the remarkable influence of the students in some of the other early universities - in such conventions as the election of rectors or chancellors (now

---

[1] Bruce Benson 1990 *The Enterprise of Law: Justice without the State* Pacific Institute.
[2] H D Ridder-Symoens ed 1992 *History of the University in Europe* CUP.

essentially ceremonial figures) by students or alumni in the Scottish universities or in Oxford or Cambridge.

Near-simultaneously, a group of northern European universities including those at Paris, Oxford and Cambridge were created by the teachers themselves, and we see the consequences of their having been founded by the staff in the academic self-governance that has survived to this day at Oxford and Cambridge (the collegiate university at Paris did not survive the Revolution).

Eventually, medieval universities were created by the Church itself (often as a development of a pre-existing cathedral choir schools) or by Kings and Emperors.

It would be a mistake, however, to suppose that the early universities initiated higher education in the medieval era, because they were actually late-comers. There were already in Europe many teachers of higher learning, but many of them were freelance, teaching where the market took them. Equally, there were already many colleges of higher or further education in Europe, but their qualifications were recognised only by local bishops or kings. The concept of the university only emerged when first Bologna, and then others, were recognised by the Pope or the Holy Roman Emperor, because only the Pope and Emperor claimed authority over all Europe. A university, was an institution whose qualifications were recognised Europe-wide.

The university, therefore, was an institution born out of a settlement with the state. Hence from the very beginning, some academics feared that universities, by settling with the state, had also compromised academic freedom and efficacy. So, for example, the prominent scholar Philippus de Grevia, who ironically became Chancellor of Paris University between 1218 and 1236, lamented that:

> when the name of the university was unknown, there were more lectures and disputations and more interest in scholarly things. Now, however, when you have joined yourselves together in a university, lectures and disputations have become less frequent; everything is done hastily, little is learnt, and the time needed for study is wasted in meetings and discussions. While the elders debate in their meetings and enact statutes,

the young ones organise villainous plots and plan their nocturnal attacks. (H D Ridder-Symoens ed 1992 *History of the University in Europe* CUP.)

And fears over academic autonomy were not groundless. Although the early universities were independent institutions, the Church and the temporal rulers soon recognised them as threats to their monopolies on thought. As Pope Boniface VIII, outraged at the temerity of the scholars at the University of Paris to think for themselves, said in 1294: "You Paris masters seem to think that the world should be ruled by your reasonings. This is not so. It is to us, not you, that the world is entrusted."[3] But by then the Inquisition - which was inaugurated during the early 12th century, and which later built on a decree of Pope Gregory IX in 1231 that confirmed life imprisonment and/or death for any questioning of the Church's teachings - was already moving in on the universities, which were forced to accept the oversight of the Church. So, for example, the Chancellor of the University of Oxford was for centuries *ex officio* the Bishop of Lincoln. That is why so many academic titles (Chancellor, Dean, Doctor, Professor, Lecturer etc) are ecclesiastical; the Church had taken over.

Of course some rulers were enlightened, and they recognised the threat to scholarship. In 1158 Emperor Frederick I Barbarossa proclaimed his celebrated *Constituito Habita* or academic constitution defending Bologna's academic freedom. But such gifts from an emperor could always be revoked by him or a successor, and eventually they all were.

Indeed, under control of the Church, the universities soon declined into absurd institutions of scholasticism, where little of importance was discussed and where Aristotelians debated (literally) how many angels could dance on the end of a pin. The culture of the day was revealed by the fate of those scholars who did question received wisdom: Roger Bacon of Oxford, who had written in his 1267 *Opus maius* that: "arguments are not enough, it is necessary to check all things through experience", was imprisoned between 1277 and 1291 for 'suspected novelties'. The recently deceased John Wycliffe

---

[3] Bernard Hamilton 1981 *The Medieval Inquisition* Holmes and Meier, New York.

(Balliol) was declared in 1415 by the Council of Constance to have been a stiff-necked heretic who had been lucky to have died of natural causes, whereupon the Church dug up his corpse and abused it. In 1600 Bruno (Universities of Paris and Padua) was burned at the stake in Rome for speculating about multiple universes (the earth couldn't be at the centre of all of them) and in 1633, for believing the sun to be at the centre of the universe, Galileo (University of Padua) was shown the instruments of torture by Pope Urban VIII. Protestantism was no more liberal, and in 1553 Calvin burned Servetus (who had discovered the circulation of the blood through the lungs) for questioning doctrines of the Trinity and Baptism.

By the 18th century, the universities of Europe had ceased to be important centres of thought, and places like Oxford and Cambridge were reduced to teaching only a few hundred undergraduates, largely studying theology in preparation for careers in the Church. Their brief 17th century renaissance in Britain, which flowed out of the weakening of central authority in the wake of the Reformation, Civil War, Restoration and renaissance (Newton in Cambridge, Hooke in Oxford) was soon crushed again by the Church of England, which required the teachers at Oxford and Cambridge to be unmarried ordained priests of the Church of England. Consequently their average age was only 23, for most of them were only marking time until a college living arose.

After Adam Smith (1723-1790) attended Balliol College Oxford, he wrote: "In the University of Oxford the greater part of the public professors have, for these many years, given up altogether even the pretence of teaching." Smith's contemporary at Magdelen College Oxford, Edward Gibbon the historian, was to write: "my tutors were monks who supinely enjoyed the gifts of the founder [endowments]. My own [tutor] well remembered he had a salary to receive, and only forgot he had a duty to perform. [My] fourteen months at Oxford were the most unprofitable and idle of my whole life." The Scottish universities were not quite so bad (Watt did good work at Glasgow) yet Hume was rejected for posts at both Edinburgh and Glasgow because his writings offended the Church, and when Dr Johnson visited St Andrews he found one of its colleges being closed and the key to the library of another lost from disuse.

People still required to be educated in useful subjects though, and different societies created different institutions to replace the neutered universities. Late medieval Italy, for example, was a ferment of small private maths schools or *scuolae d'abbaco*, which were the business schools of their day, teaching accountancy, navigation and the other useful commercial arts.[3] Those schools competed to publish research to attract students and in 1534, for example, Niciolo Tartaglia of a *scuola d'abbaco* in Venice, found the solution to the cubic equation $x^3 + px^2 = n$ where there is no simple x term; but even freelance teachers like Tartaglia found themselves being marginalised.

In Britain higher education, not finding a home in the universities, moved towards the great professional bodies such as the Royal Colleges (medicine) or the Inns of Court (law). This unsatisfactory state of affairs was rightly abused by Francis Bacon who, in his 1605 *Advancement of Learning* (which has never been out of print) argued for university reform and for the creation of alternative bodies of scholarship and research. For at least two more centuries, however, the British universities remained moribund, and Bacon's new learning had to find its home in alternative institutions such as the Royal Society (1662). Shamefully, the universities played trivial roles in two of Britain's great contributions to world history, the Agricultural and Industrial Revolutions.

To conclude, therefore, the medieval university was originally created as an independent institution, but its intellectual creativity threatened the Church and State and it was neutralised.

Revival

The revival of western universities followed three traditions, i) America's, ii) the UK's and iii) Continental Europe's.

i) America

The revival of the western university can be traced to North America, which saw no fewer than eight universities created before independence in 1776 (Harvard 1636, William and Mary 1693, Yale 1701, Princeton 1746, Pennsylvania 1751, Columbia 1754, Brown 1764, and Dartmouth 1769). Although it would be naïve to claim all eight as wholly independent institutions that were committed solely to freedom of thought (many of them were originally bound to puritan thinking and ministers' training, and they all cooperated to some degree with the state) they were nonetheless independent, founded and funded by individuals rather than governments, and they soon grew into significant and diverse centres of independent thought and scholarship.

After 1776 more independent universities were created in the US, and the individual states created their own too but (and this is important) the federal government – which believed in educational states' rights and *laissez faire* - did not. Consequently, the benchmark for quality in America was always set by the independent Ivy League.

Prior to 1940, the federal government also believed in *laissez faire* in science, and it funded very little. So, for example, the federal government's total science and research and development (R&D) budget, including for defence, was $74.1 million in 1940, compared to the private sector's total of $265 million.[4] The universities' and foundations' independent research budget alone for pure science was $31 million. And the federal government's involvement in higher education was largely restricted to certain small agricultural colleges created under the Morrill Act which were created in response to America's problem with agricultural overproductivity (not underproductivity).

But the research needs of war forced the federal government into funding vast research budgets ($1.5 billion by 1945) which encouraged Washington into seeking to place some of that research within the universities. That initiative crystalised, post-war, in the creation of a National Science Foundation (NSF). The proposed NSF was to respect the academic autonomy of the universities and the scientists, and it was to be run autonomously by the scientists and universities themselves, but the first bill was vetoed on 6 August 1947 by President Truman. His justification for his veto is instructive because it reflected conventional bureaucratic thinking:

This bill contains provisions which represent such a marked departure from sound principles for the administration of public affairs that I cannot give it my approval. It would, in

---

[4] Charles Burnett 2003 Fibonacci's *'Method of the Indians' Bolletino di Storia delle Scienze Matematiche* 23.

effect, vest the determination of vital national policies and the administration of important government functions in a group of individuals who would be essentially private citizens. The National Science Foundation would be divorced from control by the people that implies a distinct lack of faith in democratic processes.

So the situation rested until the outbreak of the Korean War persuaded the Federal Government that it simply *had* to create a National Science Foundation to boost America's supply of scientists, to create a reserve of scientists in excess of America's peace-time needs who could be mobilised in the event of total war. In 1950 it acceded to the universities' insistence that the NSF was an autonomous body, and it created an NSF on the original model. The NSF is still run by scientists and the result – America's academic science base – is now one of the glories of the world.

ii) Britain

It was America's Ivy League example that inspired the creation, 200 years later, by philanthropists, of the new British universities (London 1836, Manchester 1851, Newcastle-upon-Tyne 1852, Birmingham 1900, Liverpool 1903, Leeds 1904, Sheffield 1905). Typical was Mason College, later Birmingham University, endowed by Josiah Mason, a local industrialist. On laying the foundation stone in 1875 he said: "I, who have never been blessed with children of my own, may yet, in these students, leave behind me an intelligent, earnest, industrious and truth-loving and truth-seeking progeny for generations to come."

But preceding the new universities was the Royal Institution in London, created in 1799 by – significantly – an American, Benjamin Thompson (later Count Rumford) who argued that British industry needed more scientific research – research that should be freely available for all to access. Rumford disapproved of patents: "I desire only that the whole world should profit by [my discoveries] without preventing others from using [them] with equal freedom". But to Rumford the provision of public goods was not a matter for Government but for private philanthropy, and he wrote that: "We must make benevolence fashionable." He succeeded. Within a year of its foundation in 1799 the Royal Institution had raised no less than

£11,047. The money came from individual subscriptions, with membership costing from 50 guineas for Founders' Life Membership to 2 guineas a year for annual subscriptions. And Rumford was himself a philanthropist, who left most of his estate to Harvard University to found the Rumford Professorship. Earlier he established the Rumford medal for the Royal Society (on condition he was the first winner).

The Royal Institution was not unique as an independently funded laboratory that published science freely. Its first lecturer, Dr Thomas Garnett, was lured from Anderson's Institution in Glasgow, which was a similar laboratory; and the Royal Institution's first giant, Humphry Davy, who was appointed lecturer in 1801, was lured from yet another independent research laboratory that published science freely, the famous Pneumatic Institute at Clifton, where he had discovered the anaesthetic effects of nitrous oxide or laughing gas.

At the Royal Institution, Davy was to discover six new elements (potassium, sodium, barium, strontium, calcium and magnesium) and in 1815 he was to invent the safety lamp in 1815. His great pupil, Michael Faraday, worked all his life at the Royal Institution. He was such a great scientist that a mere list of his achievements is awesome: let us just mention that in 1831 he discovered electromagnetic induction, the process by which electricity can be generated by rotating a coil in a magnetic field, which has underlain the commercial generation of electricity ever since. All sustained on private money.

The British universities, too, remained independent organisations that received no institutionalised Government support during the 19th century. Their students often received central or local government grants, and their scientists sometimes received Government research grants, but the income the universities received from those sources was marginal. In consequence, prior to 1914, the universities flourished as centres of scholarship and research, and they attributed their success to their independence, which they even celebrated in doggerel, mocking the Germans for their obeisance to, and love of, the state:

Professors we, from over the sea,
From the land where Professors in plenty be,
And we thrive and flourish, as well as may,

In the land that produced one Kant with a K,
And many cants with a C.

Oxford and Cambridge - frightened by being overtaken by the new universities- eventually reformed, and they cooperated with the Royal Commissions of 1850 and 1871 that led to the opening of teaching positions to all qualified candidates. In 1945 Cambridge deigned to admit women to degrees!

But this happy picture in the UK changed after 1914-18. Before 1914 the universities enjoyed two major sources of income, i) fees and ii) endowments. Central government income, provided via the Committee on Grants to University Colleges, was only £150,000 annually, shared between all the civic universities (Oxbridge stayed aloof). Coupled with the local government grants to students, Government support for the universities did not exceed 20 per cent of their income.

But the Great War of 1914-18 bankrupted the universities. Their fee income disappeared as the young men abandoned their studies for the Western front, and - more gravely in the long-term - their endowment income collapsed. Between 1815 and 1914 the value of the currency had actually risen (deflation) so the universities had invested in fixed-income vehicles. But between 1914 and 1918 the pound lost three quarters of its value and inflation continued after 1918 so the universities' endowment income collapsed. Consequently, in 1918 all the universities (including Oxford and Cambridge) united in a Deputation to the Treasury. Its leader, Sir Oliver Lodge, the Principal of Birmingham University, appealed desperately for Government support: "We want a quadrupling [of the grant] at once. We cannot wait." So in 1919 the University Grant Committee was instituted with an annual budget of £1 million. It soon rose (£1.8 million in 1921).[5] By 1921, indeed, when Local Education Authority grants were included, Government support for HE in the UK accounted for more than 50 per cent of its income. Effectively, the sector was nationalised as a consequence of 4 years of total war.

Initially the UGC distributed its funds under the 'Haldane Principle' (named for the prominent Liberal politician) by which the

---

[5] T Kealey 1996 *The Economic Laws of Scientific Research* Macmillan.

money was provided by Government to academics who then – as an independent forum – distributed it on academic criteria. But the replacement of the UGC by the Higher Education Funding Councils (HEFCs) and the other *dirigiste* Government agencies has transformed the UK universities into institutions that resemble US state - as opposed to US independent - universities.[6]

Concurrently, the needs of total war between 1914 and 1918 changed government culture, and research was no longer seen as private matter for industry and philanthropists but as a national resource, and the major research councils were created. The Medical Research Council was created in 1913 in anticipation of war, and the forebear of the physical science councils was created in 1916 to meet the research needs of the Western front. But the research councils have been run on autonomous NSF lines, and they are good. The tragedy in Britain was that, solely by accident, the Great War of 1914-1918 led to effective nationalisation of the British universities.

iii) Continental Europe

The story on the Continent is completely different: it is a story of governmental activism. In France, following the direction of Colbert, who was Chief Minister between 1661 and 1683, the State created an array of schools of science and technology including the *Ecole de Rome* to teach arithmetic, geometry and draughtmanship, the *Academie Royale de Peinture* to teach painting, the *Ecole Royale Graduite de Dessin* to teach design, and the *Academie Royale d'Architecture* to teach architecture. Colbert also fostered the great workshops of the Savonerie and the Gobelins, the mint, the royal press and royal manufactory in the Louvre. The *Academie des Sciences* received generous state aid and the world's first scientific journal, the *Journal des Savants*, was created by the state. The *Jardin du Roi* was reorganised in 1671 to research and teach in botany and pharmacy. Three chemistry research laboratories were created by state, one in the King's library, one in the Louvre and one at the Observatoire.

---

[6] RO Berdahl 1959 *British Universities and the State*, Cambridge; CH Shian 1986 *Paying the Piper: The Development of the University Grants Committee 1919-1946* Falmer Press.

Successive administrations continued Colbert's policies. The school of civil engineering or *Ecole des Ponts et Chaussees* was created in 1716, the *Ecole du Corps Royal du Genie* in 1749, the *Ecole des Mines* in 1778 and the *Ecole Polytechnique* was founded in 1795. And those institutions so thrived as to produce scientists of the quality of Lavoisier, Berthollet, Leblanc, Carnot, Monge, Cugnot, Coulomb, Lamarck, Cuvier, Saint-Hilaire, Gay-Lussac, Arago, Ampere, Laplace and Chaptal. Nor were the technicians ignored. Trade schools or *Ecoles des Art et Metiers* were founded all over the country and by the early 19th Century, when it was still only a craft in England, France had established engineering as a profession, with schools, formal examinations and, after 1853, its own research laboratories in the *Conservatoire*.

Germany saw a similar pattern, following the example of Wilhelm von Humboldt who created the University of Berlin as a research university in 1810. Consequently *technische hochschulen* and other research and teaching universities were founded by the state all over Germany.

The Consequence

We have here a fascinating experiment. The US and Continental Europe have adopted almost diametrically opposed systems of higher education: *laissez faire* opposed to *dirigisme*, with the UK somewhere in the middle. Which system has flourished? The answer is almost ludicrously obvious. Every international league table of research quality is absolutely dominated by the American universities. As John Kay concluded in his 2003 book *The Truth About Markets*: "The United States is completely dominant in research and postgraduate education. The ten leading research centres in the world in virtually all mainstream subjects are found in American institutions. The eclipse of other universities, particularly those of Britain and Germany…"

Moreover teaching is manifestly better in the US, with the continental European universities now infamous for their squalor, vast class sizes and impersonal teaching. The continental universities defend their failure on the grounds of equity: tuition is free or low-cost, and entry guaranteed to all qualified candidates. Yet the same is also true of the US, where not only the state universities but also the Ivy

League (with its vast endowments) provide needs-blind admissions. And it is the American liberal arts colleges that set the international standard for quality teaching.

One major reason for the discrepancy between the US and Europe was supplied by the EU Commission itself. In its 2003 *The Role of the Universities in the Europe of Knowledge* it concluded that:- "European universities generally have less to offer and lower financial resources than their equivalents in other developed countries, particularly the USA ... American universities have far more substantial means than those of European universities – on average, two to five times higher per student ... The gap [between the US and EU expenditure] stems primarily from the low level of private funding of higher education in Europe."

Britain, interestingly, falls somewhere between the US and Europe. Oxford and Cambridge are the only two non-US universities that qualify to enter (just) the top 10 positions in the international league tables for research, while under the auspices of the UGC teaching was good too. But under the HEFCs huge damage has been done. The Universities UK 2002 submission *Investing for Success* provides the facts on funding per student in the HEFC-funded sector, concluding:

Significant damage has been done by many years of underfunded expansion, which since 1989 have seen resources per student fall by 38 per cent, following a decrease of 20 per cent between 1976 and 1989; staff-student ratios decline to an average of 1 to 17 (1 to 23 if funding for research included in the average unit of funding is excluded).

The Economist for 26 July 2003 provided a snap-shot of the state of British universities that made worrying reading:

Universities have seldom been more miserable. They are short of money. Government micro-management is intrusive and contradictory ... The financial position is certainly bleak ... around a half of English universities will fail to break even in the coming year ... a quarter admit to being in financial trouble ... 11 are in a parlous position.

The major problem, of course, is that the Government will not allow HEFC-funded universities economic freedom, and they are not allowed to charge the fees the market will bear. The situation has been eased by the introduction of fees (£1,000 pa in 1997, £3,000 pa in 2006), but until full economic freedom is provided, the British universities will never attain their full potential. Consequently, Britain will lose economically to the US (and Australia) that are beginning to dominate the international market.

The obvious solution is to create independent universities in the UK, which was why Buckingham was created in 1976. Interestingly, when Buckingham was created, the staff:student ratio in the UK was 1:9, and it still is in Buckingham. And when in 2006 the Government commissioned Ipsos MORI to poll all final year students in the UK for their views on the quality of teaching, it was Buckingham that came top of the National Student Survey.[7] Interestingly, the other university that did well was the Open University, which has long been the only other university in the UK to charge realistic fees. Independence works in Higher Education, if only because a dependence on student fees provides the institutional incentive to address the students' needs, and because that incentive need not be obstructed by alternative pressures from government.

Independence works not only because of resources but also because of freedom from regulation. The HEFC-funded universities are over-regulated. The Government's Lambert Review[8] of 2003 endorsed the conclusions of HEFCE's own review[9] and of the Better Regulation Task Force[10] that the university sector is "over-audited". Audit "is a multi-layered and complex burden that inhibits risk taking, encourages game play and costs too much [£250 million annually]". The Lambert Review lamented that "while the accountability burden is widely recognised, this has not slowed the introduction of new funding initiatives to drive central policy. In July 2002 there were 27 separate funding initiatives administered by HEFCE and the DTI. Universities are all undercapitalised ... their funding is increasingly

---

[7] J Shepherd 2006 National Student Survey *Times Higher Education Supplement* August 25 2006, p 4.

[8] www.lambertreview.org.uk.

[9] PA Consulting Group 2000 B*etter Accountability for Higher Education.*

[10] Better Regulation Task Force 2002 *Higher Education: Easing the Burden.*

earmarked by the funders for specific initiatives, leading to complaints of micro-management from the centre." This is not how Harvard, Yale, Princeton, Chicago or Stanford (or indeed Manchester United) flourish. Modern management thinking confirms that local autonomy and decentralisation are key to the optimal delivery of services.

One reason the universities are over-regulated is that, being deprived of economic freedom, they have also lost their operating freedom. Consider the case of the London School of Economics (LSE) and the Quality Assurance Agency (QAA). By 2001 it was becoming universally clear that the QAA was trying to turn itself into the universities' director, on the German state model, so in that year the LSE, outraged by its recent inspection, protested publicly that the QAA had: "infringed academic freedom and imposed its own bureaucratic and pedagogic agenda." The LSE then said that, unless the Government reformed the QAA, it would go independent, whereupon the Government surrendered. The Government removed John Randall (then the CEO of QAA) replaced him with Peter Williams and introduced a new regime of a 'light touch', which has been widely greeted as a great improvement. But the key to the story is this: the majority of the LSE's students are foreign and pay full fees, so the LSE's threat to go independent was credible, because it could afford to. Yet the LSE's economic credibility owes everything to the full fees it charges of foreign students - fees incidentally, that were pioneered by Buckingham in 1976 and copied by the Government in 1981.

Conclusion

The empirical evidence is clear: only independence delivers quality in higher education. The higher education benchmarks were pioneered by the independent institutions, first in the US and latterly in the UK. They were also the two countries to have dominated the world economy since the 18th century. To copy them, the continental countries' governments created their own state universities, but those have failed both as instruments of teaching and of research. They respected academic freedom, at least formally, and Humboldt and his liberal followers fostered ideas of *Lernfreiheit* (the right to study freely) and *Lehrfreiheit* (the right to teach freely) but in the absence of economic and operational freedom the continental universities have done poorly.

The role of the state should be restricted to that needs-blinds agency of last resort: ie, the state should ensure that no-one is denied acces to university for lack of money. But thereafter the universities should be free to run themelves as they wish in a competitive global market.

MEDDLE NOT WITH THEM THAT ARE GIVEN TO CHANGE: BATH SPA UNIVERSITY

Frank Morgan

Professor Frank Morgan is a public finance accountant who has been Chief Executive of Bath Spa University. Following his appointment Bath Spa has diversified into many new disciplines, has built up a strong local and regional identity particularly through its work with further education partners, and has established major links with local businesses. Professor Morgan has a passion for the novels of Saul Bellow and John Cooper Powys, and a love of all things Indian; he harbours long term guilt about his affection for Salford Rugby League Club (flying in the face of his commitment to Bath and its region).

Meddle not with them that are given to change: Proverbs21:24

Uncertainty may have become the only certainty, but there is no reason for the modern university to decline into dysfunctionality or for its members to groan with despair. Yes, there can be frustration when rules and regulations seem to be imposed without rationale or obvious justification. So, for example, a university must explain in its annual audit report why it departs from certain injunctions on governance while the authors of the less convincing suggestions, like some of these in the Committee of University Chairmen Guide, do not themselves defend their position. Or take my favourite: I will always remember our Director of Finance's trepidation as he explained to me that we must now have "a policy on fraud". I ponder the probability that the absence of such a policy might be deemed to imply a tolerance of fraud or even of a welcoming of it.

But these examples are mere irritants. To be more serious, when change involves the use of new tools and methodologies to improve the fundamentals of teaching, research, working with business, contributing to the local society and so on, then we should not falter. What we are offered is the opportunity to improve the very services that it is our duty as educators and administrators to deliver.

So it is at Bath Spa. As one of Britain's newest universities we are already basking in the sunshine of the Sunday Times citation as one of the "10 best modern universities". This ranking and our ambitions for the future are both based on the same fundamentals.

What are these fundamentals? First and foremost Bath Spa is proud to be a "teaching-led" university: not, emphatically, a "teaching only" university. We acknowledge that changing government policy has delivered to us both university title itself and - when due allowance is made for the size of the institution - just about the biggest grant under the Centre for Excellence in Teaching and Learning (CETL) initiative that has been allocated to any university. These developments are evidence enough that the government and its agencies endorse the value of university teaching. Indeed one Secretary of State has said that it is the most important activity of our universities. The CETL at Bath Spa serves to demonstrate most of these `fundamentals' that follow from our commitment to being "teaching-led". Our CETL, "Artswork", is directed at all our creative arts courses, thereby directly affecting three of our seven student-based schools and setting the standard for taught programmes throughout the university. Its objective is to ground our degree programmes in the relevant industries so that our graduates experience best industry practice, use state of the art equipment and facilities, and graduate with qualifications that are attractive to employers. In delivering this we must maintain strong connections with the cultural and creative industries, and while those industries are particularly well represented in the Bath area, our reach must be nationwide. Bath Spa's delivery of these programmes is often via longstanding links with regional further education colleges known as the "Wessex Partnership". The partnership is another `fundamental goal'. Every facet of this work depends on innovation and development. There can be no possibility of ever achieving a steady state, but this is part of the excitement for staff who design and teach the courses and for the students who benefit from them.

I have used our "Artswork" project as a good example of what this university is about; high quality taught provision, continuous improvement in teaching and learning, employability for our graduates, local and regional connections both economic and in terms of the social well being of our host city and region. But this is not all. Notwithstanding our teaching priority, we maintain a healthy research profile. This is particularly true of our creative subjects, and in recent years we have had, for instance, finalists for the Jerwood and Man-Booker prizes, and a winner of the Whitbread first novel prize. This and other sound research output has been maintained despite the fact that the political environment is much less supportive of our research than it is of our teaching.

Bath Spa must also maintain its commitment to the social agenda. By this we mean that we will look always to enable those who have not enjoyed early success, owing to economic, social and cultural constraints, to earn degrees of a recognised academic standard and value. The challenge of the future is to ensure that our reputation and that of UK universities is maintained at the same time as ensuring the maximum involvement from all sections of our society. On a bad Monday morning this seems more of a threat than an opportunity, but all in all it is not a merely preferred option, rather it is the essential purpose of a modern university and we are privileged to be able to help realise it.

If our fundamental goals are those shared by many universities should we be criticised for conformity or undue caution? Well, the best response to this is that if UK universities are to succeed in the next 20 years in delivering excellent and innovative teaching and research while progressing the economic and social agenda, then they must be developmental and distinctive. Also, to share a common destination does not necessarily mean sharing a common route.

What will be distinctive about Bath Spa in the next 10 or 20 years? As I have described above, the Arts - visual, performing and written - are emblematic of our ambitions. We intend to co-locate more subjects by reference to their mode of delivery (for example including digital technology or in a virtual environment) than by their traditional subject discipline groupings. We intend to secure all taught courses by reference to relevant industry practice or the nearest equivalent (such as clear identification of employable skills delivered by "academic" subjects). We believe the practical application of higher education can be an honourable objective and have embraced the introduction of foundation degrees in a variety of subjects, even where there is no obvious employer of scale. One of the many skills we must impart is the ability to gain employment even when the employment is outside the frameworks of big business or public service.

This university will unashamedly draw on the vigour and ambition of Bath and the South West so that its activities draw strength from and nourish the culture of the region. This is and will be true of our courses, but in addition our plans are to use the acquisition of a new site in order to establish this university ever more firmly into the society and economic of the sub-region.

So, I remain positive and optimistic about the ability of Bath Spa University and, indeed, UK higher education to respond to change and development. That said, there are many potential hazards ahead. I identify below four particular areas integral to our aspirations above, where my own university will face difficulties and contradictions, and may even find itself attempting to meet mutually exclusive targets: social policy, the Research Assessment Exercise, the political environment, and collaboration with further education.

The transition from a higher education system of fewer than 1 in 10 participation to one that seeks to offer opportunity to at least half of our young people was never going to be an easy one. The main issues affecting this transition have been well aired in the past. I would like now to select one particular point that has perhaps been given insufficient attention, and which bears particularly on us. Bath Spa University has a sound record of access and participation when measured against most of the common indicators. Throughout the sector participation has widened massively, and exclusion has been dramatically reduced. Many universities must take enormous credit for opening up their courses to ensure, for example, that they are welcoming to different ethnic groups. However, the pattern remains uneven between universities and between courses. But for any university to have as its long-term corporate objective its being identified as an outstanding provider for ethnic minority groups is to miss the point; it can only logically be a short-term goal. Only if the sector as a whole reaches a reasonable balance across all its institutions and across all disciplines when measured against societal averages for gender, race, disability and so on will we truly have attained a fair and balanced society. This leaves an individual university like my own with some questions to answer about how it prosecutes the social policy. There are certain indicators where it may be helpful for us to exceed our benchmark, but only as a transitional arrangement on the route to the long-term objective I have outlined above. Bath Spa will ensure that it does not unwittingly connive in a situation in which a constant minority of universities take on responsibility for the social policy on behalf of the rest, not only for its own sake, but because that would frustrate the overarching objective of a "fair and balanced society".

The Research Assessment Exercise has always been a thorny problem, not just for the post `92 universities, all of which, like Bath Spa, have a small research output relative to the big RAE beneficiaries, but also for every grouping within UK higher education. The next RAE is likely to reflect long-term government strategy: the maintenance of world-class research and the selective funding of a minority of universities to achieve it. Where does that leave a university like Bath Spa? On the face of it, we should have little difficulty: as we are a teaching-led university we could be untroubled by slow progress in attracting research funding and developing a research mission. The truth is, however, that it is unimaginable to put energy into developing a university for the long-term without securing within it a substantial research activity. There are many arguments for this and I will not rehearse them except to highlight the very pragmatic point that recruitment of outstanding teachers is unlikely to be successful if that recruitment cannot simultaneously offer opportunities for research. The majority of higher education academic staff would see the main difference between their role and that of their colleagues in further education as being the requirement and opportunity for research and scholarly activity. At Bath Spa we have wrestled reasonably successfully with this for some years. We have ambitions to maintain and develop our portfolio of advanced scholarship including research that is independent of, but not ignorant of, the RAE and its constraints. For instance, the RAE does not encourage writing textbooks for advanced learners, but it is consistent with our mission and strengths to encourage that at Bath Spa. The development of research is one of the few areas where I perceive the development and prosperity of this university as being slightly at variance with the prevailing political and funding imperatives.

Which takes me on to the political environment in general terms. It is a truism that political change will always be most difficult for an institution whose future is enabled by public funding or government recognition. Perhaps the most obvious current issue is the degree to which universities are expected to expand in the next few years. Again, many of these arguments have been described elsewhere, but as I write, the imminent change of Prime Minister, not to mention the possibility of a change of government at a subsequent election, must mean that universities, autonomous bodies responsible for their own long term future and viability, have to hedge their bets to some extent. It is my argument to my own Board of Governors that we cannot get ourselves too far out on a limb in prosecuting even the major tenets of government policy if the cutback of such a policy by a new government would render the university vulnerable. So, we are striving to add to our building stock - our current sites are very close to capacity and have space utilisation ratios that are amongst the highest in the UK sector - and are aiming to do so while balancing the associated risks. If we over-commit ourselves financially to acquire space, only to find that government policy leads to steady state or even contraction in the sector, then the university in 5 or 10 years may reap a bitter harvest of financial problems with chronic consequences. If, on the other hand, we fail to secure adequate space for our continuing expansion (we have increased numbers every year for at least 20 years) then we will no longer be a proud contributor to the UK's expansion and development of degree provision. Neither extreme scenario is acceptable. The dilemma is to gauge just what constitutes a sensible balance between them.

Finally, a particular issue connected with much that I have described above is the future of collaboration with further education. This issue has been a central ambition and objective for Bath Spa University for at least 15 years. We are quite unusual in the consistency and emphasis we have placed upon it. We work with a wonderful set of further education partners and have in a measured and responsible way developed many courses with them including, of course, Foundation Degrees. What of the future? In the first place the success and development of Foundation Degree programmes has been real but unspectacular in recruitment terms. The Funding Council on behalf of government has placed great emphasis on these programmes and we are committed to the policy. There must, however, be at least some doubt about the extent to which Bath Spa can be successful in the face of constraints, such as the requirement to provide an opportunity to enter a third year of study without concomitant funded places. Of greater significance is the question of what the future holds for the HE/FE interface. At Bath Spa we have never compromised our commitment to access routes via further education because we feared either eroding the clarity of our own university identity or because we feared we were effectively training up our competitors for the future, that is, further education colleges as major providers of higher education. So, it is not about Bath Spa's immediate tactics that I write, but to consider whether the successful partnership of HE and FE will effectively mean that from a student's point of view there will be no difference in 10 or 20 years between Bath Spa and its FE partners. What would this mean for Bath Spa, what would it mean for UK higher education, what would it mean for UK further education, and most crucially of all, what would it mean for each generation of students?

So, there is much that is uncertain and some future developments which may even be threatening. Against this universities are developing and extending their influence not just to individual students, but also in terms of their wider social and economic impact. They are at the core of developments in our cities and the rural areas. The importance of universities to all the main aspects of human society and civilisation are increasingly recognised by government and the public. This is an exciting and challenging environment for all of us.

Editors: Hugo de Burgh, Anna Fazackerley, Jeremy Black

THE MANAGEMENT OF UNIVERSITIES: MANAGERIALISM AND MANAGEMENT EFFECTIVENESS

Michael Shattock

Michael Shattock is visiting professor and founding Joint Director of the MBA in Higher Education Management at the Institute of Education, University of London. He was formerly Registrar at the University of Warwick. He is an expert on the structure, governance and management of higher education and his books include Managing Successful Universities (Open University Press 2003) and Managing Good Governance in Higher Education (Open University Press 2006). He is Editor of the journal 'Higher Education Management and Policy'. He is a member of Agora's Advisory Council.

The context of university management has changed almost out of recognition within the career span of academics now reaching retirement age. In 1960 the University of London was the only university that had more than 30,000 students, but it was a collegiate university and the students (and the staff) were managed in self-governing colleges. In 1959 a Home Universities Conference had resisted expansion on the grounds that it was inappropriate for universities to grow beyond a student population of 5,000. Fifty years later we may expect at least 15 universities to have over 30,000 students managed on a unitary institutional basis. The other institutions have grown proportionately: 15 universities (not necessarily the same ones,) have turnovers of over £300m, a figure undreamt of 20 years ago. Universities have become 'big businesses' and require 'business-like' management. In a similar period the contribution of the state for the recurrent funding of higher education has gone up many times prompting a much more rigorous public accountability regime. (Very few universities even had audit committees until the Cardiff financial collapse in 1987). Accountability regimes, whether financial, prompted by increased scrutiny from Funding Councils and from changes in corporate governance practice, or academic, arising from the activities of the

Quality Assurance Agency, have enormously increased the bureaucratic burden on universities.

Competition was essentially based on reputation until the first published league tables began to appear after the 1986 research selectivity exercise; by the time of the 1992 research assessment exercise (RAE) it was apparent to all institutions that the RAE was going to be the machinery which would determine university rankings, and competition for success in it was enhanced accordingly. The later appearance of global league tables merely added a further dimension to the nature of the competition. Competition breeds stress, demands shorter decision-making timescales and discounts equity in favour of more *dirigiste* approaches to resource allocation. At the same time the recognition of the dependence of the knowledge economy on university outputs, both nationally and regionally, has led to the creation of a 'third mission', which requires universities to maximise their community and regional contributions. These contributions need clear management structures if they are to be effective and often entail the recruitment of '*animateurs*' from the private sector whose first responsibility is to their 'customers' and not to the traditional mores of teaching and research (Goddard and Chatterton 1999). Their instincts and role are different to those of the academic community.

Financial stringency has also been a forcing house for change. This has manifested itself in two ways. In the early 1980s the then much smaller university system faced serious real budget reductions, forcing departmental closures, redundancies and considerable academic restructuring. While from the late '80s through to the mid-'90s the rapid growth in student numbers, together with the concentration of funding for research into fewer universities as a result of the RAE, led to a steady worsening of staff student ratios to levels in some universities which would have been considered completely unacceptable in a university system 20 years before. Again, the consequence has been repeated rounds of academic restructuring including some high profile departmental closures in expensive disciplines like Chemistry and Physics where student demand has fallen. From the very beginning of this period, questions were raised outside the university system as to whether managerially it could cope with change of this nature. The Chairman of Unilever doubted whether universities had "the organisational structures nor as yet the management skills" to deal with the situation (Durham 1982). The

Jarratt Report argued that vice-chancellors should be recognised as chief executives and that governing bodies should "assert themselves" over senates endemically liable to resist change and to act out of "natural conservatism" (Committee of Vice-Chancellors and Principals 1985), propositions that were given legal validity in the constitutions of the new universities in 1992. The Lambert Report condemned management in some universities as "slow moving, bureaucratic and risk averse" and commended "dynamic management in an environment that cannot wait for the next committee meeting" (Lambert 2003).

Thus size, increasing competition, accountability, the broader mission and financial stringency have in combination changed the management task in universities, not just at the institutional level but down in the basic academic units of the faculties and academic departments. Does this mean that management needs to become managerialist to get the job done? Can universities retain collegiality in management when the management task has so changed? Many people do not think so, and in many universities a much more executive style of management has been introduced. Stephen Schwarz, the then vice-chancellor of Brunel, argued against consensual appointments of senior academic managers:

"Academics are not going to vote for a manager who advocates cutting their programmes. The result is that only those people with no plans or those who promise everyone whatever they wish to hear are elected. University managers, including deans and heads of department should not be elected but should be selected for their management ability. This will give them dignity and authority. Also managers who are hired can be fired – a key element of accountability." (Schwarz 2003)

The logical end point of such an approach could be seen in the structure described as operating at DeMontfort University, a post-1992 institution, towards the end of the 1990s:

"A small Board of Governors working closely with a Chief Executive...who really is the Chief Executive and has considerable delegated powers; the Chief Executive runs the institution with the Senior Executive including four Pro-Vice-Chancellors, two Associate Vice-Chancellors, the Director of

Finance, the Academic Registrar and the Director of Personnel." (North Report, University of Oxford 1997)

Both statements could be described as 'managerialist'. The DeMontfort structure with variations of details, and perhaps without quite the emphasis contained in this quotation, is not untypical of the style of management that arises naturally from a literal interpretation of the 1992 structure given to the 'new' universities (which has also influenced to various degrees the structures of many pre-1992 universities). To emphasise how far this represents a shift of opinion it is worth comparing these statements with a quotation from a senior vice-chancellor from the 1960s:

> "It is clear that the optimal distribution of responsibility for academic management is not the most economical of time and effort. A much smaller and more authoritarian oligarchy with a tight hierarchy of subordinates could reduce the size and complexity of the committee system. It would, however, be unacceptable for the valid reason that under it academic freedom would be restricted and academics would carry out research and teaching less well. The academic does not produce best performance to order". (Aitken 1966)

Of course we have no way of telling how Aitken himself would have responded to the pressures on universities described above, but it is worth asking whether the values to which he subscribes still carry force?

We can attempt to answer this in a number of ways. The first is to try to evaluate university performance. Here the evidence looks pretty clear that whether we use the international (Shanghai Jiao Tong or the *Times Higher Education Supplement*) or the UK league tables published in the media, those UK universities which are towards the top end of the ranking lists place a high priority on participative management structures, while those at the bottom, like DeMontfort, do not. It could be argued that the inherited wealth of Cambridge and Oxford rather overbalances the evidence were not York and Warwick, both 1960s universities, and both strongly collegial in management style, not so high up in the UK league tables. (Shattock 2003a). Similar evidence is provided by the US with highly collegial universities at the top of the rankings and 'vest pocket' institutions at the bottom. Ehrenberg, writing about the top private universities. says that: "It is hard to think of any decision made by the university in which faculty members do not feel they have a legitimate interest". (Ehrenberg 2002).

University management is often judged by external commentators through analogies with business, ignoring the fact that the functions of universities and companies are remarkably different. However, even by this yardstick the evidence we have is that collegiality works well and particularly in crisis situations. In spite of the strictures of the Chairman of Unilever, no UK university went bankrupt, or even looked like going bankrupt in the period of severe cuts of 1981-84. The university which faced the heaviest cuts (44%) dealt with them by asking every professor to tender his/her resignation to the vice-chancellor (not a single one demurred) and when the re-structuring was agreed, by the senate as well as by the council, some letters were handed back to their authors and some were accepted. The university even bounced back, and created space to appoint some young new staff. Hardy, in case studies of how Canadian universities handled similar sharp budgetary reductions in the '80s, identified different institutions' approaches as bureaucratic, technocratic, political and collegial; she concluded that collegiality remained the most effective mechanism to manage competing pressures and was "more likely to encourage creativity and innovation" (Hardy 1996:183). Creativity and innovation are precisely the qualities that are sought by most successful companies, which is why leading business researchers argue that strategy is best formed by bottom up rather than top down methods (Ghoshal and Bartlett 1993), that the role of senior management is more as a "retroactive legitimiser" than in providing charismatic leadership (Quin 1985) or that the task of top management "is less to spot and solve problems than to create an organisation that can spot and solve its own problems" (Hayes 1985: 116). Professional and partnership organisations similarly work more on the basis of concensus than direction: Clifford Chance manages some of its corporate decision-making on the basis of referenda amongst its 5000 partners world-wide; McKinsey's elect their top post by a ballot amongst the partners. The belief that business or accountancy or law firms operate best on a hierarchical managerialist basis is a notion that dates back to the age of manufacture rather than to the knowledge industries of the present. Kets de Vries notes that trust is an important element in leadership and "with trust comes candour, the willingness of people to speak their minds. When people are reluctant to discuss their ideas and thoughts openly realism disappears and the quality of decision-making deteriorates" (Kets de Vries 2002)

The consequences of managerialist approaches to university management could be said to be evident in some institutions. In 1997 the Dearing Committee commissioned a report on academic staff experiences and expectations. The report, which was based on over 1000 responses, was revealing: 48% of respondents under the age of 35 indicated they were unlikely to stay in the academic profession, and even when research staff were stripped out of the data, some 32% of 'tenured' staff under 35 said they were unlikely to stay and 19% of 35 to 50 year olds; the report notes the "large number [of respondents] who, unprompted, mentioned problems of deprofessionalisation and lack of morale and direction" and that this was more often mentioned by staff in post-1992 universities" (NCIHE 1997). A more recent study (Bone and McNay 2006) based on a questionnaire addressed to members of the Higher Education Academy's Learning and Teaching Networks (therefore quite senior academics) makes even worse reading. 78.8% of 274 respondents expressed agreement or strong agreement with the statement that: "There is a fear of sanctions against those who 'speak truth to power', with corporate management approaches verging on a culture of 'bullying and blame"; 84.6% agreed or strongly agreed that "The emphasis within universities is 'now more on systems rather than on people, and much of the humanity and excitement has been lost'". These responses were 8:1 from staff in post-'92 universities although the differences in responses between pre and post-'92 were not significant. This was a much smaller sample than the Dearing exercise but of a more senior group of professionals; the two samples are not, therefore, technically comparable. They do, however, suggest that, at best, the management style of some universities is anything but collegial and this, together with continued financial stringency particularly at the lower end of the rankings, has seriously impacted on the morale of the academic workforce. One thing is abundantly clear, that institutions where morale is low, and where to quote Kets de Vries, 'trust' and 'candour' are not present, are irrevocably handicapped in seeking to raise their game.

If managerialism is ineffective in managing institutions whose core business is teaching and research, where creativity and innovation are at a premium, are there approaches to management which can be described as effective? I believe there are, but only if one accepts that universities are organisationally *sui generis* and have to develop a style of management which is true to their own key functions. Such a style will seek to combine the virtues of collegiality and the politics of consent with the disciplines of timeliness in decision-making. Senates or academic boards and governing bodies meet too infrequently and are usually too large and too inexpert to manage institutions effectively. Many institutions have therefore created what Clark has called "a strengthened steering core" (Clark 1998); this may either be a senior management team-- that is, a group of full time managers answerable to the chief executive-- (common in universities which have gone down the managerialist route) or a body comprising both academics and administrators which is constitutionally answerable to senate and the governing body. A critical element in this latter model is whether the deans are members of the group or not. If they are, academic management becomes a central concern of the group and the deans have the task both of reflecting faculty opinion to the centre and of representing central decisions to their faculties. If they are not, the group's decisions tend to become more centrist, and less academic, and the deans to become advocates for their faculties, rather than key participants in institutional policy-making. The interrelationships between such a 'steering' group, which will probably meet weekly, and the senate and the governing body on the one hand, and the faculties and/or academic departments on the other will define the organisational culture of the institution.

Where does the vice-chancellor/chief executive's role sit in this new context of university management? Leadership can be expressed in various styles, but Collins, examining a group of companies that had radically improved their performance, found that their chief executives were not charismatic leaders in the conventional sense and had no public profile at all (Collins 2001). Goodall has found that: "The higher the global ranking of a university the more likely it is that the citations of its president will also be high...better universities appoint better researchers to lead them" (Goodall 2006). This ensures that such presidents possess what Ramsden sees as a key university leadership skill: "an understanding of how academics work and an ability to enter into their world" (Ramsden 1998). Leadership in collegially managed universities will be distributed and not concentrated in a single person and the task of a vice-chancellor will be to build robust structures and strong teams, not to lead the charge (Shattock *ibid b*). "It's about listening, then deciding and then leading forward" and not about managerial direction and confrontation (Midgley and Macheod 2003). Indeed, the ideal is perhaps summed up in the Chinese Taoist saying:

"The wicked leader is he who the people despise.The good leader is he who the people revere. The great leader is he who the people say, 'We did it ourselves'". (Lao Zhi, quoted in Fan Yihong 2004)

This should not be taken to imply that vice-chancellors do not need financial skills, managerial foresight, and toughness under pressure, but it does emphasise that in institutions where teaching and research are the core business, enabling and motivational skills are more critical to the achievement of institutional success than top down direction.

References

Aitken, R. (1966) *Administration of a University* London: University of London Press page 77

Bone, J. and McNay, I. (2006) *Higher Education and Human Good* Bristol: Tockington Press page 76

Clark, B.R. (1998) *Creating Entrepreneurial Universities Organisational Pathways of Transformation* Oxford: Pergammon

Collins,J.C (2001) *Good to Great* London: Century

Commission of Inquiry (the North Report 1997) *Commission of Inquiry Supplementary Volume* Oxford: Oxford University Press page 90

Committee of Vice-Chancellors and Principals (1985) *Report of the Steering Committee on Efficiency Studies* (the Jarratt Report) London: CVCP page 24

Durham, K. (1982) "Foreword" in Oldham, G.(Ed) *The Future of Research Leverhulme Programme of Study into the Future of Higher Education*, Guildford: Society for Research in Higher Education

Ehrenberg, R.G. (2002) *Tuition Rising: Why College Costs So Much* Cambridge, M.A.: Harvard University Press page 22

Ghoshal, S. and Bartlett, C. (1993) *The Individualised Corporation* London: Heinemann

Goddard, J.B and Chatterton, C (1999) "Regional Development Agencies and the knowledge economy: harnessing the potential of universities"

Environment and Planning C: *Government and Policy* Vol 17. No 6 pages 665-699

Goodhall, A. (2006) "The Leaders of the World's Top 100 Universities" *International Higher Education* No.42 Winter pages 3-4

Hardy, C. (1996) *The Politics of Collegiality Montreal and Kingston*, London and Buffalo: McGill-Queen's University Press page 183

Hayes, R.H. (1985) "Strategic planning-forward or reverse? Are corporate planners going about things the wrong way round?" *Harvard Business Review* 63(b) pages 111-119

Ket de Vries, M.F.R. (2002) "Beyond Sloan: trust is at the heart of corporate values" *Financial Times* 2 October

Lambert, R. (2003) *Lambert Review of Business – University Collaboration, Final Report* London: HMSO paras 7.2 and 7.6

Lao Zhi, in Fan Yihong (2004) *From Integrative World view to Holistic Education Theory and Practice* Chengdu: Southwest Jiaotong University Press page 32

Midgley, S. and Macleod, D. (2003) "Vice-squad" *Guardian Education* 1 April

National Committee of Inquiry into Higher Education (NCIHE) (the Dearing Report) Higher Education in the Learning Society Supplementary Report 3 *Academic Staff in higher education: their experiences and expectations* London: HMSO pages 121-124

Quin, J.B. (1985) "Managing Innovation: Controlled Chaos" *Harvard Business Review* 63(3) pages 73-84

Ramsden,P (1998) "Managing the Effective University" *Higher Education Research and Development* 17 3 pages 347-370

Schwarz, S. (2003) "Can you pinpoint your boss?" *Times Higher Education Supplement* 7 March

Shattock, M.L. (2003 a) *Managing Successful Universities* Maidenhead: Open University Press page 9

Shattock, M.L. *ibid* b page 92

THE STUDENT EXPERIENCE?

Gary Day

Gary Day is a principal lecturer in English at De Montfort University. He is a graduate of the universities of Essex, Sussex and Cardiff and is the author of two books; Re-Reading Leavis: Culture and Literary Criticism (1996) and Class (2001). His Literary Criticism: A Polemical History will be published by Edinburgh University Press next year. He is a columnist for The Times Higher Education Supplement.

The Sodexho University Lifestyle Survey 2006, conducted in association with the *Times Higher*, has given us a picture of how young people view higher education.[1] By and large they go to university to improve their employment prospects.[2] So it's surprising to learn that what mainly determines their choice of institution is not its academic reputation, nor the career destinations of its graduates but how friendly it is. The desire to experience a different way of life comes bottom of the list of reasons for going to university. This may explain why so many choose to attend their local university rather than seek a fresh challenge but a more likely explanation is money. Students say that is their biggest concern. A good number have to survive, once their rent is paid, on between £40 and £50 a week. Some struggle on as little as £30 or less. Not surprisingly, the vast majority of students expect to leave university in debt. They support themselves, during the degree, with a mixture of loans, parental hand-outs and part-time jobs. Some 53 per cent work between 11 and 20 hours a week which might be good for the curriculum vitae but it is not so good for the curriculum. If students cannot study full time, then the amount they are expected to learn will reflect that.

---

[1] A summary of the report is available at http://www.sodexho.co.uk/ULS06-summary.pdf

[2] But see Alison Woolf, *Does Education Matter? Myths about Education and Economic Growth* (Harmondsworth: Penguin, 2002), especially chapter 2. She questions the government's claim which lies behind the increase in student numbers, that there is a link between a highly educated population and economic growth.

What with study, work and little money it would seem that students do not have a great deal of time for socialising. But Laura, a sociology student at York, measures out her university life in precisely those terms.

> "The first year saw a lot of clubbing, drunken deviance and events attending (all good fun). The second year saw more house gatherings, a lot less clubbing (instead the local pub was of choice) and generally being flopped in front of the television."

She intends to make the most of her final year. Laura, who was not part of the Sodexho study, is one of those students who did want to study away from home. While the growing trend for attending the local university reduces the opportunity to mix with different people, it has minimised the traditional divide between town and gown, potentially making the university a more integral part of the community.

Apart from money, students are pre-occupied with balancing their various commitments. This is probably good preparation for life but whatever happened to 'the gift of the interval,' the opportunity to grow and explore? Because students have to pay for their studies and because they believe a good degree is essential to securing a good job, they are now far more anxious about its classification than certainly my generation were. As one student remarked: "If all I'm going to get is a 2:2 there's not much point my being here". And in a sense he was right. If a university education is defined purely in economic terms then the student will want at least a 2:1 as return on his or her investment.

The Sodexho study offers interesting insights into why students go to university, what makes them choose a particular institution and the challenges they face in completing their degree. But, because it is concerned with the student experience in general, it does not pay a great deal of attention to how that experience varies from one institution to another. The media is fond of saying that we live in a classless society but class is an important factor in education.[3] The

---

[3] The increase in student numbers has largely come from the middle class. Working class participation in university life remains fairly constant at 26 per cent. But the

University of Wolverhampton has the highest proportion of working class students in the country, Oxford has the lowest.[4] And its research income is 100 times higher than that of Wolverhampton.

But let's look at how this difference is embodied in two individuals. Emily is studying Politics, Economics and Philosophy at Oxford. She was given a reading list and told that she would have to cover most or all the books that were on it. How many? For politics she thinks it was about 30. And that was just for the term. She is expected to be fully prepared for her weekly tutorial. She and another girl discuss their work for an hour with an expert in the field. Her experience is quite different to Eric - not his real name - at Wolverhampton, who is often taught by a part timer. He is studying English and is given a reading list but it is considerably shorter, some six books per module. He is provided with a booklet of extracts of secondary material but 'doesn't bother' with it. Eric is taught in seminars of about twenty-five students though the numbers fluctuate widely from week to week, depending on commitment, interest, or job. Emily also works but says "quite a lot" of her peers at Oxford don't need to because they have very wealthy parents. Like Eric, she is in debt.

The big difference between them is that she is more highly motivated. Why? Because Emily comes from a middle class background that instils attitudes of hard work, perseverance and respect for education. She has also been immersed in high culture since she was a child. Eric comes from a working class background. He freely admits that study is a chore and that he finds some books bewildering because they seem to require a prior knowledge that he doesn't have. He requires more teaching because he knows less and more support because he has not had the opportunity to develop habits of independent study. Both will get degrees but Emily's chance of employment is much greater than Eric's because many firms would rather recruit from the older universities than the new ones. I recall chatting to a representative from a highly respectable firm of

---

point to stress is that working class students are concentrated in the new universities. See Chloe Stohart, 'Access Drive has Failed to Bridge the Class Divide' and 'Student Cities Skew the Data' *Times Higher* 17 March, 2006

[4] 'Highest/Lowest Participation Rates from lower social class groups' *Times Higher*, 1 October 2004

accountants who said that they would never consider attending a careers fair at a new university because they did not consider the students good enough for their training programmes. Given such views it is not surprising that the gap between well paid and less paid graduates is growing and that "less than half regard their degrees as being useful for work".[5]

Ethnicity is another factor that complicates the simple notion of the student experience. Here too we can see a stark divide. According to a recent report in the *Guardian*, 60% of students at London Metropolitan University belong to ethnic minorities while the figure for Bristol is 7%. Drawing on research from the Higher Education Statistics Agency the article goes on to say that the 1,575 students of black Caribbean heritage at London Metropolitan is more than in the whole of the Russell Group of elite universities.[6] This kind of separatism can reinforce ethnic divides. One of the recent plane bomb suspects was head of the Islamic society at London Metropolitan. Even when the student body is mixed divisions still manifest themselves. This is apparent in seminars where the different groups tend to sit in their own enclaves. Attempts to integrate the class must be handled very sensitively and the various cultures represented in the seminar can potentially affect what can and cannot be taught. It is very difficult, for example, to teach Mark Ravenhill's *Shopping and Fucking* (1996), which contains graphic scenes of gay sex, to a group that contains orthodox Islamic students - or Christian ones for that matter.

This is an issue that needs confronting if we are to maintain the principles of social cohesion and open enquiry. Hayley, who graduated in 2006 from East Midlands University, talks of the tensions that can arise between British and Asian students. "This came to a head," she writes, "when there were complaints from many of the Asian students that it was unfair for the university to have a Christmas ball." It had to be renamed "The Snowball". And yet, writes Hayley, the Asian Ball was allowed to go ahead unchallenged, despite the fact

---

[5] See Alison Goddard, 'Degrees do not pay for all' *Times Higher* 6 July 2001and Alison Utley 'Marks in class county less than class marks' *Times Higher* 20 February 2004

[6] Polly Curtis 'Segregation, 2006 Style' *Education Guardian* 3 January 2006

that it was made clear "whites were not welcome". Sameera, not her real name, feels that white students are racist, that they do not respect the Koran or her beliefs because they eat pork in front of her. Neither of these views can be considered representative, indeed many students from different backgrounds seem to co-exist quite happily even if they do not mix, but the possibility that a free exchange of views may degenerate into a clash of cultures is very real. Hayley describes angry scenes in shared houses when male friends would drop by and see, quite by accident, Muslim girls with bare hair. But this is not just a problem between British and Asian students. There are also conflicts within and between different ethnic groups that occasionally erupt in violence.

One wonders how overseas students view this situation. At present they represent 13.4% of undergraduates and 33 per cent of postgraduates. [7] The proportion of international students on postgraduate research programmes recently rose from 36 per cent of the total cohort to 46 per cent and this figure is expected to rise. The number of UK enrolments has not increased.[8] This overseas presence in our universities brings obvious benefits: it introduces much needed income to our cash-starved institutions, it promotes understanding between different cultures and establishes potential trade links. But if a number of universities decide to focus on post-graduate education with an emphasis on overseas recruitment what will happen to the indigenous undergraduate population? Where will they be trained? And what will happen to the cultural heritage by which a nation partly knows itself and which is its basis for negotiating change?

Despite glossing over problems of class and ethnicity the Sodexho study does capture one fundamental truth about the student experience; namely that it is about consumption. This is a consequence of the transformation of British universities from an elite to a mass system of higher education. Once funded largely by the state but now increasingly having to generate their own income, universities are more like corporations that have to make a profit than communities dedicated to the transmission of culture. Hence their main aim, particularly those institutions at the lower end of the market, is to

---

[7] 'International Cohort Grows' Times Higher 15 September 2006

[8] Britons Spurning Postgraduate Research' Times Higher 15 September 2006

please students not to educate them. For the first time in history what the student wants, not what the student needs to know, has apparently become the driving force of education.

The idea of student choice is enshrined in the principle of modularity. Because modularity presents every subject as self-contained, it discourages students from making connections between different topics. Here is a concrete instance of how the principle of choice erodes intellectual analysis. And here's another. To be appealing modules must, at least in the humanities, be up to date and relevant to the modern world. Twenty-first century cinema will be far more popular than metaphysical poetry. Ideally students have a free choice but they choose in ignorance because they do not know which combination of courses will yield the best view of their subject. Hence, at least until recently, they could do a degree in English concentrating almost entirely on contemporary literature. Even then the content of modules is changed to accommodate student preferences. Reading is reduced, the choice of books is made easier, exams are avoided. In this climate, students do not aspire, they expect. As customers, they have little sense of the value of intellectual life or the discipline required to understand complex ideas and issues. Laura feels that her ten hours contact time at York is not sufficient considering what she is paying for her degree. Although she enjoys her subject, sociology, there are many students whose interest in their course extends only so far as what they need to know to obtain a good grade. And they are adamant that it is the lecturer's responsibility to make sure they achieve it.

Although students see themselves as consumers, particularly now with the advent of top up fees, and universities encourage them in that view by such mechanisms as the module evaluation form-whose worth is called into question every time students say they were not well informed about assessment dates when these dates are clearly printed in their module handbook - the picture is in fact more complicated. The idea of the consumer implies freedom and power, freedom to choose and power to make business bend to their needs. But students are also citizens with a responsibility to their society's traditions, institutions and way of life. For them to accept that they are first of all consumers not only circumscribes their social and political identities, it also serves the interests of those corporations whose power and profit depend upon the 'free' market. Looked at in this way the university's various feedback mechanisms deepen the student's sense of him or herself as a consumer instead of getting him or to reflect critically on that role.

As well as reinforcing the students' identity as consumers, universities also prepare them for the discipline of work, not so much by providing them with skills as by normalising a culture of targets, performance reviews and continuous development. There is nothing wrong with this in principle, but when it becomes the sole focus of higher education we need to worry. Why? Because it saps the student's initiative, discourages them from thinking for themselves and renders them incapable of improvising when faced with the unknown. This is hardly the best training for dealing with a dynamic economy. Shortly after the student arrives at university he or she is given a personal development plan. This consists of four stages, "self appraisal, target setting, implementation of plan, and review and evaluation". [9] These terms effectively frame their course. Consequently students do not examine ideas, only their own shortcomings; they do not question aims and outcomes, they meet them; they do not explore, they follow a prescribed path; and they do not analyse, they assess according to fixed criteria. Thankfully, in my experience, many students ignore this ideological imposition and are as anarchic as ever but many more are insecure and cling gratefully to this guide rail. In their desire to legislate for all areas of the student experience, universities are becoming more and more like schools.

What, then, is the student experience? The term is questionable since it eclipses differences between institutions and issues of class and ethnicity, not to mention gender, sexuality and even disability. [10] These all affect how students see higher education. At the same time the increasing dependence of the universities on the market has led to them adopting a more corporate character that decisively alters how students study. We often hear about the distinction between knowledge for its own sake and the knowledge economy but the real issue in universities is not about the status of knowledge but about the

---

[9] For a typical example of a personal development plan see http://www.pdp.uhi.ac.uk/docs/cspdp.pdf

[10] According to HEFCE statistics, the ratio of men to women at university is 1: 1.3 and the ratio of disabled to able bodied students is 1: 13

means to achieve it. Students are drilled in the mind-crushing idioms of learning and teaching and quality assurance which, as result, assume a far greater importance than anything they actually study.

But perhaps the most salient characteristic of the student experience, at least in the humanities, is one of which they are least aware and that is of how, ceaselessly prompted by government, universities encourage young people to identify themselves exclusively in terms of their usefulness to the economy. But students won't just work in an economy they will also live in a society, and this requires that they be more than their job or profession. To help them realise that simple human fact, they should have the opportunity to read great thinkers, to engage with tradition and to debate cultural values. "The true and adequate end of ...a university" wrote Cardinal Newman, "is not learning or acquirement, but rather thought or reason exercised upon knowledge."[11] Sadly that ideal seems out of place in our society where the relentless rhetoric of economic modernisation takes no cognisance of the misery of overwork or the social and religious divisions opening in our society. Newman's vision was never more relevant.

---

[11] John Henry Cardinal Newman, *The Idea of a University* (New York: Chelsea House, 1983: 150

Part 4

MICKEY MOUSE AND THE DEATH OF SCIENCE:

WHAT SHOULD UNIVERSITIES BE TEACHING?

Editors: Hugo de Burgh, Anna Fazackerley, Jeremy Black

WHAT IS THE NATIONAL INTEREST?

Jeremy Black

Jeremy Black MBE is Professor of History at the University of Exeter. He is a senior fellow at the Center for the Study of America and the West at the Foreign Policy Research Institute. He is author of over seventy books, and an expert on eighteenth century British politics and international relations. He graduated from Queens' College, Cambridge, with a starred first and then did postgraduate work at Oxford. He held a chair in history at Durham before moving to Exeter in 1996. He has lectured extensively in Australasia, Canada, Denmark, France, Germany, Italy and the USA. He is one of the founding trustees of Agora.

Goals and means. If we were starting anew, we would not devise the current higher education system, and, in considering the national interest, it is possible, in that context, to think in terms of blue-sky prospects. Heady thoughts, but maybe better applied to framing the parameters within which the hard task of the adaptation of the existing system can be assessed.

These heady thoughts are best approached in the light of realisation of the many different constituencies that exist in higher education. This is not just a question of students, universities, and the economy, but has to include other constituencies such as parents and others paying for the system, as well as the variety of interests entailed by 'students' or 'the economy' and so on. For students, for example, we need to note the differing range of abilities, of courses pursued, of outcomes sought, and of personal circumstances. A model of university life designed for eighteen year olds with two As and a B living away from home, but able to call on family support, is probably going to be completely unsuitable for mature students whose circumstances are very different. As a consequence of this and other factors, it is particularly inappropriate to imagine that one size will fit all, although that is the drive of public policy, social assumptions, and legal threats. Instead, however unwelcome the idea might be to a practice of government focused on standardisation, it is necessary to accept that the availability of different universities, doing different things, and at different standards, will be not only a good in its own right, providing both variety and flexibility, but also a characteristic that furthers the response to these different constituencies.

At present, for Conservatives in particular, but not only for them, there is an emphasis on the market, as the source of demand for academic services, and the means of providing them. This approach indeed has many attractions, not least because consumerism is an adjunct to democracy, but also because state provision has been compromised by its tendency to centralisation and uniformity, as well as by its openness to politicisation. This is readily apparent with repeated Labour pressure on student access and prescriptive quotas across much of the European Union. There, despite recent attempts at improvement, for example in France, jobs are frequently filled as a result of political connections, and universities are key to the patronage structures of politicised intelligentias. This pattern transferred readily from the autocratic systems of state control to more democratic times, for example in Spain.

In such a context, there is scant care about teaching or research. I can recall years ago meeting the head of a history department at an Italian university who remarked as a matter of course that he taught no undergraduates. When I asked what he did, he said that he was responsible for keeping his department politically loyal. This entailed excluding those of a different political persuasion, making regular visits to the Ministry in Rome, and entertaining the senior civil servant every two months, with both a slap-up meal and the services of a very good prostitute. However attractive to those on the gravy train, it is scarcely surprising that this system has few attractions to anyone else.

There are, however, problems with a simple market solution. One rests in the question of whether we permit the market to drive the entire system, or whether we take a national view and ask what should be provided by higher education and what we want the universities to be turning out. In short, if sixteen-year-olds think science is boring should that lead to the limitation of university provision or are there other goals and means at stake? Indeed, there are more general issues posed by this question. The degree to which those educated should shape the system is unclear, and doubly so because they will be shaping it not only for themselves but also for future generations. If a physics department is closed down in 2008 because there is insufficient student demand, that reduces the options thereafter. There is also something peculiar about a system that assumes that eighteen-year olds require education, then simply responding to their requirements. That may well be more appropriate at the level of mature students and postgraduates, but the bulk of undergraduates do not make their choices about subjects or courses in a particularly mature fashion. This issue has not been satisfactorily addressed in public discussion.

A second problem arises from the nature of the market at the international level. This is heavily volatile as a result of political and technological developments. The market, for example, may well be transferred by the digitisation of Higher Education, a process that will make trans-national study far easier. Digitisation may lead to a e-university system in which individual students rarely, if ever, meet others, and in which there is little serious interrogation of what students are doing or thinking. This risks reducing education to a series of skills, rather than allowing it to be central to a process of self-development.

Furthermore, far from transnational study leading to a rising of standards that will benefit Britain, it is as likely to lead to a volatility that will be damaging, as well as to downward-price pressures that will challenge established systems of provision, especially in residential universities. In this, as in other possible changes arising as a consequence of political and technological developments, there is the question of whether the result will be appropriate in terms of any sense of a national interest.

The last is of course open to contention. Indeed, this is part of the stuff of both politics and ideology. The term the national interest is usually understood in a functional and utilitarian fashion, a long-standing practice, but, first, it is necessary to note that this interest should also be understood in a cultural sense. The cultural role of universities does not play much of a part in the discussion of their future, but is in fact central to their place. Higher education encourages people to think and to express themselves. Each is central to education understood as a process of more than simply the repetition of lessons; and each is crucial to cultural life, understood both as an individual activity and as a collective process and affirmation.

Editors: Hugo de Burgh, Anna Fazackerley, Jeremy Black

Universities have become more important in the public and cultural life of the country, both as the numbers going through them have dramatically increased, and, possibly more significantly, as the cultural life of Britain itself has become more plastic and far less a case of the apparent continuities that were fatally shattered in the 1960s. Because it is difficult to assign a measurable value for these activities, they are apt to be underplayed, and this has become very serious as the debate over universities has been conducted in quantifiable terms.

In part, this is an aspect of the triumph of means over goals in the discussion of higher education, a triumph particularly noticeable in the case of the current government; but, in part, it is a case of a sense that cultural activity and value are unworthy of serious attention. The latter view has been driven, in part, by the primacy of research-linked funding issues, and by a view of the economic value of education propounded in narrowly utilitarian terms. This is, at once, limited as an account of education, as it deliberately neglects the cultural dimension, and also mistaken as an account of economic issues, as the cultural health of a society is in large part important to its capacity for economic progress. That might strike some as a curious vitalist statement, but culture relates directly to the spirit of inquiry, and the desire for improvement, and these are important to a bottom-up concept of economic development. A functional defence of the cultural role of universities does not, however, suffice. It is also necessary to see this cultural role as inherently valuable both in the sense of present realisation and with reference to the long-term development of society. Indeed, as with expenditure on the arts and heritage, there are fundamental questions of value and worth involved.

For an historian, there is a strong sense of discontinuities in discussions of national interest, as well as a feeling of transience when considering higher education. It is, for example, notable that the circumstances and values of the recent past are enshrined by each generation, and without any sense that these circumstances and values were not themselves integral to the system or longlasting. This can be seen, for example, with notions about funding, or about the desirability of universities providing residential accommodation, of students encouraged, and even funded, to travel for education to the other side of the country. These may, indeed, be desirable, but to treat them as inherent values is dubious.

CAN THE PRIZES STILL GLITTER?
The Future of British Universities in a Changing World

These discontinuities will be accentuated as national 'solutions' for higher education become increasingly implausible in an age in which education is increasingly traded as a commodity, not only because of digitalisation, but also due to the general culture of globalisation. For defenders of the present situation this will be fatal as global demands are unlikely to respond positively to national attempts to fix provision. However, if the one-size-fits-all approach will not work at national or international level, the state can also play a role as a purchaser, supporting study in particular areas as it currently supports research in specific fields. These areas will have to include subjects in which there are clear national needs, such as medicine, as there is no guarantee that international 'trading' in graduates will fill gaps. Furthermore, governments ought to have the confidence to support study in particular areas that are culturally important. For some subjects, this will be a case of postgraduate study, for others undergraduate; but support there should be. A market-only approach is as inappropriate as the one-size-fits-all and statist approach that is currently dominant in Britain.

Editors: Hugo de Burgh, Anna Fazackerley, Jeremy Black

KILLING SCIENCE IS KILLING OUR CULTURE

Harry Kroto

Professor Sir Harry Kroto was awarded the Nobel Prize for Chemistry in 1996 for his co-discovery of C60 buckminsterfullerene, a form of pure carbon better known as "buckyballs". Sir Harry is Francis Eppes Professor in the Department of Chemistry and Biochemistry at Florida State University. He left the University of Sussex after 37 years in 2004. He is a former President of the Royal Society of Chemistry and a passionate advocator of science communication and education. He is a co-founder of the Vega Science Trust, which produces science television and web broadcasts.

Introduction

There is food for thought in the fact that, after a decade of Labour Government, at the same moment that the Prime Minister was making a speech about how important he considers science, The University of Reading announced the closure of its Physics department. Thirty per cent of physics departments have either been closed or merged in the last 5 years. What is one to make of the deafening silence of Government ministers when last year, the small Sussex Chemistry Department - a fantastic department to work in where I had stayed for some 37 years and which has housed some 12 Fellows of the Royal Society, 3 Nobel Laureates and a Wolf prize winner since it was created in 1962 - was under threat of closure? It was only through the concerted efforts of staff and students that a U-turn occurred.

Does no one in the Government care or is there a hidden agenda? Some government measures, such as those that concentrated on the research/industry interface aimed at improving technology transfer and the encouragement of start-ups, have been successful. However, nothing effective has been done over decades by this government, or for that matter the previous administration, to improve the situation on the science education front and indeed several measures introduced have exacerbated the problem. The laissez-faire attitude to science education has now resulted in a disaster exemplified by the fact that more young people are opting for media studies than physics. As a new five story chemistry building nears completion here at the Florida State University (where I was wanted!) the jaws of colleagues drop with incredulity as news crosses the Atlantic of each successive UK science department closure.

As I finish writing this article I note that - out of the blue - HEFCE has suddenly pledged support for strategically important subjects such as chemistry. But is it too little too late and will it ever materialize? One notes that according to the Broers' Report, the £200m previously pledged by the Government to improve school science facilities has '...yet to emerge'!

The Need for Science Education

All of this matters because the need for a general population with a satisfactory understanding of science and technology (S&T) has never been greater. We live in a world economically, socially and culturally totally dependent on S&T not only functioning well but being wisely applied. Unfortunately the numbers of young people opting for scientific training has dwindled frighteningly all over the developed world, not just in the UK. It is worth noting that over decades the US has been spectacularly successful in making up its home-grown S&T shortfall by draining first Western European scientists and now Eastern European and Asian scientists. Most importantly as well as trained engineers and scientists we desperately need a scientifically literate general population capable of thinking rationally – and that includes lawyers, businessmen, farmers, politicians, journalists and athletes. This is vital if we are to secure a sustainable world for our grandchildren.

The fact that a) we use in one year an amount of fossil fuel that took a million years to accumulate, b) we may be on the verge of a climate change catastrophe of global proportions and c) powerful technologies may soon fall into the hands of disturbed individuals with minds riven with those twin cancers nationalism and religious fanaticism, seems to concern the scientific community a lot more than it does politicians or the media (the latter seems more concerned about a wedding in Italy at present). As my Sussex colleague the Nobel Laureate Sir John Cornforth has written (cf www.vega.org.uk) "...if you are a scientist you realize before long that if the world is in anyone's hands it is in yours".

The failure of our general science educational policy is manifest in the fact that so few are aware of the true level of our dependence on science and technology or the truly humanitarian contributions that S&T has made to society: from raising the health of the population (half of all 18th century children died by the age of 8) to the advanced technologies which pervade our everyday lives (the Internet and mobile phones being archetypal examples).

The personal reasons for choosing an S&T education are also overwhelming. A Royal Society of Chemistry/Institute of Physics study indicates that graduates with Chemistry and Physics degrees earn, for the most productive 15-20 years of their working lives, some £15,000 more annually than most other degrees, including psychology, that seductively popular subject which is diverting a large proportion of our best young people into dead-end, uncreative careers. It is actually a triple whammy as in addition the Government gets greater investment return in tax from this better-paid workforce and there are S&T industries for graduates to enter. The chemical industry posts a 50 billion pound annual turnover with a 5 billion profit - which is more than can be said for Law.

At a time when China and India are producing the hordes of scientists and engineers on which they know their futures depend all we hear from our government is that it is not its job to interfere with a secondary or tertiary education system that is graduating ten times as many psychologists, linguists, historians and media people than there are jobs for. Too bad if young people are not going to be qualified for the careers available and commensurate with their abilities, forcing many to settle for poorly paid, uncreative jobs.

The Cultural Nature of Science

Many think of the sciences as merely a fund of knowledge. Journalists never ask scientists anything other than what are the applications of scientific breakthroughs. Interestingly I doubt they ever ask a musician, writer or actor the same question – I wonder why? In addition to numeracy, the main values of a scientific education are the acquisition of the skills to solve problems and uncover new knowledge, but more importantly to be "at one" with the modern environment which is suffused with wall-to-wall scientific inventions and technology, as well as with environmentally important issues. The "Scientific Method" is based on what I prefer to call "The Inquiring Mindset". It includes all areas of human thoughtful activity that categorically eschew "belief", the enemy of rationality.

This "mindset" is a nebulous mixture of doubt, questioning, observation, experiment, and above all curiosity, which small children possess in spades. I would argue that it is the most important intrinsically human ability we possess, and it is responsible for the creation of the modern "Enlightened" portion of the world which some of us are fortunate to inhabit. Curiously, for the majority of our youth, the educational system magically causes this capacity to disappear by adolescence. Without it we have no instinctive ability to assess the importance of many of the technical issues that impinge on our everyday lives and are unable to accurately gauge the validity of fears over such issues as climate change, the immensity of the looming energy crisis or the socio-economic and humanitarian importance of new genetic technologies.

Scientific education is by far the best training for all walks of life because it teaches us how to assess situations critically and react accordingly. It gives us an understanding based on reverence for life-enhancing technologies as well as for life itself. If we do not know how things work, how can we fix things, and how are we going to use these powerful technologies wisely? It is this need for everyday scientific common sense and wisdom about our environment that our forefathers developed and which in the modern context we shall need to improve if we are to survive.

The Misunderstanding of Science

The level of public misunderstanding of science can be gauged by the overwhelmingly negative response to Genetically Modified foods in the UK, stem cell research, and nanoscience and nanotechnology (N&N). N&N is basically chemistry and thus as old as life itself, indeed almost as old as our Universe. In fact that ardent opponent of GM and N&N, Prince Charles, is not only the result of an infinitely long sequence of genetic modifications but also the product of N&N – atom by atom, molecule by molecule, bottom-up assembly on the basis of a DNA blueprint. The discovery of this blueprint is arguably the greatest advance in knowledge of the 20th Century, and a British one at that. N&N is just a new name for a vast swathe of immensely varied Chemistry in fields where this discipline overlaps Physics, Biology and Engineering. The claim that N&N and GM are innately bad is as inane as saying any one or all of Chemistry, Physics and Engineering is or are bad for us. Those who campaign against N&N do not understand what it is and in any case there is no doubt that trying to stop it is a futile exercise. To paraphrase Moliére in "le Bougois Gentillehomme" – "Cor blimey Guv we've bin doin N&N since Dalton discovered it in 1803 and didn't know it!" If indeed it were possible to curtail N&N we are very likely to lose massive future advances. It would be comparable to having stopped all Chemistry in 1906: stopping the discipline that led to the fertilizers feeding 70% of the world's population, penicillin, anaesthetics, plastics, silicon chips and computers, paint, pure water, false teeth and fillings. N&N promises comparable benefits in the 21st Century.

Of course there are going to be serious attendant problems as all powerful technologies can be beneficial or detrimental, depending on how wisely society decides to use them. However it seems that a population with a good understanding of S&T is more likely to use the new technologies more wisely than one that is ignorant of the sciences.

Science is fundamentally based on doubt, a concept orthogonal to faith which is presently providing some motivation for certain disaffected individuals to undermine our moderately democratic world. Here in the US such ignorant "beyond belief" belief, unbelievably, is resulting in theme parks which encourage the scientifically illiterate to "believe" that human beings and dinosaurs inhabited the Earth at the same time!

Reasons for the Disappearance of Science Students

There may be many reasons for the dearth of S&T students. One less discussed one that I think is important is the fact that in my lifetime a profound paradigm shift has taken place in our everyday technologies. Mobile phones, digital watches, DVDs, camcorders, and Ipods have become totally impenetrable to understanding without significant scientific background knowledge. That was not the case in the past, when young curious children could enter the world of S&T fairly easily to find out how a clock, gramophone, telephone and even a radio worked. How could a child today be moved by the inner workings of that modern miracle - the digital watch - as was I by the elegant gold and silver inner workings of the pocket watch my father gave me - when I finally managed to prize the back off? As one TV, mobile phone or game player is ditched to be replaced by the latest version, so our children have no chance of gaining understanding by fixing them and most importantly never develop reverence and awe for the technology they use incessantly. Whenever I see a young person on a mobile phone – it seems to me that most are never off them – I wonder how many ever wonder how they work. I was staggered to meet someone in science education recently (in the US but born in Britain) who told me they did not care how mobile phones worked! Because I knew a bit about how they work, some years ago I wondered about the possible effects of a pulsed radio signal emanating from a source located a few centimetres from that delicate object called the brain and worked hard to put together a significant funding to produce a TV programme about the possible health hazards of mobile phones (cf www.vega.org.uk). It seems to me a good thing that some people do care about our technologies.

Why are there not hordes of UK students eager to follow in the footsteps of those British and Irish giants of Science, Mathematics, and Engineering: Newton, Hooke, Dalton, Watt, Brunel, Hamilton, Faraday, Maxwell, Whittle, Darwin, Dirac and Crick, some of whom have graced our money and our stamps? Perhaps we should not be surprised when the media overflows with wall-to-wall sport, cooking, trivial quiz-shows and inane so-called-reality shows. There are TV channels devoted to sport, religion and films but next-to-nothing of cultural value in general and science in particular. It is thus hardly surprising that there is very little incentive for our kids to get stuck into the demanding intellectual rigours associated with calculus, differential equations, and the complexities of chemistry and physics subjects whose values only become apparent at a later stage.

Everyone knows that education is the key to a healthy economy and a creative population and yet governments show their contempt for scholarship by not paying teachers anything like what they deserve and certainly not enough to ensure sufficient numbers of gifted people with a passion for science enter the profession. Not only is there is a serious shortage of trained science teachers teaching children during the pre-16 period when they start to make career choices but they are often up against teachers who have excelled in non-science subjects.

The Science Department Cull

The situation is further exacerbated by present policy, which actively encourages vice chancellors who know the cost of everything and the value of nothing to eliminate science departments in favour of trendy cheap courses. These VCs bleat about how important is their freedom to do whatever they wish with taxpayers' money, and steer funds earmarked for the sciences into softer areas which students prefer. Just as cheap fast food has resulted in unprecedented levels of obesity, so this McDonalds approach to cheap, trendy, seductively soft courses designed for mass consumption in tertiary education has resulted in a plethora of students trained for nonexistent jobs.

Another major factor, encouraging VCs to close science departments even if, as at Exeter, they have plenty of students, is the inadequate provision made by the Government to cover the real cost of science education. The unit of resource ratio for an arts graduate versus a science graduate is 1:2 when a more realistic ratio is at least 1:4. It is thus no wonder that VCs who fail in their primary role – to bring in outside funds – are encouraged by such manifest governmental disdain for science education to eliminate science departments. I understand that at a university with which I am somewhat familiar, a building construction policy based on half-funding by Government, in the vain hope that matched funding would fall like manna from the heavens, has brought this once outstanding institution with outstanding departments across the arts and sciences and humanities to the brink of relegation to a second division arts college. There is a simple rule for universities: the first priority is to invest in the brightest young talent available and new buildings are nice to have but must be secondary.

Peer Review and Research Funding

I know few successful scientists who have a good word to say for the peer review process. It is a process in which a disparate bunch of overworked scientists has to plough for hours through piles of the interminably repetitive arguments inserted into ineptly designed research grant application forms in a vain attempt to asses the relative merits of the various proposals. (It is, by the way, no better here in the US – probably worse.) Then a committee attempts to grade the applications on the basis of these assessments using some arbitrary numerical voting system - more ludicrous than that used to grade Olympic skaters and gymnasts. Often a tenth of a percentage point can mean the difference between being funded and not. As a young scientist I once complained to an eminent elder colleague that it was impossible to construct a proposal for good research project, which by its very nature must entail the unexpected. My colleague, in a tone that indicated I should know the bleeding obvious, told me to apply for funds for good research already done and use the grant for a new project!

Instead of this system research funds should be downloaded to the university departments on some flexible scale that is graded to help the less well performing institutions that exhibit promise. The funds should be divided into three not necessarily equal amounts – the first to adequately support young people starting up. The institutions have done the work in finding the young people on whom they have placed their hopes for the future so why not leave it to them to disburse the funds? They have done the work - why do it all again in such a half-baked fashion? The second portion should be distributed to those whose last research projects have been rated excellent on the basis of the final research report. If they have done well once there is a good chance they can do it again. This is basically the bookie's approach to backing racehorses. The third amount to be distributed to part-fund researchers who did satisfactorily the last time, encouraging them to trawl for matching funds from other source such as industry. Some sort of peer review could be applied only for this group. This approach would save a lot of precious time that is better spent actually doing the research. Something akin to this was at the heart of the dual support scheme that was responsible for helping me to make a start as a young researcher in the 1960s.

Conclusions

Do I think there is any hope for UK? I am really not sure. It is beyond belief that in the 21st Century, our Prime Minister and the Department for Education and Skills are diverting taxpayers' money to faith-based groups intent on propagating culturally divisive dogma that is antagonistic to the secular "Enlightened" philosophy that created the modern world. One need look no further than Northern Ireland to see the results of a sectarian segregated educational policy. It is a scandal that the present system is enabling a car salesman to subvert significant government funds to propagate dogma such as "Intelligent Design" in our schools. State funds are also being used to support some schools which abuse impressionable young people by brainwashing them into believing that non-believers will burn for all eternity in the Fires of Hell and that it is their duty to undermine the last few democratic freedoms left in UK law. This policy is a perfect recipe for the creation of the next generation of home-grown and state-educated suicide bombers.

The resurgence of inter-religious prejudice and its incursion into education, politics, law and the media is as disturbingly anti-democratic as it is anti-scientific. Unless the UK (and the USA) wakes up to the imminent dangers, not only will the Enlightenment be extinguished but also the UK's capacity to survive in a world that looks increasingly likely to be dominated by the Eastern Tigers who do not seem to have such ridiculous anti-scientific hang-ups. I think there is every likelihood that the lack of scientifically educated and aware young people in the UK will result in ever-poorer performance on a global scale and a takeover by the next generation of young Chinese and Indians, which is ravenous for the scientific spirit that will free them from the shackles of present poverty levels. This new generation is being actively encouraged by their governments, who understand that the future lies in a scientific education based on doubt and questioning, rather than on belief. Paradoxically, this philosophy - pioneered in the West since the time of Galileo and responsible for the modern way of life - is now being undermined by an ignorant anti-science movement in the West. It is truly disturbing that a well-funded cohort of religious groups aided, abetted and condoned by this government is undermining our science education (in the US also). If they achieve any more success in their subversion of the intrinsic secular safeguards embodied in our democratic institutions and our educational system, there can be no doubt that there is major trouble ahead. So my final message is - "Do Panic!"

Editors: Hugo de Burgh, Anna Fazackerley, Jeremy Black

MICKEY MOUSE DEGREES: UNIVERSITIES AND THE CREATIVE INDUSTRIES

Sally Feldman

Professor Sally Feldman is Head of the School of Media, Arts and Design at the University of Westminster. For many years she was editor of BBC Radio 4's Woman's Hour, as well as a stable of related programmes. She is associate editor of the New Humanist magazine and sits on the council of the Media Society.

In this chapter I argue that the traditional mistrust between the universities and the creative industries has gradually, often grudgingly, been diluted.   But the mutually harmonious and constructive relationship that should enhance both depends upon the recognition of a globalised world that requires the industries and the academy alike to adapt to meet its rapidly changing demands.

A shockwave shuddered through the British media industry when a puckish television arts editor became Controller of BBC1 in 1990. It wasn't just that Michael Jackson was the youngest ever executive to be appointed to such a hallowed position. And it wasn't just that he had not graduated from Oxford or Cambridge, nor even from a University at all, but from the Polytechnic of Central London. Far, far more perplexing was that he was the product of the country's first ever degree in media studies. And it got worse. Soon after that meteoric rise he rocketed even further skyward to become Head of Channel Four. A fitting destiny, really, since his degree dissertation had been about Channel Four scheduling.

Jackson's career was a symptom of two major shifts in British cultural life: in the media and in higher education. Both of these changes were central to the policies of the Thatcher era, designed to break what was regarded as a pernicious triumvirate: the stranglehold of the unions, the perniciously critical BBC and the non-productive elitism of the universities. So it is no coincidence that the launch of Channel Four itself in 1982, heralding the wholesale deregulation of the media industries, happened at the same time as the 18-month industrial dispute at *The Times* which ended the traditional protectionist employment practices in the newspaper industries, making way for a leaner workforce facilitated by the new technologies.

In 1992 the new legislation granted university status to the country's polytechnics, bringing a new recognition to the kinds of degree courses the polytechnics had made their own: photography and film, fine art and fashion design. And, of course, media studies.

The collision of these great transformations set the tone for the uneasy, sometimes openly hostile relationship between higher education and what have now come to be termed, in a somewhat clumsy phrase, the cultural industries. At its root, this tension is something peculiarly British: a combination of conservatism, snobbishness, a passion for quality in both culture and education and, above all, a conviction that its own way of doing things is best. That is why the alarm and suspicion that greeted the advent of the new wave of creative courses were shared more or less equally by the traditional universities and these industries.

It is, if you like, a perfect paradigm of the wearying conflict between theory and practice: the Tom and Jerry sniping that has always plagued practice-based courses and particularly media studies. While much of the early hostility from the industries has now been broken down, and while the older universities are beginning to accept the inevitable and mounting similar courses themselves, these deep divisions do still persist and will continue to contaminate both sectors unless we can arrive at a more rational and trusting rapprochement between the two.

The precarious status of creative degree courses is underlined by the attitudes of some leading commentators. When she was Minister for Higher Education in the early years of this century Margaret Hodge regularly derided the trend towards what she called "Mickey Mouse degrees" – by which she meant courses like media studies. At about the same time the subject was dismissed by Chris Woodhead, former Chief Schools Inspector in England, as a "one-way ticket to the dole queue". Alan Smithers, Professor of Education at Buckingham University, believes that media studies is a "soft option", lacking the rigour of traditional subjects. In 2006 Cambridge University advised applicants that media studies was not a sufficiently academic A-level, unless combined with "proper" subjects.

Opinions like these are still regularly seized on by the British press, who adore belittling media and journalism degrees, portraying them as covering nothing but soap operas, football reports and celebrities, and also feeding an annual panic about the rising numbers of applicant to such courses. If it's August, I know some newspaper is going to phone up and ask me to "defend" media studies because the summer application rates are about to be published.

There are many reasons why this kind of lampooning is still a standard response in our press. It's partly jealousy, from journalists who wish they could have studied something as interesting, and partly defensiveness: journalists who spend so much of their professional lives intruding and probing don't much like it when they're the ones being scrutinised. And then there's snobbishness, of both the traditional and the inverted variety. The BBC, for example, for most of its existence has favoured those from Oxford and Cambridge, while newspaper editors would habitually mistrust anyone with a degree at all. So both forms of media, from their different perspectives, were unlikely to welcome the new breed of creative and practice-oriented courses.

The media would also have reason to resent a discipline which has traditionally been so openly hostile to it. Originally media studies, in the UK at least, grew out of sociology, which had been itself derided for similar reasons when it first emerged. Marxist in orientation, strongly influenced by political thinkers like Althusser, Gramsci and Adorno, it was an approach which regarded the media as deeply ideological and set out to expose its relations with power and capitalism. When I first moved from the BBC to higher education, a colleague explained that I needed to understand that while film scholars love film, media studies hates the media.

By the 1990s a rather different form of media criticism had begun to take hold, strongly influenced by the French post-structuralists and increasingly concerned with gender, race and colonialism. This led to the questioning of assumed values and hierarchy, and the growth of the notion of cultural relativism. If the political economy approach to the media was regarded as hostile because it was seeking to overthrow the system, cultural studies suggested it wasn't worth the fight. One interpretation was castigated as leftist propaganda; the other for daring to suggest that Bob Dylan was as good as Beethoven.

Both of these caricatures downplay the real value of media theory: that it is a mode of academic inquiry, like other branches of the social sciences, which seeks to understand political, social and cultural dynamics through analysis of one of the most influential forces of modern life. Over the last 30 years the study of the media has developed in areas which are patently beneficial to the industry. Several of my colleagues, for example, especially those working in the fields of media policy and audience research, have acted as consultants to government departments, regulators and broadcasters. At the same time, a considerable body of highly sophisticated media scholarship has emerged which has given the discipline increased credibility in the wider academic community.

What has not been so acceptable to the traditional universities is the practice-based teaching which is an important component of most media studies degrees. Even now, many continue to dismiss it as a vocational rather than an academic education, typical of the upstart polytechnics and art schools that have had the temerity to encroach upon their high ground.

But this aspect of media education is the one that, ever since the 1980s when employment practices were being revolutionised, the industries have gradually come to regard as most obviously valuable. The casualisation of the workforce meant that traditional apprenticeship routes for producers and journalists were being eroded and the industry began to look to the universities to provide the training that used to be their prerogative.

Creative courses emerging from the polytechnics were ideally suited to the task. A jaded news editor may not relish the kind of media studies graduate who will castigate her for her role as a gatekeeper culturally programmed to support the status quo. Broadcast heads may not be impressed if challenged on the intertextual potentialities inherent in the narrative hybridities of the latest reality show. But what they have come to welcome and exploit is the growing talent pool of media-literate, technically competent trainees who can turn around a vox pop or bash out a report, research a story, brief a presenter or drive a radio desk.

That is where the new breed of creative degrees has always excelled, even though the teaching of practice can sometimes appear to conflict with the traditional hard-headed analysis of the more extreme reaches of media theory. At times, even now, the two can sometimes be in danger of cancelling each other out. Students may find themselves writing an essay deconstructing the notion of objectivity in the press one moment, then being assessed for the quality of their fact-finding on a documentary the next. Journalism tutors will tell them to seek the truth...media analysts will warn them that it will always be elusive. To one lot the big conglomerates are the enemy...to the other they are the goal.

Nonetheless, the successful creative courses have managed to navigate the rocky waters between the two by ensuring that well-grounded academic teaching supports and enhances practical studies. On the best of these courses, practical work is taught by industry professionals in well-equipped, up-to-date studios and with considerable contact with the industries through work placements, guest speakers, advisory panels, mentors and potential employers.

The closer their involvement, the more likely employers are to value our graduates, which is why, increasingly, universities are seeking the public hallmark of industry approval – through accreditation. This strategy can bring its own hazards. Sometimes the relationship can be positive. Journalism degrees, for example, have traditionally sought the badge of recognition from bodies like the Periodical Training Council, the National Council for the Training of Journalists and the Broadcast Journalism Training Council. Recently, though, the powerful accrediting body Skillset has been flexing its muscles, increasingly seeking to influence and, in the opinion of some, to control all media education.

Skillset is the Sector Skills Council for the Audio Visual Industries (broadcast, film, video, interactive media and photo imaging). Set up ten years ago, jointly funded by industry and government, it claims that its job is "to make sure that the UK audio visual industries have the right people, with the right skills, in the right place, at the right time, so that our industries remain competitive."

This means that not only does Skillset have the authority to give accreditation to higher and further education courses in a very wide range of disciplines; it has also assumed the prerogative to badge a chosen few as centres of excellence. It has already awarded the status of Academy to some film departments, and is now planning to extend a similar distinction to media.

Higher education institutions are concerned that the climate of competition which Skillset is creating through its particular method of kitemarking accords exceptional advantages to some providers without acknowledging the strengths of the sector as a whole. Even more worrying is Skillset's over-mechanistic view of media education, stressing technical and practical skills above those of reflection, inquiry and analysis. In other words, it is more concerned with training than with education, which means that many excellent institutions and courses would not conform to its somewhat narrow criteria. Criteria that appear to ignore the established forms of monitoring set down by the Quality Assurance Agency and administered through the internal processes of individual institutions.

This attempt at standardising media training within a somewhat arbitrary set of vocational competencies undermines or at least fails to understand the most fundamental values of higher education: to nurture through teaching and research the intellectual, creative and personal growth of their students.

In keeping with these values, higher education courses in media and communications underpin technical skills training with the ability to understand and analyse social and cultural life. Their purpose is defined by the QAA's own subject benchmarking statement: "Whilst these programmes are committed to enabling students to meet the challenges of employment (including self-employment) in a society in which the cultural and communications industries play an increasingly central role, they emphasize that the fostering of employability requires the development of students' creative, intellectual, analytical and research skills."

This broader educational remit gives students the transferable skills that equip them for employment rather than the purely instrumental ones that may meet their sector's immediate skills and business needs but would not prepare them to predict more long-term ones. Indeed, the employment prospects of media students are considerably higher than average. The cocktail of technical, creative and theoretical education that characterises these practice-oriented courses is ideally suited to the new requirements of industry.

All across this sector, from fashion to music, animation to broadcasting, the old distinctions between technicians and producers, operatives and designers, are disappearing. These industries now require multi-skilled employees who can present a radio show and studio manage it; devise an animated sequence and complete its production; create not merely the music for a CD but the cover design and brand concept; report, photograph and file a story straight to page. At Westminster, we've launched a Masters course for fashion designers which also requires enterprise and media skills so that they can not merely start their own businesses, but make them succeed. My School has launched a BSc in Computer Games jointly with the Harrow School of Computer Science, reflecting the requirement for a combination of technical and artistic skills.

Working in teams, building business plans, developing negotiating techniques, giving and taking briefs – these are the hidden new skills that today's creative graduates acquire on their courses. But they also have the backbone of research, scholarship, analysis and academic rigour which allows them not merely to enter the creative industries but to lead and change them.

The theoretical model which characterises media studies today has changed and developed, too. With the impact of the internet as a major force in communications and the possibilities of the new technologies becoming ever more ambitious, the media can no longer be usefully studied as a local, homogenised force. It is global – in its production, reach, distribution and ownerships, and that is how it must be approached and studied.

This crucial shift of emphasis was underlined at a recent conference on Global Media organised by my colleagues in Westminster's Communication and Media Research Institute. Scholars from more than 50 countries were welcomed by the organiser, Professor Daya Thussu, editor of the journal *Global Media and Communication,* who remarked: "The globalisation of media combined with the globalisation of higher education means that the research and teaching of the subject faces immediate and profound challenges, not only as the subject of enquiry but also as the means by which researchers and students undertake their studies."

The papers presented at the conference, he continued, were "a blazing testament to the richness, diversity and vitality of the media studies landscape and the value of such an endeavour". There were contributions on the role of the media in Turkey, Latin America, China, Australia, Russia, Africa, Iran and South Asia, with a huge range of more specific inquiries: peace journalism in North Cyprus; the treatment of media workers in Taiwan; neo-conservatism in the European press; young people's response to the media in Thailand; reality television in Sweden; news-making in Hong Kong; Arab and Israeli coverage of the Middle East.

All of this excitement and energy demonstrates just how far media studies has developed. It has shed its earlier ideological trappings to become a powerful and illuminating force for international understanding. This approach characterises the focus of media studies at Westminster. In addition to our established specialisms in media policy, audiences and history we have made a deliberate move on to the international stage. Two years ago, we launched our highly regarded China Media Centre, offering research, consultancy, teaching and collaboration. We have now established an Arab Media Centre along similar lines. Our research community also includes scholars from Africa, India and the rest of Europe.

This approach is of value not merely to our media industries but to a far wider social and political community. The media is the most acute barometer of any society. It offers myriad insights into different cultures, values, politics and, perhaps most fascinating of all, the way that populations think and feel. An understanding of the world's media can be a key to international diplomacy, trade, business and knowledge exchange, and that is what the higher education community is able to provide.

Media studies has come of age. An international perspective will once and for all do away with the old antagonisms and suspicions that have dogged it. Instead, universities and the creative industries can work together as partners rather than combatants. Mickey Mouse, in true cultural studies tradition, can shake hands with Shakespeare and scuttle up the trousers of Bill Gates, transforming a mischievous little rodent into a vibrant world-class brand.

THE FUTURE OF LANGUAGES AND CULTURES

Susan Bassnett

Susan Bassnett is Professor in the Centre for Translation and Comparative Cultural Studies at The University of Warwick, which she founded in the 1980s. She was educated in several European countries, which gave her experience of diverse languages and cultures, and began her academic career in Italy, lecturing in universities around the world. She is the author of over twenty books and a regular contributor to national newspapers. She is a trustee of Agora.

The start of the twenty-first century has seen an unprecedented movement of people around the globe. Millions are displaced by war, famine and natural disasters, millions seek new lives in countries that appear to offer more than they might have expected had they stayed at home. When the Twin Towers were destroyed by terrorists on September 11th, 2001, the death toll of thousands included men and women, from many different countries, who were employed in New York . Some three quarters of a million Polish citizens arrived to work in the United Kingdom once Poland became a member state of the EEC, a mass exodus that is radically changing the economy of their home country in less than three years. As the Chinese economy prospers, Chinese citizens appear in ever greater numbers in Rome, Paris and Berlin.

These great economic and political movements have been assisted by ever cheaper flights, prompting travel on an unprecedented scale. Leaving home, once an adventure fraught with unknown dangers, is further facilitated by the ease with which the traveller can communicate with the place he or she has left, through mobile phones and the ever-present internet.

Implications for Higher Education

This phenomenon has also had an impact on the world of education. Studying abroad is perceived by many students as a necessary developmental step. Universities in Europe, North America and Australasia have set out to recruit students from countries with less well-developed education systems, and there has been extensive traffic from China and India, for example, to universities in all those regions. Fifteen years ago, relatively few students from Mainland China could afford to study abroad, but that picture is now completely different and many universities have recognised the importance of the expanding Chinese market.

Some institutions based in the English-speaking world have opened campuses in China and in Singapore, which has a stated policy of aspiring to be an education hub for South-east Asia. Leading British public schools have also been developing branches in China.

To assist students in making a choice between universities, international league tables have sprung up. The criteria for establishing an hierarchical league table vary enormously, with some basing their judgements on the quality of research, established through quantification methods such as citation indices and listed priority journals, and others opting for evidence based on a more student-centred holistic approach. The international league table culture has appeared almost out of nowhere in the last three years and seems set to have considerable impact, regardless of defects, for some time to come.

In the 1980s and more so in the 1990s in the UK, as funding of higher education shrank, universities of all kinds came to view the international market as the key to their survival. Large overseas student fees were imposed, and the composition of the student body started to change, though not every university was as thorough in vetting the quality of applicants as they might have been, given the financial incentive. Predictably, however, this period was short-lived. Today, there are signs that leading universities in China and India are rapidly catching up with the best in the world and are starting to offer strong competition. Moreover, assured of better quality at home for less expense, ambitious Chinese students are opting to study in their own country and take advantage of the networks that they can develop during their period of enrolment. For the disadvantage of going abroad to study for four or five years or in some cases longer is that there is a risk of losing touch with what is happening at home and, where there is rapid economic and political change, there is a risk of finding it difficult to adapt upon return. In Japan, there is a term for those citizens who have spent periods of time abroad and are perceived to have lost touch in some way with their Japaneseness.

Global English

A spur to students to study in the UK, in Australasia or in North America has been the advantage of becoming proficient in the language that has become the language of global business, news and diplomacy: English. The boom in English language learning began in the 1970s, and accelerated rapidly. Knowledge of English is now seen as a pre-requisite for advancement in many professions, and the ease with which people who have acquired good English can find employment in international institutions such as finance companies, law firms and businesses testifies to this. Where once it was important to obtain a good degree and acquire a driving licence and excellent computer skills, now a sound knowledge of English can be added to the list of essential requirements.

Confident in the growing interest in studying English, the UK and North America have basked in the surety offered by their native speech. The world wants to learn English: the British and Americans already have English, hence they are one step ahead by birthright. Unfortunately, this blinkered and biased view has been enshrined in educational policy. The decision taken in 2002 to abolish compulsory foreign language learning in schools for English pupils over the age of fourteen was seen by many educationalists as an act of sheer folly. Granted, the government intends to bring in compulsory language study in primary schools by 2010, but meanwhile foreign language departments in universities have been shutting down as demand plummets and they become unviable. By the time the primary school policy is set to be implemented, there may be nowhere to train foreign languages teachers, without a massive injection of funds. Lord Dearing's enquiry into the decline of foreign language learning in schools that reported in March 2007 has revealed nothing that was not already glaringly obvious to teachers and academics in the field. The government has demonstrated contempt for foreign language learning and ignored warnings for years. Dearing's proposal to introduce languages in the primary school curriculum comes late in the day and without any strategy to increase language provision in secondary schools the primary initiative will be useless.

For the reality is that though demand for English globally has increased, this has led to millions of people becoming bilingual, trilingual, often multilingual, while native English speakers are becoming increasingly monolingual. This means that those with more than one language have a competitive advantage over monolinguals in a plurilingual world. Given the option of employing someone with expertise in two or more languages in addition to a good degree and all the other necessary skills and all things being equal, the linguistically endowed candidate is likely to be preferred.

Awareness of Cultural Difference

Even more significant than the competitive edge provided by being able to operate in several languages is the awareness that knowledge of another language provides a key to understanding cultural difference. Language is effectively the heart in the body of culture; what we say and how we say it, our very patterns of behaviour are conditioned by the framework of the languages we use. The instant anything is translated the gulf between languages opens up and the excitement students show when recognising the extent of the differences even in what appear to be the most banal situations is always rewarding. So, for example, the casual greetings system that English speakers use is light years away from the more complex and sophisticated system of greetings in Japan and other parts of Asia. What constitutes rudeness and lack of care in one culture can be ordinary polite behaviour in another. The current debates across Europe about the use of the veil in Islamic countries is a good example of the gulf that opens up when one set of cultural practices collides with another.

The problem with monolingualism is that it inevitably implies monoculturalism, and in an increasingly globalised world it is vital to recognise that not all cultures are alike. Politicians may use generalised terms such as ' the international community', but in reality there is no such thing: perspectives on the world differ with different environments, histories, religions, traditions, and cultural expectations. The very word 'democracy', held up as a universal model by the

CAN THE PRIZES STILL GLITTER?
The Future of British Universities in a Changing World

Anglo-American alliance has no common meaning. We only have to remember that Communist East Germany termed itself the German Democratic Republic to see that vastly different notions of what constitutes democracy exist. The Iranian journalist, Amir Taheri has argued that democracy as a concept is incompatible with Islam, and notes that the term itself only started to appear in Muslim languages in the late nineteenth century. Islam, he claims, is based on a concept of certainty, while democracy is based on doubt and hence the need to have systems in place that can be amended and changed according to changing circumstances. [1]

In the world of higher education, cultural differences need to be recognised and understood. The Anglo-American idea of student-centred teaching, with lecturers often on first name terms with their students, is unthinkable in many parts of the world and causes considerable discomfort to students who are unfamiliar with the practice when they arrive in the English-speaking world. In Britain, contact hours in many Arts and Social Science subjects are minimal since the assumption is that students will use their time productively for independent study. The seminar is premised on the idea of students sharing their ideas and learning from one another. But for students used to more than thirty or forty contact hours a week, and accustomed to respecting the authority of the lecturer even to the point of reproducing that lecturer's opinions as gospel, a practice deemed often to be plagiarism in the West, it is easy for them to feel disorientated and disempowered.

There are other interesting implications also. Women students from South-East Asian countries have often told me about their concerns at how they would manage to reintegrate at the end of their period of doctoral study in the UK, since they had spent four years learning how to argue a case, express their own independent views and be critical of other scholars, none of which would be acceptable once they returned home, where an hierarchical model with the university professor at the top and the student (especially the women) very definitely at the bottom was the only acceptable norm.

---

[1] Taheri, Amir, *The Sunday Times* 23, May 2004

Changing Perspectives

Understanding cultural difference involves making a quantum leap into the world of others. It does not necessarily mean abandoning culturally specific practices that have pertained in a dominant culture for decades, but it does mean being aware that one size does not fit all and that increased diversity in any population necessarily involves different perspectives on the same issue, hence a potential for misunderstanding. Interestingly, in the world of international business, there has long been recognition of the importance of inter-cultural awareness. There is a whole industry of publications and training programmes designed to give succinct and speedy information on diverse cultural practices to businessmen. Hofstede and Trompenaars pioneered this kind of work back in the 1980s, showing how it is possible to acquire a degree of knowledge and understanding about other cultures even without knowledge of another language, though obviously the language is an essential tool for in-depth knowledge. It seems as though recognition of cultural difference is a vital first step to entering into another culture, and if this can be linked to acquiring another language as well, then the risks of miscommunication are radically reduced.

So far, the predominant pattern in the UK has been for students to travel here to study, and this too has reinforced over-confidence in the importance of English. However, there is no doubt that this one-way traffic will not continue indefinitely. Not only are students in the Far East opting in greater numbers to study in their own improved universities, but many European universities are starting to offer programmes taught in English. The advantage to a student from outside Europe who opts to study in Germany, for example, is clear: the fees are lower than in the UK, and in addition to learning English , there is the opportunity to acquire another European language as well. This is bound to have an impact, particularly since the heightened security situation in the UK has led to increased visa charges and a growing climate of uneasiness.

Meeting the Challenge of Internationalism

The Bologna Declaration of 1999 is designed to facilitate the movement of students around European Community member states.

CAN THE PRIZES STILL GLITTER?
The Future of British Universities in a Changing World

UK students, like their mainland counterparts, have the option of spending part of their period of study somewhere else, familiarising themselves with another set of university practices in another context. The problem is, however, that the take-up of UK students opting to study elsewhere in Europe is minuscule in comparison with the numbers able to study in the UK. Explaining why this should be so involves consideration of many factors, including the cost of study for UK students as fees have risen, the tight timetable of the traditional three year degree programme and its relative rigidity, the tradition of UK students leaving home at 18 for university, which is not common practice elsewhere in Europe, where students tend to live at home during their studies. But it is also clearly linked to the inability of UK students to work in another European language, because of the deficiencies in their schooling.

For the moment, there is little sign that anything will change. The international student market is still buoyant, even though it is declining, English is still a dominant world language and there are still going to be large numbers of people aspiring to study in Britain. However, the first uneasy stirrings are evident in the government's belated recognition that something needs to be done to halt the demise of foreign language learning in the UK, as merely knowing one language, even if it is English is going to put future generations at a competitive disadvantage.

Moreover, as can be seen from the daily bulletins emanating from the Islamic world, it is becoming imperative that all governments endeavour to increase the awareness of their citizens that cultures are different. Those of us who watched the destruction of the Twin Towers with horror, watched, with both horror and bewilderment, the news footage of scenes from parts of the Islamic world later that day of children and teenage boys celebrating the event. Yet understanding something of why mass murder could give cause for celebration is vital if we are to move forward in what has already shown itself to be a century promising to be every bit as bloody as the last century, the bloodiest hundred years ever recorded.

I would like to see all British children taught another European language when they start school, gradually building on that basic knowledge to learn about the cultures that use that other language. This means creating a curriculum at secondary school level that includes teaching history, literature and politics of that other culture, and abandoning the facile rote learning conversational method that has bedevilled British foreign language teaching for so long.

At university, I would like to see compulsory modules on intercultural awareness, along with leadership skills and other forms of training that are increasing in importance for all students. Ideally, students would want to develop their languages skills acquired at school, but a valid alternative that would also be an enhancement to the more linguistically gifted would certainly be the acquisition of knowledge about how other cultures operate. Issues such as the importance or not of religious observance, attitudes to time-keeping, the system of social hierarchy, politeness strategies, social attitudes to minority groups and their visibility or invisibility, systems of control, including issues of freedom of speech and the role of the media differ radically from country to country and in quite unexpected ways. Having even the slightest sense of how such differences might be encoded in someone else's culture is surely a necessary objective in our increasingly pluralised world.

UNIVERSITIES AND VOCATIONALISM

Alison Wolf

Alison Wolf is Sir Roy Griffiths Professor of Public Sector Management at King's College London, a regular columnist for the Times Higher Education Supplement and author of "Does Education Matter? Myths about Education and Economic Growth". Her interest in education and Labour market policy stems from work as a policy analyst in the US government, and she continues to undertake regular consultancy work for a range of government departments, here and overseas, and for professional and examining bodies.

When I was growing up, I remember people being very disdainful about American universities and the way they offered all sorts of degrees which were not in 'real' subjects at all. Subjects like sports science, nutrition and event management were given as examples of the way American higher education – at that time the only truly mass system around – had become something that was not 'really' a university system at all.

The unspoken sub-text was that we, in the UK, had higher and better standards. Degrees were for 'proper' subjects, such as physics, or history or French. There were some engineering degrees as well, of course, and a fair number of undergraduate lawyers, plus a lot of medics (mostly out of sight in specialised training hospitals, in London, Edinburgh or Glasgow). But universities were, and should be, about training minds through in-depth study for one of those aforementioned 'proper' degrees.

Yet British public figures were then, as they still are, also queueing up to preach the importance of 'parity of esteem' for vocational education. It was, apparently, a particular failing of the British not to accord the same status to vocational as to academic subjects and degrees, and one we needed to rid ourselves of. We were (and are) told that we should recognise how much more open-minded and unprejudiced our European neighbours were in this respect, and how good this had been for their economies. Writers such as Corelli

Barnett castigated the British for their 'pseudo-aristocratic' frivolity, and for destroying the British economy with their addiction to education removed from the requirements of 'life and work' and refusal to give adequate respect to vocational education. (Barnett 1986: 301) The Labour politician Tony Crosland, launching the polytechnics in 1966, did so with a speech praising the French for the high status they awarded to the vocational through their network of *Grandes Écoles*.[1]

The need for parity of esteem between the academic and vocational remains a staple of political speech making, though in recent years it has been argued less with respect to degree courses than to education and training for teenagers. The promise that, under the latest reform, vocational learning will be 'a positive choice' with 'equal status' is the same whether the reform in question is a Youth Training Scheme, General National Vocational Qualifications, Vocational A levels or (currently) a new set of vocational Diplomas. 'Academic', in this context, becomes anything which leads to a university course, while 'vocational' may mean something practical, non-degree based, but tied to a specific skilled job. But it can, and increasingly often does refer to something more limited; namely whatever is taught to or proposed for young people who are failing academically, and who are thought to be better off with a 'practical' curriculum.

There is a good deal of muddle here, as well as a good deal of hypocrisy. We seem, in the UK, to be arriving at a point where vocational education is actually understood to mean low-status education for non-academic students, even though everyone is also busily denying this. If vocational education is so valuable in its own right, why downgrade HNDs and launch new, specific, work-related qualifications as foundation *degrees*?

And yet, if vocational studies means instruction designed to equip someone with specific skills of relevance to a specific job, then a good deal of university-based education is highly vocational. It is also vocational education that has plenty of prestige already, with no need for governmental help. Far from lacking 'parity of esteem' with

---

[1] In doing so he either inadvertently or wilfully mis-represented the nature and role of the *Grandes Ecoles* in the French education system.

academic courses, medicine, law, and, in many countries, engineering, attract the best students, and send them into the best-paid and most elite careers. These degrees have been high status throughout the last century and a half, and remain so, and though their relative desirability varies across countries and time, it does so within a fairly narrow range.

Meanwhile, for all our erstwhile disdain for American higher education, ours has become more or less identical in its embrace of ever-more degree subjects. Many are in areas that no-one had ever heard of a century ago, let alone regarded as suitable for university study. Media studies, peace studies and women's studies are offered, and so are physiotherapy, exercise science, game design and such esoteric favourites of the media as golfing studies and herbal medicine. Teacher training colleges are an extinct species, even for primary school teachers, who now take Education degrees (or a post-graduate certificate) instead. Nursing won its battle for degree status in the 1990s (with the transfer of Nursing Colleges into the higher education sector complete by 1997). Professions which once sang the praises of an articled apprenticeship are increasingly graduate-only, from law and architecture through to accountancy and chartered surveying.

It seems that every occupation which can possibly secure itself a specialist degree is doing so, and in a university, not some other type of institution. For many years, Camberwell School of Art, the London College of Fashion and St Martin's School of Art were top destinations for young people who wanted to make careers in their respective specialties. When the current senior team set out to secure the position of a newly federated group of 'arts' institutions, which included these long-established institutions, one of their first and most important acts was to secure a change of formal status and of name, to the "University of the Arts."

Left to itself, the university sector seems set, in its usual entrepreneurial fashion, to extend the range of degrees (and the size of the student population) as far as it possibly can. Why stop at 50% participation? Why not 60%? 70%? Why not everyone? Why not have every form of post-school education and training based in universities and rewarded with some sort of a degree?

Editors: Hugo de Burgh, Anna Fazackerley, Jeremy Black

There are two major substantive arguments which can be mustered against allowing (let alone encouraging and subsidising) universities to expand and, in effect, take over all post-school education and training, and they are very different in nature. The first argument addresses what a university 'ought' to be; the second what it is actually any good at. The first states that the core functions and mission of a university get undermined and devalued by the presence of vocational courses. The second sees the expansionist university as a threat to effective vocational training, doing badly what could be done much better elsewhere, but able to spread its embrace because of the excessive status awarded to academic study in modern societies.

In its purest form, the argument about what universities 'ought' to do traces its origins back to Newman's classic text on the 'Idea of a University' (Newman 1852). Those who oppose vocational degrees on these grounds argue that universities should not be in any sense about vocational training, but rather about the pursuit of knowledge for its own sake and the training of young minds in argument, logical thought and reason through such pursuit. However, there are a number of serious problems with this argument, which have been discussed in depth by another contributor to this volume, Gordon Graham, in his book, *The Institution of Intellectual Values* (2005). As Graham points out, the idea that we should value 'knowledge for its own sake' is a very peculiar one. Why would we think that it is particularly valuable to, for example, become an expert on the sorts of bus tickets issued in the world's metropolises? A degree in such a subject would surely attract quite as much ridicule as one in golf course design, without even having the benefit of some obvious relevance in the labour market.

Living creatures, including humans, do things for a purpose. Their activities may include pursuits which do not have any obvious economic benefits; but in that case, they will be related to other values and objectives – including ideas of what it is to be a 'better' or more virtuous human being. Modern universities trace their descent directly from the mediaeval institutions of Bologna, Paris, and Oxford, which arose within a civilisation which saw the care and salvation of the soul, by the Christian Church, as the single most important aspect of human life, and in which universities became the foremost mechanism for training Christian priests. This aspect of the mediaeval world-view is not much in evidence in modern British society; but we do continue to share other values of the mediaeval university which co-existed from the start with their mission to help save souls.

Mediaeval universities regarded reason and reasoned argument as desirable, and 'good', and believed that the pursuit of truth through reason was something which human beings ought to embrace – as a matter of value and principle and not because they might be economically useful. So do we, today, though it would be more accurate to say 'and not *just* because we think they might *also* be economically useful'. Of course, in the case of the Church there was a consistent tension between theory and practice, between encouraging the application of reason and coping with results which posed major problems for and challenges to Church authority. The case of Galileo, forced to abjure his scientific conclusions in order to save his life, is merely the most famous single example of this tension.

Nonetheless, the development of students' reason *was* a core principle of university education from its early years. There was nothing necessary or inevitable about this. The vocational training of soul-savers could perfectly well have been divorced from any concerns with critical analysis. By contrast, the reasoned argument in which students were trained in Plato's Academy and its successors was available only to a very few of the affluent young of the time, and had no links to the process by which Greek religion trained its priests, any more than it does in the case of many of our planet's contemporary religious training schools.

The development of universities which valued and nurtured reason was extraordinarily important for world history. Because of it we can and do see it as an essential part of universities to promote understanding. That means, more specifically, fostering understanding through the free pursuit of rational argument and inquiry – that is, argument based on principles of logic and empirically-based claims for causality; and instilling the relevant values and capacities in university students, as part of what it is to be a worthwhile individual in a worthwhile society. Courses which do not do this should, on this view, not be a part of a university's offerings.

However, we can also, equally reasonably, see vocational training as an essential and permanent part of universities as well. Universities were always about the training of the non-military part of the social elite, which in the beginning meant priests and lawyers and senior state bureaucrats (many of whom were also churchmen). If universities had not had this vocational function, their students would not have attended them. These were poor societies and the number of people with both a thirst for scholarship and study, and the means to pay for it irrespective of its pay-off, was vanishingly small. For an example of how necessary vocational education is to universities' survival, we can look at the history of Spain. In the Golden Age of the sixteenth century, the numbers of universities and of students soared. (Kagan 1974) Students aspired to jobs in the expanding royal administration and courts, as churchmen and above all as lawyers. Then, in the seventeenth century, came economic decline, sale of offices by a cash-strapped monarchy, domination of appointments by noble families, and with these, a near-total collapse of the university sector.

Given the amount of money spent on higher education today, whether directly on teaching and research, or on the living expenses which are often students' major headache, we can hardly be surprised that vocational preparation still figures large. In comparison with early universities, far more students now study for degrees that do not have a one-to-one fit with a specific job or profession. This is probably fortunate, given how many jobs in the modern UK economy, even at the highly skilled end, do not require much in the way of very specific preparation, and/or morph with remarkable speed. But graduates in 'non-vocational' disciplines still command a high wage premium, and the graduates of the traditional high-status 'vocational' degrees continue to command very high wage premia indeed.

Overall, it is very hard to argue that vocational degrees are in any way fundamentally at odds with what a university should be about: rather the contrary. What of the second argument: that universities are a threat to effective vocational training, because they do badly what could be done much better elsewhere?

This may seem a slightly odd argument. If universities are not very good at doing a particular form of vocational training, why would anyone want to do it there in the first place? However, there are two good (or perhaps bad) reasons why this might arise. The first is that, in many societies, university-based programmes enjoy a higher level of financial subsidy than non-university, post-school training. It therefore becomes financially more attractive for students to attend university-based courses, rather than vocational courses offered elsewhere, even if the former are less well aligned with employment needs. And if universities are where students go, universities are where employers will hire.

Universities' financial advantage over other forms of post-secondary provision is only to a small extent associated with the tax advantages of charitable status, and very largely with the differences in direct payments they receive. For example, in the United States, government financial aid has often been more generous for students attending universities or four-year state/not-for-profit colleges than for those attending proprietary (profit-making) vocational schools. This is true even though the latter are often very close to the vocational and industrial sectors they serve, and tend to provide a given vocational training for less money in total (since they are not also supporting research, extensive libraries, or the various sports, leisure and arts amenities increasingly expected of Western universities.)

In the United Kingdom, the last few decades have seen a steady falling-off in the level of employer spending on post-secondary training within further education colleges, and the virtual disappearance of the part-time National Certificates and Higher National Certificates which were once central to technical and engineering education, and in large part employer-financed. Employers get criticised for not spending more on such training; but it is not obvious why firms should have become more short-sighted about their skill needs in the last few decades, than they once were. The much more obvious explanation for these declining expenditures is that, if employers are being provided with an ever-expanding graduate population for free, then university training has to be very bad indeed before it becomes rational to pay for it under the National Certificate model.[2]

---

[2] Why governments so often provide universities with preferential funding is an interesting question in and of itself. Probably it is a combination of politicians' own belief that university education is economically more critical, especially in the 'knowledge economy', universities' lobbying power, a desire to woo middle-class voters whose children make up the bulk of university students, and even, to some extent, a belief in the value of making university education, in the sense of an education designed to advance general understanding, available to more people.

The second reason why training might migrate to universities, even though they do it less well, is the 'labelling' role that universities play. There is a large literature on the extent to which employers reward those with higher levels of education because that education bestows skills, as opposed to doing so because education labels the educated as clever and desirable employees. The evidence suggests that it is a combination of the two. (See eg Jenkins and Wolf 2005) The skills people acquire in education are genuinely valuable, since an illiterate genius is not much use in your modern workplace. But a high level of education also attests to the fact that someone will probably master job-specific skills quickly, and also has the self-discipline required to turn up to work reliably and on time.

Among educational institutions, universities are seen as demanding the highest entrance standards, and give the highest level awards. This means that more and more employers use possession of a degree as a first-line screening device when recruiting. Having a degree may not guarantee you a job, but not having one shuts many doors in your face. Universities are thus well placed to expand their recruitment and the range of their offerings, colonising areas of vocational education and training which were traditionally the preserve of apprenticeship or of vocational schools and colleges. Young people may reasonably feel that a degree in a given vocational area will give them an advantage if they seek a career in the specific field concerned, and will still be useful if they decide on something else – in both cases because of the 'labelling' phenomenon which marks a university graduate as somehow superior to someone without a degree.

The absolute value of a degree obviously tends to diminish as it becomes more common; but getting one may still be a good bet, because not having one is so much worse. However, what needs emphasising here is the impact that university expansion may have on the intrinsic quality of vocational education in a number of fields.

There are two key characteristics of universities which undermine their ability to provide good education and training *in some areas*. First, they are self-contained and separate from the workplace. They cannot, for either financial or practical reasons, possibly keep up with all the changes which take place in a fast-developing industry – the new machinery and techniques, the new markets, the emerging competitors. And because they are separate, their instruction takes place in environments which are not like the workplace. Universities use classrooms (even if the classroom may be fitted out as a lab). They assess and mark people individually, which is the only fair thing to do – and what students, very reasonably, demand - since people then go out into the world as individuals, with their individual degree results. University rhetoric about developing teamwork is consequently not worth very much. When people in work are asked about the type of training they have found most valuable, 'on-the-job' training, with others, invariably comes out top by a mile; and it is what universities cannot, by their nature, provide.

Second, university teachers, however 'vocational' their speciality, are making their careers as academics, not as practitioners of whatever profession, trade or calling they teach. The tension, in university life, between teaching and research is a permanent one. Teaching is, ultimately, what universities exist to do. But research is what academics like to do, it is what helps to maintain the universities' (and their teachers') ability genuinely to promote understanding, and, critically, it is something on which one can reach fairly objective judgements about people's quality and abilities. You cannot sit round a table looking at direct evidence of teaching skills in the way you can with research publications. So research publications inevitably get the most attention from the ambitious and able.

These are facts about university life which we just have to live with, at the aggregate level. But what they underscore is that universities will always be an imperfect place for acquiring certain vocationally-related skills; and the further removed those skills are from the print-based interactions and the research values of academics, the worse a place they will be. In a world of ever-expanding higher education, the major problem of vocationalism and the universities is not really that vocational degrees are bad for universities. It is that universities are bad for the future of many of our vocational skills.

References

Barnett, C (1986) *The Audit of War: the Illusion and Reality of Britain as a Great Nation* (London: Macmillan)

Graham, G. (2005) *The Institution of Intellectual Values: Realism and Idealism in Higher Education* (Imprint Academic)

Editors: Hugo de Burgh, Anna Fazackerley, Jeremy Black

Jenkins, A and A. Wolf (2005) Employers' Selection Decisions: the Role of Qualifications and Tests in S. Machin & A. Vignoles eds *What's the Good of Education?* (Princeton and Oxford: Princeton University Press)

Kagan, R. L (1975) Universities in Castile 1500-1810 in L.Stone ed *The University in Society*, volume II. (Princeton: Princeton University Press)

Newman, J. H. (1852) *The Idea of a University* (London: Longmans Green & Co)

FOSTERING INNOVATION: ARE BRITISH UNIVERSITIES ENTERPRISING?

Alec Reed[*]

Alec Reed CBE is the founder of Reed, the UK's leading recruitment specialist. Their website, www.reed.co.uk, is currently Europe's largest commercial job site with over 300,000 jobs and one million job applications each month. He was formerly Professor of Innovation at Royal Holloway, University of London and Visiting Professor of Enterprise at London Metropolitan University.

Right now the Reed jobs website has 240,000 graduates registered on it, all looking for work. Every graduate job will have at least ten applicants, higher than any other category. But are these graduates qualified in the right things? Has their university education given them the skills they need? Unfortunately all too often the answer is No. University education as it stands does not adequately prepare graduates for future employment.

Undergraduate skills are not comparable with business skills. A survey of where graduates end up by the Association of Graduate Careers Advisory Services in 2004 proved sobering reading. On the plus side, it found that 11 percent of geography graduates became managers in the public or business sectors and 11 percent gained professional jobs in business or finance. However, they were the lucky ones. Ten percent were serving customers in a bar or restaurant or working in retail, and a hefty 21 percent had secured clerical or secretarial jobs. Did any of these students really need their degree?

There is no doubt that university plays a valuable role in young people's lives. For one thing, it occupies you until you grow up – it gives you the chance to mature. But what else? Bright, gifted teenagers go into a university, and bright, gifted young adults come out. Which begs the question: what is the added value of universities?

---

[*] Alec Reed spoke to Anna Fazackerley.

The failure to produce the right sort of graduates – which is not a personal bugbear of mine, but a complaint heard across the working world – can be traced to a lack of forward thinking inherent within the entire education system. Schools behave as though everything ends at the age of 18, and universities behave as though everything ends at 21 or 22. No one is regarding the process as a continuum. They aren't thinking about the end product, which is not the degree ceremony so beloved by parents; it is the employment market. Students aren't asking themselves what skills they will need in the real world and universities are neglecting to engage properly with the world of work.

There are different ways of building the skills you need to be successful and the alternative of not going to university can be quite attractive. In many ways I had a tremendous advantage not going to university when I left school. At the age of 22 I was working as junior accountant at Gillette. I had already been working for four years and I'd been in the army for two. I think I was more mature and certainly better qualified for work than a graduate of my age. I also had the opportunity to be trained by, and learn from, a department of experienced adults who were transferring their skills every day. You wouldn't get a similar teaching ratio at a university; a student can be one of hundreds.

There is a false assumption – as demonstrated by my employers at Gillette who favoured Oxbridge graduates - that brand is what matters when it comes to choosing a university or university alumni, and if you have the right institution on your CV your work is done. But funnily enough, it's the universities with the strongest brands that seem to do least in preparing graduates for the real world. They also have the least focus on enterprise. It astonishes me that Oxford only launched a business school relatively recently. It seems to be the metro universities that have the most innovative approaches to education – maybe because they can't rely solely on their brand to generate applications and have to make a real effort to attract people. As a result, they have thought about what they are offering and how it differs from other institutions.

We are entering an era where brands worldwide are dying. People no longer trust the manufacturers of a product because of their brand; they look to the product itself. The same applies to universities. What they are offering is a commodity – education – and they need to think long and hard about the product they are offering. If they do, it will force them to dig deep and find something of real value in their offering.

So, what should added value from a university look like? Well, universities should be looking to turn out graduates that are truly enterprising. This does not mean that institutions should be trying to churn out thousands of Richard Bransons. It means simply that they should be developing people with a can-do attitude, who are capable of original thinking.

You would hope by the time someone got to university they'd be proficient in the 3Rs. This means universities have the opportunity to take education to another level; one that will prepare young people for employment. I'm not necessarily talking about hard skills here – the type of knowledge that someone on a business studies course would gain – but rather soft skills that will stand people in good stead for operating in the world when they graduate.

We need to foster the 7 Cs: communication, courage, creativity, cooperation, criticism, community and culture. These personal skills can be woven into many courses and universities should be striving to feed them into every aspect of their teaching. Universities are perfectly placed to teach more than facts; to teach a new way of thinking. They should be aiming to foster a spirit of enterprise in their students that will contribute to their success beyond the educational arena.

However, this won't happen without a serious effort to train the trainer. At the beginning of the millennium I founded a trust that promotes enterprise education in schools and discovered that one of the main obstacles to cultivating enterprise in the children was that the teachers weren't thinking in an enterprising manner. We therefore need to foster a spirit of enterprise in university lecturers. This would have two positive effects on universities: first, it would make them better equipped to instil an enterprising attitude in their students; and second, it would inject an enterprising attitude into the university as an institution.

The effects on business would be staggering. As I have written elsewhere [1] Capitalism is dead and we have entered a new era of Peoplism. People are everything in business now and everything must change in recognition of that fact. In this new economy knowledge is extremely important, but what is absolutely essential is the ability of an individual to build on that knowledge. And that is where universities currently fail their students. Intelligence is vital, but it is intuitive intelligence that is truly valuable to a company. To survive in this new world you need more than a degree certificate: you have to have something special between your ears.

---

[1] Alec Reed, *Capitalism is Dead: Peoplism Rules; Creating Success Out of Corporate Chaos*, McGraw-Hill Professional, 2003

ACADEMIA, INDUSTRY AND SCHOOLS: HOLY TRINITY OR MENAGE À TROIS?

David Lathbury

David Lathbury is Director of Process Chemistry R&D at AstraZeneca. After obtaining a PhD from Southampton University, he began his research career in academia, working at Cornell University and then Bath University. His first industry job was at Shell Research. Before joining Astra in 1998 he worked at SmithKline Beecham.

Almost every week there is one article or another decrying the fall in both the quality and quantity of science taught in our country's classrooms. My own discipline, chemistry, has become something of a lightning rod for this debate with several recent, high profile, closures of university chemistry departments hitting the headlines.[1] Does this mean traditional chemistry and physics have reached the end of their useful lives? Are people like me just acting like old king Canute, raging against the inevitable tide of educational progress? Is this passion for my subject some half-baked romantic attachment to a glorious past that's had its day? I don't think so. The molecular sciences are, however you label them, vital to the future prosperity of the UK. Indeed if we keep retrenching to new more trendy enterprises sooner or later there won't be anywhere left to run to. More crucially, if you look at many of man's current and future challenges, advances in science and technology may well be the difference between business as usual and significant declines in living standards or even mankind's extinction.

So, let us start where it begins, in education. Last year saw an increase in chemistry undergraduate numbers, and I hope that this is maintained in future years, although we are still some way below the high water mark of 4,300. However, there are some key issues that

---

[1] The views that I express, which are take form my Society of Chemical Industry Hurter lecture in 2005, although focussing on Chemistry would apply to science in general. They are personal views and although I am sure one would find many other scientists in industry who share my views, these shouldn't be seen as those of industry as a whole or AstraZeneca specifically.

will continue to exert downward pressures, if they are not addressed. And it is not just a numbers game. If the chemical and life science industries are going to succeed in the future, we need to make sure that out brightest and best students are attracted into studying chemistry and the physical sciences, but also that they are then attracted into careers in these areas. This could be the single most important future issue for these industries. The molecular sciences and related industries will, I believe, be the dominant growth industries in the 21st century. We should remember that bright kids have choices - lots of choices - and if science isn't attractive they will simply choose something else.

What has driven the recent decline? The first problem is the school syllabus. Most of us are in agreement that exposure to more practical experimental science would go a long way to enthusing students, but I think there are some more fundamental problems. If you are designing any large programme, such as a new drug research programme, you normally start at where you want to get to and work backwards. It is the only way you can really ensure that all the individual pieces of the plan all link together. The problem with the syllabus is that it seems to be designed from the bottom up. Naively I would have thought that the main objective in setting the syllabus for GCSE should be preparation for A-level, and for A-level it should be preparation for a degree. Some people might argue that this does not make sense because most A-level chemistry students do not take chemistry at degree level. Yet if you pursue that logic then accountancy firms should be devising the chemistry degree course, because more chemistry undergraduates go into accountancy than chemistry. For me, education is about providing individuals with choices. If students are prepared well at GCSE they have a choice about whether to do A level chemistry or not. If they are not prepared, they cannot continue and have no choice. So I want to see an end this see-saw argument about whether we need to enthuse or enable students: the obvious answer is that we have to do both.

How much influence should industry have in designing A level courses? In my view they should have very little. At this stage in the education process industry should be much more involved in enthusing students. However, universities should have a much greater influence than they currently appear to have.

CAN THE PRIZES STILL GLITTER?
The Future of British Universities in a Changing World

There has been a worrying shift to modular exams and courses. Again, there are some good reasons for this, both logistical and to reduce the pressure of one off end of year 13 exams. Yet this has introduced a culture of learn, pass exam and forget. For some subjects this is fine, but for science, where each level builds on the previous one, it is disastrous. It causes universities major problems later on when some students are outraged that one might expect them to remember something they were taught in their first year.

We have to try and move away from a situation where higher education and science education policy is being set by the likes and dislikes of 17 and 18 year olds. Too many schools and universities are encouraged to see students as their customers. For universities I can understand this as they now have to pay tuition fees, but UK PLC and the taxpayers are the true customers: despite the increase in fees, the tax payer will still be picking up the lion's share of the cost of higher education. Another disturbing manifestation of the student customer phenomenon is the proliferation of hybrid or vocational-sounding degrees. Many medicinal chemistry degrees have appeared recently. Some use medicinal chemistry examples to illustrate and enhance the core subject, whilst others simply dilute it. These courses confuse students, who mistakenly assume a degree in medicinal chemistry gives them a better chance of gaining a research and development position in the pharmaceutical industry, and it frustrates employers when deficiencies are exposed at interview. A similar charge could be levelled against forensic science degrees.

The interfaces between the various stages in education are key and they need to be managed much more effectively than they appear to be currently. I also believe we need more flexibility in the system. The recent debate on reading strategies made me think. What seems to happen is that we introduce a system then after a few years we notice a sub set of students, around 15 per cent, are failing. We then look at what these students need and introduce a new system. A few years later we still have 15 per cent failing, but it is a different 15 per cent. If you have a single approach, I think you will always fail some children, so let's not have one. Making a student like me study English or French post 16 would have been a total waste of time, (although it would have made my PA's life much easier,) but for others it would have been great. Some students know exactly what they want to do post 16 and some don't. The brightest should be fast-tracked, perhaps going through a three-year degree. Others will take longer but as long as they get there is there a problem? At one end of the spectrum there are some students who will never be remotely interested in science, and at the other there are students who aren't interested in anything else. The group in the middle, the undecided, are the group who may benefit form a more general education post 16, yet for the others it is of questionable value. If you want to alter the proportion of these groups, assuming that is possible, then we need to focus on the key stage 3 part of the process in secondary schools.

In the higher education arena there are some key national problems that need to be grasped. How many chemistry departments does the UK need? I have no easy way to answer that. I have seen estimates ranging from 25 to 6 and I have heard reasonable arguments to support the entire range. The case for consolidation is a strong one. Science is getting more expensive. There is a growing gap between equipment in industry and equipment in universities. This will increase if we do nothing. At some stage it all comes down to funding, so if we want better-funded departments we may need fewer of them.

Of course, this is all very logical, but there are a few things we have to understand before we make what will probably be irreversible changes. When some people look at undergraduate chemistry numbers they tend to fall in to the trap of seeing a chemistry degree as a vocational one. This is not true. Last year one or two of us in the pharmaceutical industry did a back of an envelope calculation of the total number of UK chemistry undergraduates who wanted to work in synthetic chemistry in the pharmaceutical industry and who were of the required calibre. The result was less than 100 out of an intake of over 3,000. This phenomenon is well known to academics and it is called attrition. I am not unhappy that chemistry undergraduates go off into all types of careers. However, until we understand attrition, its causes, how much is actually predetermined (which incidentally I think is probably most of it,) we should tread very carefully.

A few years ago I asked the Universities and Colleges Admissions Service to give me a list of all the schools in England who had provided five or more chemistry undergraduates over the previous three years. Seventy per cent of the schools were north of Leicester. I don't know why this is, but it tells me that geography is also important

CAN THE PRIZES STILL GLITTER?
The Future of British Universities in a Changing World

and that any consolidation must take this into account, especially in the age of tuition fees.

We recently reviewed our recruitment data. If we looked at our PhD entry employees then this roughly followed the Research Assessment Exercise league tables, with 5 and 5* departments the main source of recruits. However, when we looked at where the PhD level candidates had studied for their first degree the picture was very different. Many more 4 rated departments were present, and in fact when we looked at our undergraduate intake it really didn't follow any pattern, showing a much wider span of institutions and varying tremendously year on year. We have a complex web of interdependent universities - some of which don't even realise this.

I'm not against consolidation, but it has to be thought through and it should have the single objective of strengthening UK research and teaching in chemistry or it will simply become a back door opportunity for some vice chancellors to balance their books. In fact to implement changes of this nature will probably require significant extra investment in the short term. This is why the Stone report in the 1980's sank, to quote original members of the committee, "in an ocean of fudge". The current HEFCE funding formula for laboratory-based science is not sustainable, because science teaching at our universities is, in most cases, being cross-subsidised by research activities. This cannot carry on.

So I come to the old question, what does industry want? The fact that this is always being asked worries me. It suggests to me that government think of industry as one big homogenous body. Nothing could be further from the truth. I hear all sorts of comments about the need for chemistry graduates to understand business, and to be entrepreneurial, whatever that means, and a whole load of other things. I disagree. The above are all nice-to-haves, but not at the expense of core skills in chemistry. There will be a need for at least a sub-set of our future staff to be able to operate at the boundaries between disciplines, such as chemistry and chemical engineering or chemistry and biology. However, this isn't a plea for hybrid qualifications, either undergraduate or postgraduate. We need collaborations between scientists who are excellent in their particular discipline but can talk to each other, catalysed by one or two polymaths. Again industry can and should be showing academia how to do this. We've been doing it for years. People have to realise that students have a finite amount of time for studying, and many of the nice-to-haves will have to be delivered in the workplace, whether smaller companies like it or not.

Returning to the HE sector, a crucial problem is accountability. It is not clear who owns undergraduate and postgraduate chemistry training. Assuming we could derive a national strategy for chemistry, it is not at all apparent who would drive it. Who is accountable for our national planning? The answer, right now, is no one. No one government organisation spans the entire education pipeline. PhD training is funded jointly between the Higher Education Funding Council for England and the research councils. Regional Development Agencies are also beginning to have an increasing role to play in the funding of research and higher education. Perhaps there isn't a simpler way of managing what is a very complex system, but there seem to be too many players involved, and at the very least this must increase administration costs. I think the same comments could be made about the plethora of professional bodies and other NGOs and examination boards that currently exist. If we have multiple voices reporting to multiple government organisations the result is chaos. But, more importantly, this complexity makes it hard to identify and deliver strategic objectives quickly. That is where China really has the edge. If the Chinese government want to deliver a strategy for the physical sciences, the plan can be drafted on Friday and start to be delivered on Monday morning, (actually, probably Saturday morning, or even Friday evening). How long would it take in the UK? This is the flip side of having a democratically elected government.

Industry has some way to go in its relationship with academia. It always surprises me that much of academia only really view industry as a source of cash. Few academics see industry as true scientific or educational collaborators. The Engineering and Physical Sciences Research Council has provided funds for many years to enable academics to spend time in industry. But, such is the dominance of the RAE, I have only seen two examples where this has been taken up. Yet in both these cases the benefits to the individuals' subsequent research were immense. If nothing else, industry will continue to provide a great source of important scientific problems worthy of study and as intellectually challenging as any currently being worked on in academia. In contrast to the schools arena I think that industry has a role to play in the enabling side of the equation. There are numerous skills and technologies that could be passed on from industry to senior undergraduates and postgraduate students.

Yet it is important to understand the reality of the UK Pharmaceutical industry today. When I was looking for my first job in the mid 1980s, I applied to three medium-sized UK Pharmaceutical companies: Glaxo, Beecham and Wellcome. Now these companies are one and I don't think there is a single big Pharmaceutical company with its R&D headquarters in the UK. This changes the landscape with respect to investment. It's much more competitive getting funding as we are now competing with US and other international academics, and although I understand the reasons behind the introduction of full economic costing for universities in this country, it is going to make this competition harder. If the extra money is fed into the research department then that is acceptable, but if more and more of it seems to be going back to the centre to expand what, in my opinion, are inefficient and oversized central bureaucracies then both I and my *foreign* senior management will have a big issue with supporting UK investment versus investment in the US, France, Sweden or Canada.

In the UK we have all have the ingredients for successful pharmaceutical R&D. We still produce some top class graduate and PhD chemists, and in the synthetic organic community we have some very good young academics coming through. However, with all the focus on university education have we inadvertently endangered the vocational path? Re-establishing a true vocational path of entry into R&D would, I believe, be of huge benefit to both the pharmaceutical and the fine chemicals industry, but this would require a great deal of collaboration between a range of higher education institutions and industry, and a great deal of effort. Of course this path will only work if it is seen as a gold standard and a true alternative to the traditional full time HE route. We tend to like stability within industry as a whole and perhaps that's why foundation degrees haven't taken off within Pharmaceutical R&D chemistry: we do not really understand them or how they correlate to previous qualifications.

The key message is that academia, schools and industry all have the same interests in making the system work. We still have enough good will on all sides to really engage, but I'm not sure if there is an adequate national forum where this can happen.

Certainly with the rise of China and India time is running out. When I am at events for schools or universities, I often wonder whether I am doing this for the benefit of UK PLC or for my company. In the age of the multinational I suspect that the answer is the former. However I think that there is an argument that by strengthening local (UK) education, we will strengthen our companies, whether they are foreign multi-nationals or small regional companies.

The final most important question must be: who should be responsible for reversing the decline in my subject? Having thought about it extensively over the last year, the answer I would give is everyone: the school teacher who works overtime to organise an industrial visit, the examination bodies that actually have a dialogue with the academic institutions on the receiving end of their decisions; the academic institutions that bother to ask industry what should be taught in a medicinal chemistry degree; the industrialist who volunteers to help out with a school or university activity, or his boss who encourages him; and the government department or professional body who decides to collaborate with a competitive organisation for the greater good and put aside vested interests. I can point to examples of most of this going on within the UK but we need to do more.

The heritage we have in scientific discovery is a proud one - but it is in the past. As a country we will only attract high tech investment if we have the scientists to use it. If we do not, high-tech industry will follow many other former UK industries and leave. The big difference between this and the textile industry is that because of the high level interdependency this will in turn greatly damage the university sector and have a knock on affect on schools. All of us who work in the science arena have to realise that if this happens it is highly unlikely any such changes will be reversed. If you do not want your grandchildren to work in call centres I urge all readers to get involved.

UNIVERSITIES AS IDEOLOGICAL TRAINING INSTITUTIONS

Kenneth Minogue

Kenneth Minogue's The Concept of a University (1973) was republished last year by Transaction Publishers in the US. He is Emeritus Professor of Political Science at LSE. Born in New Zealand, and educated in Australia and Britain, his other books include The Liberal Mind, Nationalism and Politics: A Very Short Introduction. He has edited several books, including most recently "Essays in Conservative Realism" (1996). He is a director of the Centre for Policy Studies and a trustee of Civitas.

For hundreds of years, British universities were lively and valuable self-governing corporations. They have now lost their autonomy and fallen into the role of mere instruments of the state. This change dates from the Robbins Report and the 1960s conviction that economic prosperity was closely correlated with, and probably caused by, the spread of something called "higher education." Such a political takeover was achieved in the same way as bureaucracies in liberal-democratic states reduce some area of civil society to a servile status: first subsidise, and then call for central control and accountability. Universities were first showered with generous subsidies by the British Government, and then very rapidly – already in the 1970s - called to heel. They lost all power of independent movement, and were subjected to alien targets for their teaching practices and their research output. It made little difference whether the Government was Labour or Conservative: the imperative of control lay with the Ministry. There's quite a lot of ruin in any established tradition, but this event may appropriately be described as the collapse of British universities. I take all this for granted, but my concern here lies elsewhere.

Contemporary British universities, unlike their predecessors in earlier times, pay lip service to the value of critical thought and breadth of opinion, but in fact they have come to disseminate an orthodoxy in the form of a set of admired doctrines. Further, these doctrines are not academic but rather practical – in fact political. To enter a British university today is to become engaged in a world where alternative opinions can only be held at the cost of a certain fashionable derision. My concern here is not with the pieties of the thing called "political correctness", which merely intimidates the feeble, though its official agents dispose of significant legal power. What concerns me is a more insidious form of orthodox thinking that involves universities in ideological convictions. In order to explain this view, let me first engage in a simple thought-experiment, and then move on to suggesting a few reasons why the experiment would come out as it does.

Let us consider a young person, of either sex, in late teens going up to a university to study the social sciences or the humanities. The courses chosen are relevant here because the ideological pressures are considerably less in areas where the technical preconditions for study are more demanding. Mathematics and science are obvious examples, though even here, ideology is not unknown. Let us posit that our Candide figure is a person of entirely conventional virtues. Such a person may well be religious – and for this purpose the actual religion does not matter. What does matter however is that whether our Candide is a Christian, Sikh, Muslim, Jew or other, he or she must have absorbed the feelings and experiences appropriate to the particular conviction. Our Candide, or Candida, in being religious, is tolerant enough of other religions, but not some breezy ecumenical who thinks that everyone worships the same god in different symbols. Our Candide is also a patriot, attached to Britain, the flag and the state as embodied in the monarchy. And finally, our Candide has managed to get through to the late teens while still holding to what used to be conventional views of how one ought to conduct one's life. He (or she) believes in sexual restraint, and a future involving marriage and family life, along with the need to learn about some occupation that would sustain the resources needed for such a life.

I have no idea whether such paragons still exist, though the plural character of our society is such that many young people fit at least part of this prescription. Nor do I know whether such a constellation of attitudes is entirely to be desired, particularly in contemporary life, with its endless invitations to indulge impulses and its ceaseless distraction of mind towards trivial things. But our model is perhaps explicit enough to allow us to ask what would happen to such a person going to a university. Religious belief would clearly be one vulnerable area. Modern academic life is rightly concerned with evidence, and the evidence that trumps most argument is facts that can be sustained by observation. What cannot be evidenced in this way is distrusted. Religion as a cultural tradition that has generated everything from our moral attitudes to the art and architecture of public life is reduced to a few simple "killer" questions. ("Do you believe in God?" "In miracles?" etc.) Christianity in particular is further subjected to supplementary attack as an anachronism. Unless our student becomes philosophically sophisticated, then science will become scientism, and belief erodes into secularism.

Mere scepticism, of course, would be something any believer would have to accommodate in a university, but academic scientism has become itself a quite positive doctrine. In distancing oneself from religious belief, runs the doctrine, a person is rejecting many sources of fanaticism and intolerance, and abandoning wishful fantasies of divine involvement in human affairs. Religious belief is a crutch allowing those who cannot face the realities vouchsafed to us by science (that we are a small and fragile set of developed organisms living in a tiny corner of a pretty unhelpful universe) to be consoled.

At issue is not, of course, merely the validity of competing beliefs. Our thought experiment must necessarily consider two levels of response. There is, firstly, the question of whether such and such a belief is plausible, and secondly, the question of what I am revealing about myself in affirming such a belief. Some beliefs, to put it vulgarly, have cachet, others do not. Religious beliefs, in the modern West do not, which is why Islamic religious beliefs generate a culture shock among us: here are people who take religious convictions very seriously indeed.

The positive doctrine involved here is often called "secularism", and that will do for us, though behind secular attitudes will be found many strange enthusiasms, often of a pseudo-spiritual kind. Secularism is in part constituted by the principle of tolerance, but like all abstractions, tolerance can produce unexpected results. Secularists are not at all tolerant of something they call "fundamentalism", for example. Strange reversals often occur. The ideal of toleration may be rejected as a cold and patronising virtue that demands to be replaced by something called "acceptance", another case in which what purports to be merely a sceptically virtue of tolerance is unexpectedly found to involve very positive approvals, of unorthodox sexual conduct, for example. Tolerance leading to acceptance may also demand that we approve of some rather strange practices of other cultures. In general, we may observe that the strength of secularism depends basically on presenting itself as merely a refusal to embrace things that seem absurd, but it actually conceals a very strong positive programme.

Our Candide is thus likely to lose his religion at the university, and his virginity will not be far behind. Academic life over the last couple of generations has been experienced much less as an immersion in scholarship and research than as a form of liberation from conventions that restrict one's inclinations. No doubt quite a lot of the more entrenched moral virtues – integrity, honesty, courage etc. – will survive this transition, but Candide is soon likely to find that his moral passions are taking a new direction. He will find that he exhibits his goodness in this environment less by courage and integrity than by supporting a set of admired political causes. These causes include peace, protecting the environment, lifting Third World poor people out of poverty and working for social justice in Britain and other Western countries.

In his religious days, Candide would not have been surprised at the fact that the world, and even our part of it, contains violence, ignorance and folly. Religions recognise the world as an arena lacking divine perfection, or having fallen from it. But Candide will now begin to acquire the idea that the many defects of our society result not from human folly but from bad social conditions, things that have arisen because they suit the interests of the rich and powerful. He will thus pick up almost insensibly the idea that the status quo being bad, change (in the abstract) must be good. It is the thing one ought to work for. The state of the world which he previously thought to be a moral and religious question will now come to seem political and technological.

The grand cause requiring us to improve society, Candide will come to understand, is a politico-moral task to which we can bring increasing rationality, something clearly lacking in the outmoded religious passions of the past. Such passions will be associated with the Inquisition, sectarian persecution, the problems of Galileo, and similar evils. It may not be immediately evident to Candide that improving society according to some ideal plan has created horrors that leave religious fanaticism far behind. The Nazis tried it and ended up killing millions. So did the Bolsheviks, and as we move to the prodigies of social improvement attempted by Mao and Pol Pot, the stomach certainly heaves. The idea that improving society, or trying to perfect it, is an innocent piece of virtuous idealism could only be entertained by the most simple-minded secularist.

In the course of his burgeoning enlightenment, Candide will also lose his patriotic attachment to Britain. He will identify flags and national sovereignties with nationalism, perhaps indeed with militarism, and his view of Britain's past will be distinctly curate's eggish. Britain gets few credits for having abolished slavery in the Western world, and many debits for imperialism. Candide will learn that in politics as in morality, the only guide he ought to follow is to be found in the set of abstract admirations he has acquired during his education. Mere loyalties and concrete identities will be seen as minor and contingent aspects of life compared with the exhilaration of judging everything in rational terms, where rationality is constituted of a set of abstractions. Candide's allegiance and identity will be in large degree fragmented, so that he now supports supranational organisation (such as the EU), international organisations (such as the UN) and a variety of international declarations of policy regarding human rights, refugees, targets for the improvement of the poor and much else. Candide has thus largely discarded his British identity and become a kind of cosmopolitan. Whereas before he might, in religion, have imagined a far away salvation, he will now be persuaded that there is a potential political salvation in using political power and international law to release us from the basic evils that plague our world. Since the 1960s, the universities have been the main suppliers of feet for protest marches affirming uplifting slogans.

Here then is the content of the current orthodoxy disseminated in various explicit and implicit ways in universities. It is likely to turn Candide into a secularist, a socialist and an internationalist. One might, of course, respond by saying: "what is so very wrong with these views?" and I would have to agree that within their rather unsophisticated limits they are plausible, defensible and (up to a point) benign. But the essential point about them is that they are practical, and that they constitute a kind of orthodoxy, and neither practicality nor orthodoxy have much place in universities.

A critic might well ask: "What is the evidence for this reading of current undergraduate experience?" As with many such judgements, the ultimate test is by looking to one's own experience, and of course that will vary. But supplementary support will be found in abundant studies showing that, for example, the overwhelming majority of professors in universities in the West support social democratic political parties. Occasionally they break cover by issuing collective letters of supposedly expert advice, regretting the increase in inequality, or the defects of economic policies designed to free up markets. Who that loves truth finds it easy to put up with error? This is why a special kind of intolerance is to be found among dons. But we are all fallible, and can get things wrong, as economists did for many decades after 1945 when the Hayekian criticism of central direction of economies was regarded as beyond the pale of truth.

My question is, then, how we have come to this interesting pass? The causes are no doubt immensely complicated, so in this short discussion I want merely to point to several allegiances that have impelled universities in this direction, and they happen to interest me because each of them seems to me to be a betrayal of what it is to be academic.

The first of these is the belief that the essence of academic life is criticism. In a sense, of course, criticism is exactly what we find academics doing. But the banner of criticism became in time a slogan, and slogans popularise and simplify. In the 1960s a wave of unsophisticated people turned up in universities who had picked up Marxist notions of social criticism. And it was as being supposedly critical of society that a whole raft of intellectual lobbyists – for proletarians, women, homosexuals, supposed victims of colonial oppression and others – succeeded in according their publicity materials a place in universities. An institution devoted to the study of human life as a universal succumbed to a Babel of rather shrill partisan voices. A deformed version of criticism came to reject the very civilisation from which it had emerged. Again, it was often thought that criticism would spread toleration, because it was assumed that critical reason would target intolerant passions resulting from prejudice, superstition, bigotry and so on. But criticism is also an exposure of the contingent and partisan features of ways of life, part of the creative tension of Western life. To criticise another ways of life, then, can lead to actual intolerance, universities being as we have observed in some respects highly intolerant places.

The university in the past was indeed often a rather crabbed place full of quarrelsome pedants, but it was only by such protective colouring that universities could distinguish themselves from the popularisation found in the intellectual journalism of the media. The literary scholar F. R. Leavis is now remembered as a ridiculous figure who detested book reviews in the Sunday papers of the time – but it was only by marking out academic scholarship as quite distinct from popularisation that its independence could be sustained. Popularisation, or the conversion of science and scholarship into cliché and metaphor, happens as universities come to be populated largely by students whose interest must be stimulated by sugar coating because they have never been taught the disciplines of study.

A second betrayal of the academic results from teachers developing the conviction that the hope for a better future rests in their hands because they have the power to mould the minds of the young. Those who believe in progress may want to "teach" the young that (in their belief) violence never solves problems, or that we must take care of the planet, or many another improving belief. University teachers still no doubt exhibit real passion for their subject, but they have also picked up a weakness for crusading, usually but not always sotto voce. Some historians have been known to sacrifice pedantic accuracy of report in favour of dramatising the past in ways likely to induce corrective change in society. Academic integrity may come to be shadowed by a sense of moral responsibility thought desirable in a democratic citizen. Thus does the philosopher turn into the philosophe. Such corruptions have corroded the whole notion of education to such an extent that we no longer flinch when someone says that we must "educate" the young not to drink and drive. There's nothing new about this vulgarisation, of course; it has been around since at least the beginnings of the Enlightenment in the eighteenth century.

Such are the attitudes Candide (or Candida) is likely to pick up from Professor Pangloss, and we can only hope that experience of life will then be no less dramatically "educational" here than in the case of Voltaire's hero. And it is Voltaire's message we may end by recommending. "Il faut cultiver son jardin" is wise advice for dons no less than for Candide. The basic betrayal of the academic tradition results from trying to make it the instrument of <u>any</u> practical purpose. Practicality – the attempt to achieve an end, satisfy a need, solve a problem etc. – inevitably narrows our intellectual focus, and the essence of the university (if it may be said to have one) lies in the widest possible focus. Many things, of course, narrow that focus, including the idea that the point of an education is to get a good job. Few things darken the spirit of inquiry more than the careerism of someone seeking to conform to some pre-fabricated idea of what he, she or the state ought to be doing.

If I had to specify what makes a university different from other activities, I would be inclined to nominate its inculcation of "thoughtfulness" – but only then immediately to disavow the whole idea immediately. As we have seen with the idea of criticism, any formulation of the academic will turn into a slogan and get itself vulgarised. We may hope that our hero Candide will find in the university some valuable distance from the hot and steamy controversies of practice and politics, in order that students may find some perspective in which reflectiveness or thoughtfulness becomes possible.